ESSAYS IN EXPERIMENTAL PSYCHOLOGY

EDINBURGH STUDIES IN SOCIOLOGY

General Editors: Frank Bechhofer, Patricia Jeffrey, Tom McGlew

The *Edinburgh Studies in Sociology* series publishes sociological works from the Department of Sociology at the University of Edinburgh. The majority of the books in the series will be founded on original research or on research and scholarship pursued over a period of time. There will also be collections of research papers on particular topics of social interest and textbooks deriving from courses taught in the Department.

Many of the books will appeal to a non-specialist audience as well as to the academic reader.

Titles published

Kathryn C. Backett: MOTHERS AND FATHERS: A Study of the Development and Negotiation of Parental Behaviour

Frank Bechhofer and Brian Elliott (*editors*): THE PETITE BOURGEOISIE: Comparative Studies of the Uneasy Stratum

Tom Burns: THE BBC: Public Institution and Private World

Anthony P. M. Coxon and Charles L. Jones: THE IMAGES OF OCCUPATIONAL PRESTIGE: A Study in Social Cognition

Harvie Ferguson: ESSAYS IN EXPERIMENTAL PSYCHOLOGY

John Orr: TRAGIC DRAMA AND MODERN SOCIETY: Studies in the Social and Literary Theory of Drama from 1870 to the Present

John Orr: TRAGIC REALISM AND MODERN SOCIETY: Studies in the Sociology of the Modern Novel

ESSAYS IN EXPERIMENTAL PSYCHOLOGY

Harvie Ferguson
*Foreword by Antonio Negri,
translated by Gianfranco Poggi*

© Harvie Ferguson 1983
Foreword © Antonio Negri 1983
Translation of foreword © Gianfranco Poggi 1983

All rights reserved. No part of this publication may be reproduced or transmitted, in any form or by any means, without permission

First published 1983 by
THE MACMILLAN PRESS LTD
London and Basingstoke
Companies and representatives throughout the world

ISBN 0 333 28113 6

Printed in Hong Kong

For Sandra

Contents

Foreword by Antonio Negri   ix
  Translated by Gianfranco Poggi
Acknowledgements   xvi
Introduction   xvii

PART ONE   CONFINEMENT

1   The Existence of Confinement   3
2   The Appearance of Nothing   11
3   Self-Destruction   49
4   The End of the World   76

PART TWO   CHILDHOOD

5   The Art of Recollection   101
6   The Golden Age   117
7   The Prehistory of Nostalgia   154

PART THREE   CONCLUSION

8   Metaphysical Polarities   175

Bibliography   186
Index of Names   191

Foreword by Antonio Negri
Translated by Gianfranco Poggi

We are in our cell. A comrade says, 'Now I know how to make money when we get out of jail. We'll build a prison just like this one, and we'll take in as paying guests all those who keep asking us: "What's it like in jail, how's life there?".' We all laugh. And I find myself reflecting on that mixture of compassion and curiosity often addressed to us prisoners.

Is also philosophy inclined to such a mixture when it contemplates the prison condition? Sometimes; but it is not, in that case, good philosophy. Harvie Ferguson, however, is neither compassionate nor curious. Instead, he gathers diligently a substantial mass of documentation about confinement, and then dissects, with an anatomist's pitilessness, the prisoner's psychological condition. Of course, this angers me as I read him; for, how can he claim, from the outside, to be able to grasp what it's really like to be a prisoner, no matter how many mirrors he focuses on his subject? And as I sit here, writing in the midst of the constant, ear-splitting din of each prison day, I review the absurd variety and cruelty of the condition that has been mine over nearly three years. 'Judicial isolation' - meaning, months in solitary confinement, in total silence, amounting to utter sensory deprivation, broken only by those infrequent, disconcertingly formal, occasions when the inquiring judge finds the time to interrogate the prisoner. 'Maximum security jail' - here you may be searched any minute of the day: take off your trousers, strip naked, bend over. The 'punishment treatment' - I had a whole month of this after an inmate revolt, wounded, twenty of us in a cell with four beds, not enough to eat. Or the 'special prisoner' condition in smaller prisons, where you are segregated from all other inmates, and the guards have total discretionary control over you. I also review the moves from one jail to another: they awaken you suddenly at three o'clock in the morning, dump all your possessions into a blanket, which you then fold and carry around on your shoulders during the endless trips from one end of the country to another, chained, surrounded by a number of fearful armed guards.

I have seen men survive, others die or get killed, others rebel, others wound or kill themselves. I have experienced the terror of armed guards rushing into a cell in the middle of the night, beating up inmates, who then invariably end up in solitary. I have lived with people sentenced to life imprisonment, with political prisoners who never yield an inch, with drug addicts who scream in the agonies of forced withdrawal. I have lived through an inmate revolt: police helicopters landing on the roofs, commando troops (S.W.A.T.S.) blowing-up makeshift barricades, submachine guns fired in the direction of inmates who had already surrendered, then the harsh justice meted out by guards who had previously been seized, on their captors. This catalogue of horrors is but a partial account of three years of prison experience. How can one bring all this under one abstract category, 'confinement'?

Yet Harvie Ferguson tries quite successfully to do just that, for he distances himself or his reader greatly from concreteness. His are, indeed, 'concrete abstractions'. On the strength of the attempt I have just made to convey some of the lived particulars of my own confinement, I must acknowledge how coolly and penetratingly he engages his topic. To a considerable extent he owes his success to his determination to avoid starting the usual, benighted hare - the nature of legal punishment, the moral justification for confinement, the ludicrous paradox of claiming to improve an individual and fit him out for society by reducing him to utter misery and total segregation. Unconcerned with such diversionary themes, Ferguson elects to see confinement as a metaphysical condition, 'a primitive experience which we must acknowledge as an immediate intuition' and which can be used to throw light on very general features and quandaries of man's estate. Basically, in the metaphysical condition of confinement the spatio-temporal dimensions of existence are abolished, together with the horizons of fantasy and communication, and, ever increasingly, with the subject's own forms of resistance. Ultimately, the subject is annihilated: 'something, we begin to realise, of a philosophical masterpiece'. Confinement is a principle and a form of internalised self-negation, selflessness; and manages to be this all the more because it is filled through and through with noisome events, with collective cruelty, with expressions of violence.

One must point out that, no matter how sophisticated, a phenomenological approach does not amount to a metaphysical statement. As Ferguson works through his insights, the drive toward nothingness characterising the logic of confinement is shown to be identical with a general feature of existence, and a distinctive polarity of contemporary consciousness: the negation of subjectivity and the consciousness of that negation. Ferguson does not carry out this exercise in phenomenological reduction by following the dialectical scheme adopted by Hegel in the *Phänomenologie des Geistes*, and leading up to 'the dialectic of master and servant' there; rather, he appeals to Kierkegaard. In the latter's intuition, men attain the discovery of subjective difference via the experience of absolute indifference (whereas in Hegelian dialectics that which is determinate is positively implicated in the absolute). 'The self strives to defend itself against the encroachment of the absolute and tries to maintain a human corner where it can resist the "transcendental" power of confinement. But it cannot succeed; it is forced to compromise, to cooperate, to resist and in the end to capitulate to the negative synthesis. The self is penetrated by an alien substance but with such cunning that at the very point where it is about to decompose the last remnant of the human, it can appear in all the seductive glory and spirituality of life's ultimate secret.' (p. 75).

With an eye to the respective metaphysical imports, and with a healthy disregard for common-sense objections, Ferguson chooses to assimilate to the negative indifference of confinement the positive indifference of childhood. The latter's empty fullness, focused on play and possibility, appears as a further principle and form of negation of the subject, of selflessness; it, too, must evolve into the attainment of subjective difference. 'The selflessness of confinement is one of absolute negation, a void left by the annihilation of the subject; that of childhood is one of unformed potentiality'. I see no need, here, to offer examples from the phenomenology of childhood; this, unlike confinement, is everybody's experience, and everyone may submit his/her own evidence. If I chose to add to what Ferguson writes on this topic, I could only emphasise the depth of his insights and the vigour of his analysis.

It is however possible to raise some objections, concerning not so much Ferguson's phenomenological account, as its metaphysical implications (or assumptions). Well schooled in Kierkegaard, Ferguson sees consciousness as grounded on indifference. On one side the void of prison and solitude; on the other, the unformed fullness of childhood; between these two extremes, difference stands as the very ground of the subject's irreducibility, its uniqueness. And this may be true, at any rate as against all those philosophies which treat the subject as the plaything of the absolute spirit, or of some other canny transcendental force. However, one might place this emphasis on difference within a positive conception of being instead. It would make sense to me, at any rate, to see subjectivity as a moment within a collective circulation process, an aspect within an ontological horizon, within a solitary enterprise in the course of which humanity becomes constituted.

Personally, I am impressed by the use made of this approach in a text by Giles Deleuze with a Kierkegaardian title, *Différence et Répétition* (P.U.F. 1976). As I read Deleuze over, against empty repetition (as in Ferguson's confinement) or a full repetition (as in Ferguson's childhood), only the production of difference allows an understanding and a resolution of that nothingness which a rationalist philosophy simply produces and an irrationalist philosophy simply transcends. With repetition we are never confronted with an utter nothing, since those repeated are always events; at the same time repetition shows up the real irreducibility of such events. It constitutes a scandal, it points to difference as the horizon of being. A concept of difference adequate to this task cannot, then, encompass only a conceptual difference (amounting to a specific difference within a generic identity); it directs attention instead to the existential concept of the production of difference, as the material condition of an advanced sensuous being.

Lest this objection be seen as purely an epistemological one, consider again confinement as I experienced it. The miracle of the prison experience lies in the possibility for the inmates of countering all steps taken toward their own subjective annihilation, and to change them into something positive. Sociality, cooperation, solidarity - a wealth of aspects of shared living lies revealed. The weakest can find protection, the most ignorant, instruction. The destruction of space may be gainsaid; with some cigarette packs and a bit of glue one can build boards, tables, toys and tools with which to differentiate all that blank space. The vacuous rush of time may be stopped, and time may reappear as the locus of lived experiences, albeit imaginary ones. Foucault has written an interesting preface to the French translation of the accounts of prison by B. Jackson (*Leurs prisons: Autobiographies de prisonniers et d'ex-détenus américains*, Paris 1972). Here, understandably, he finds a plausible ground on which to develop his ideological vision of the world as a network of circuits transmitting command, exclusion and violence (also advancing, parenthetically, a frightening, and possibly questionable, view of capital as prison). However, Foucault is also struck with astonishment and enthusiasm at the extent to which rebellion, independence, communication, self-realisation keep taking place within jails. Both the idea and the felt experience of power, of law-and-order, which pervade prisons and account for the horrific experiences reported by the inmates, at a certain point seem to falter. The regularity and sequentiality of events are fractured, and new possibilities open up. It would not be instructive to characterise what happens as a 'dialectical' process; for dialectic, with its fake logic, its static reversals, its rigid inversions, thwarts the imagination of new possibilities; whereas what we are confronted with is a whole, open horizon. For instance, processes of segregation/separation which phenomenological analysis interprets as steps toward the annihilation of the subject, can be countered by an active strategy whereby they appear as moments of emancipation, and subjects confined and constrained actively seek self-realisation. Is it utterly inconceivable that, under such extreme conditions, the concept of self, its possibility, may unfold an irrepressible power of its own? Would it be out of place, here, to appeal to Spinoza's concept of 'potentia-conatus', power-possibility? (Ferguson gives too narrow a rendering of that concept.) One might then construe the positive significance of difference not as an a priori datum, but as a product, an accomplishment, which can come to characterise existence even under conditions as unpromising as confinement.

These, then, are some of the problems Ferguson's book raises for me. I feel, incidentally, that only its author's attachment to Kierkegaard's own phrasing justifies his subtitle, 'essays in experimental psychology'. In fact, the ancestry of Ferguson's book is to be found in that great tradition of metaphysics of the psyche which indeed first Schopenhauer and Kierkegaard, but later - and more systematically - Dilthey and Husserl have developed, and which in the bourgeois era has always constituted the theoretical base for a thorough critique of the philosophical enterprise. Ferguson's book is worthy of that tradition, and makes a significant, salient contribution to it by its sustained focus on some of the most distinctive experiences of our own time. On the one hand, confinement - which stands also for the Gulag phenomenon, for the militarisation of production relations by the socialist regimes, or the use of information and nuclear technology as means of social control under capitalism. On the other hand, childhood - which stands also for the experiences of youth revolt, the crisis ensuing upon the defeat of the struggles of the sixties, the demise of the aspiration to *l'imagination au pouvoir*. These collective experiences are central to our historical circumstances, and point up the problematicity of our culture and our daily existence. We can only live within the constraints of these problems, even when we anticipate, hopefully or fearfully, positive or negative solutions. Ferguson shows this with an impressive wealth of arguments and a keen sense of reality. Yet, I repeat, as I read them in jail his essays seem to me explorations in critical philosophy rather than in experimental psychology. At bottom, they amount to an effort to determine the new conditions of possibility of this world, to work out a new 'transcendental aesthetics'. Why should not one hope that such an effort may begin to produce a solution to the antinomies of 'transcendental dialectics' and thus power a new thrust toward emancipation?

I am well aware that such a prospect transcends the scope of Ferguson's inquiry, as well as that of any Christian dialectic of 'Nada-todo', whereby existence can open up only as new boundaries are set to it. Yet, it is the force itself of Ferguson's effort which suggests that prospect. I also feel that the understandings of the contemporary world derivable from the metaphors of confinement and of childhood are in the process of becoming inadequate in the face of such phenomena as the correct transformations in the State, in the destructive dialectic of capitalist rationality, in the catastrophic prospect of war. Together, such phenomena diminish the possibility of getting a hold upon wider philosophical problems in the light of individual experience. In this context, I do not find what Ferguson has to say on Canetti convincing. Given the enormity of the danger, one may have to postulate a transcendental aesthetic, rather than aiming toward it in a roundabout, uncertain fashion.

As I read Ferguson's manuscript, I find myself engrossed also in *Der Stern der Erlosung* (Frankfurt 1921), an unaccountably forgotten book by the great Hegelian scholar Franz Rosenzweig. This, in its own way, epoch-making book, seeks the root of the contemporary tragedy, rather than in the experience of confinement as Ferguson does, in that (still fresh at the time of writing) of trench warfare, of poison gas. Rosenzweig's itinerary is similar to Ferguson's: it leads into the depth of solitude and the desperate surrender of any dream of totality. However, to the Christian experience of meditation and redemption, to Kierkegaard and the whole bourgeois and romantic tradition, Rosenzweig opposes the Judaic experience of the chosen people's lonely witness, sacred time over against historical time.

Personally, I do not believe in sacred time, nor do I believe in redemption or hanker after totality. Yet, for all our differences, it should be possible for Rosenzweig, Ferguson and myself to join in the aspiration toward an experience of life and freedom no longer grounded on the emptiness of time, the solitude of confinement, the stolidity of childhood, or the destruction of war, but at long last seized and enjoyed within freely constituted time.

Antonio Negri
Carcere di Rebibbia (Roma)

FOREWORD

TRANSLATOR'S NOTE

Antonio Negri is an Italian political philosopher, and the author of several academic and political works, a number of which have also appeared in other languages. He holds a chair at the University of Padua; but on the 7 April 1979 he was arrested (together with a number of others including some of his junior colleagues) and put into custody on grave charges of terrorism and other illegal political activities. Some of the charges have since been dropped, and Negri and his associates were on trial at the time of going to press. He has been asked to comment on this book from his current standpoint as both a philosopher and the inmate of a prison.

'. . . However, on April 7, 1979 the police in Padua announced they had captured a 'master-mind of terrorism' who was Professor Antonio Negri, then accused of involvement in the Aldo Moro kidnapping. The Moro charges against Professor Negri have been dropped. He remains in prison, without trial, and Italian terrorism has got along without him . . .' - *Guardian*, 11 January 1982.

Gianfranco Poggi

Acknowledgements

I would like to thank the following individuals for their encouragement, generosity, practical assistance, patience and example: Jimmy Boyle, Tom Burns, Zoë, Sophie and Rex Ferguson, John and Bridget Fowler, Pru Larsen, Ilya Neustadt, Paddy O'Donnell, Gianfranco Poggi, Tom McGlew.

H. F.

Introduction

Confinement and Childhood are occasionally likened. John Holt indeed has titled one of his books, *Escape from Childhood* to draw attention to one side of just such a comparison. We are just as familiar with its other side, with the characterisation of prisoners, mental patients, old people in care - the confined in their perplexing variety - as 'merely' childish or 'just like children'; requiring, and deserving, however much of a nuisance they become, to be 'looked after'. And both children and the confined are more discreetly equated in their common metaphorical existence as wild animals, sharing to the same extent, though in somewhat different combination, in the naturalness, violence, simplicity, unpredictability, naiveté and charm that simultaneously attracts and repels those in their charge.

Such a direct equation, however, attends too much to the immediate character of behaviour and not enough to the types of social relationship they signify or to the quality of experience contained within such types. Even more it ignores the larger historical and cultural context that makes such superficial attributions of likeness plausible.

Confinement and Childhood share a commonality beyond the 'regression' of the captive towards infantile behaviour or the feeling common among children that they are prisoners within an adult world. They are conjoined also, and more fundamentally, in being relationships of dependence; and are alike, in a certain formal sense, in creating their own inner-world as a means of defence against this relationship. Neither children nor prisoners participate in the fundamental activities of our social life. They are not simply awarded, by virtue of their powerlessness, an inferior status, but are denied altogether the privilege of a personal social identity. It is this absence which has encouraged a certain confusion and allowed children and the confined, when they have been compared, to appear more alike than, in reality, they are or can be. Confinement and Childhood exist outside of the individuated selfhood which we still take to be essential (in our kind of society) to normal experience. Both are constituted, in other words, as forms of selflessness.

We should not be tempted, however, to deduce a common world of experience where none exists. The selflessness of Confinement is one of simple negation, a void left by the annihilation of the subject; that of Childhood is one of unformed potentiality. The prisoner in the end ceases to remember 'who' he is, the child, as yet innocent of who he is to become, has nothing yet to remember.

It is this quality, however opposed in the two instances, which makes so fascinating a tour of a prison or long-stay hospital and the hidden observation of a group of children at play. It is not that we are attracted by the one and repelled by the other; our feelings on coming into contact with these alien subjectivities are, in both cases, deeply mixed. They challenge, in their very presence, our personal identity and cherished selfhood; they abolish, or threaten to abolish, all our settled ideas and conventions about ourselves; they excite, in a quiet profound way, our dread.

It makes sense, then, to compare Childhood and Confinement, and both to the world of individuated experience we think so 'natural'. The experience of being a captive or a child can be described, then, in terms of the way in which it departs from what we take to be 'normal' to the self. It is for this reason that the writings of Søren Kierkegaard have come to play a central role in these essays. Kierkegaard did not write directly about either Confinement or Childhood but, in providing the first really convincing account of the emergence of the 'self' in modern society, should be considered the real starting point for the present discussion.

The centrality of Kierkegaard explains, too, the somewhat archaic subtitle which is borrowed directly from his unique little book, *Repetition: An Essay in Experimental Psychology*, published under the pseudonym of Constantine Constantius in Copenhagen in 1843. It is as a response to his book that the present work was conceived, the notion of 'repetition' is its *leitmotif* and the key to describing the inner-world of captives and children.

It is not intended in adopting Kierkegaard as a master, to defend a view of individualism which should more properly be regarded as an historical curiosity. Sociologists have quite rightly rejected individualism as a false starting point for reflecting upon experience. It has proved, none the less, a tenacious ideology which, however mistaken, has by now become rooted in the experiences it was designed originally to explain. It has become, in other words, part of the institutional complex of the modern world which in being accepted uncritically as an obvious truth continues, in fact, to order the world of experience for us. Most attempts to overcome the despair of individualism offer nothing more alluring than the metaphysical abyss of Confinement on the one hand, or the nostalgia of a misremembered Childhood, on the other. Trying to think critically about such alternatives should not be construed as an apologia for the common unhappiness from which, in different ways, they depart.

PART ONE
Confinement

1 The Existence of Confinement

How does it feel to be locked up?
   We have all experienced the minor irritations of confinement – housebound for two or three days with a bad cold; restricted, by some accident or other, to a week in bed or, perhaps, suffered a fortnight in hospital. Can we pursue some such incipient personal classification to its logical conclusion and discover for ourselves, simply by reflection, the inner world of its more extreme forms? Such a method would be misleading, less because of individual variety in our experience of constraint, than because of its inability to anticipate those qualitative changes and the more complete re-ordering of our subjective life effected in its 'advanced' stages, and because of the distortion, common to everyone, in the recollection of such experiences after they are restored to a normal condition of freedom.
   We cannot rely either upon a method of direct, objective observation. That not only refuses to define confinement as an experience and avoids by this scientific tactic the personal struggle which is its real subject matter, it employs a whole variety of analytical 'frameworks' (political, economic, historical, psychological, anthropological, etc.) for its observation, defines its world from so many different angles, that it cannot even reconstruct the inescapable and simple totatilty which it constitutes for those it encloses. The basic fact of confinement, that is to say, is not an 'objective' fact at all, but a primitive experience which we must acknowledge as an immediate intuition.
   Observation none the less is vital, and our personal experience is no less so, if we are to grasp the reality of confinement. It is conventional nowadays to regard personal interests, intuition and moral commitment as so many distorting influences upon the scientific method, to be either purged by suppression or exorcised by open admission and public debate, from our search for knowledge. The stunning negativity,

of confinement however demands a reversal of this judgement, and places understanding in the perspective of a personal encounter.

We can begin, therefore, directly with a quotation from one of George Jackson's prison letters contained in Soledad Brother. In it he admonishes his father for sending an indiscreet letter that referred to his son being 'bent on self-destruction'. This was seized upon by the prison authorities as 'proof' of Jackson's proneness to violence. In consequence the letter, Jackson adds matter-of-factly, 'caused me to to be put in a cell that has the lock welded closed'. That little phrase, 'welded closed', is not a piece of information upon which we reflect, it is simply a statement that makes us shudder.

And here is something from Volume Two of Solzhenitsyn's Gulag Arhcipelago; he is describing the first Soviet labour camp, on Solovetsky Island in 1918:

> And here is how they kept the prisoners in the punishment cells: poles the thickness of an arm were set from wall to wall and prisoners were ordered to sit on these poles all day . . . The height of the poles was set so that one's feet could not reach the ground. And it was not easy to keep balance. In fact, the prisoner spent the entire day trying to maintain his perch.

This response, at once moral and physical, addresses itself to the universal character of confinement. A response, localised in the viscera, which is aroused by the appearance of confinement in all its forms; in the personal and particular, in its vast historical presence, and in the invented plight of its imagined victims.

The welded lock and the poles take confinement to an extreme. They perfectly isolate the pure principle of confinement from the encumbrance of utility or rationality. They are imposed as punishments to which the prisoner is forced to submit because he has not already submitted to the pitiful life allowed him in prison or labour camp. This refusal is met by releasing upon him the full force of confinement. It is the purity, rather than the harshness of this alien condition to which our moral nausea is a response.

George Jackson was already restricted to a solitary cell for twenty-three-and-a-half hours of every twenty-four; the prisoners on Solovetsky Island were already lost to the world. Yet a further extremity is reached, a more perfect constraint devised. This extra half-hour, this last half-hour, and with the lock 'welded closed', it is this absoluteness that creates such a shudder in the reader. And, if we could be honest, it creates in the same instant a kind of breathless, suppressed admiration for its perfection. Our aesthetic and moral response, in fact, is more complex than the simple repulsion with which we first encounter its otherness from life.

These passages leave the reader in a complex state of dread. How must it leave its victims? Would it be possible not to imagine oneself entombed; like the epileptic in one of Edgar Allan Poe's stories who, on awakening from a seizure to the darkness of a small cabin and the smell of the damp pine boards of the upper bunk inches from his face, imagined himself prematurely buried?

And these poles. What a lucid apprehension of the principle of confinement taken to a limit of bodily immobility. More certainly and painfully than a straitjacket these poles clarify the absolute alienness of confinement. They signify its otherness and reveal at once its enjoyment of a profound paradox – in literally doing nothing it forces its victims to destroy themselves.

Part of the horror as well, no doubt, lies in acknowleding the practical and circumstantial details. Someone has thought this out, someone else has carefully calculated, measured and installed the necessary apparatus, and someone watches to ensure the punishment is carried out according to the regulations. They must beat the prisoner who stupidly allows himself to slip, or burst open the welded lock to prevent a too sudden and visible suicide. But these horrifying particulars leave no lasting taste in the mouth; they slip quietly into the great reservoir of misery with which we manage to live. We can forget the names, the dates, the history and geography of terror, but there is something mentally indigestible about the pure condition of confinement, and something just as absolute and compelling in our gut reaction to it.

This visceral reaction is less, to be sure, than a method of enquiry, but more certainly than eccentric individual reaction. An apprehensive tightening in the chest, a slight dissolution of the internal organs; these are the personal signs that can guide us through the 'literature of confinement'.

It is to this 'literature of confinement', memoirs, recollections, letters, fictional reconstructions and accounts – rather than to objective, academic studies – that we must turn first of all for a description of the 'facts' of confinement. This literature is all too depressingly extensive, yet that it should exist at all is puzzling. If confinement does contain such an abyss of otherness how can anyone, present within it or in recollection of it, tell us about its intimate experiences? Logically such a gulf seems unbridgeable by language. Dostoevsky, who has left us one of the most sensitive and at the same time most deceptively straightforward accounts of confinement in The House of the Dead, admits to such limitations and can describe the movement across its boundary to freedom only as an 'unspeakable moment'. Yet, in a sense obvious to any reader of his book, Dostoevsky has succeeded in communicating to us something of the feel of confinement. Dostoevsky trusts both his own and his reader's intuitive powers, allowing the synthesis he has to describe to take shape in the mind, rather than according to some system of deductive rules. He refuses, in other words, to analyse and reduce to a few neat principles the mechanisms of that particular world; an analysis which would not only render its potent totality into a series of disparate elements, but would, in this same process, conceal much of its horror.

The 'literature of confinement' which describes such an existence establishes its truth through the most intense personal struggle rather than by the shaping of 'evidence'. And this is no mere literary convention or device, but a necessity born of the peculiar reality it describes. This literature when we read it (as much with our stomach and heart as our head) reveals to us, in a way scientific studies never can, the real impossibilities of which confinement is composed.

Jean Genet, whose luminous and disturbing contribution to the 'literature of confinement' will have to be confronted later, suggests in his 'Introduction' to George Jackson's letters, that 'a certain complicity links the works written in prisons or asylums'. This should not surprise us since they share in the task of exposing, without being able to do so directly, the nature of confinement.

Any of the major works of this genre might, then, serve as a prototype, and be read as exemplary of the experience as a whole. But think first of Jacques Casanova, in 1732 imprisoned under the

Leads (so called because the cells were unconventionally situated immediately beneath the leaded roof of the Doge's Palace in Venice). His account remains more than an historial curiosity. Themes emerge in his description which recur with refinement and elaboration in many later writers.

Casanova confronts confinement with the naive optimism common among the lesser eighteenth-century philosophes. He not only fails to realise, at the outset, the simple physical horror it will become; he also lacks any sensitivity to those circumstances which can intensify, as it were, its absoluteness. For though we have begun by saying confinement is an absolute, it rarely occupies, initially at least, our entire experience. The victim finds some foothold, manufactures some form of life within it, to weigh against its awful emptiness. Poor Casanova however, so used to the life of freedom and its natural aristocratic pleasures, even thanks his gaoler for providing him with the relative luxury of a solitary cell. Lawrence, his gaoler (we are still in the period when gaolers have names) has to impress upon the innocent that his lack of companions is intended as an additional punishment. Confinement, however, is in itself a powerful demystifier. 'The fool was right, and I soon found out', Casanova admits with some bitterness.

He was restricted to a small, very dirty cell, infested with rats and insects, especially fleas 'which held high holiday over me'. He could not walk upright and saw Lawrence only once a day when his food was brought (we are also in the days when prisoners could pay their gaolers to receive additional and better food, than that normally provided. Within a matter of days isolation and squalor reduced him to 'the most wretched of men'. He declares he 'would like to be in hell, if he believed in it, for the sake of the company'. Deprived even of the paper and ink which he rather optimistically estimated would 'take away nine-tenths of the torture'.

Over a period of weeks he began to develop some insight into his new, and alarming, situation. Interestingly enough this insight is due, in large measure, to reading a book, containing the 'revelations' of a Spanish nun. This work, thoughtfully provided by Cavalli, who was responsible for his incarceration, was his sole diversion. Casanova realised that it was the nun's enclosed life – still not a life in confinement proper, her religious exclusion from the world lacks an element of involuntariness we associate with confinement (though doubtless it is more difficult to leave than to enter) – that is part responsible for the hallucinated and extravagant fantasies she committed to paper. She was 'devout to superstition, melancholy, shut in by convent walls, and swayed by the ignorance and bigotry of her confessors'. From such a state there arise 'the dreams of a visionary who, without vanity but inebriated by the idea of God, thinks to reveal only the inspiration of the Divine Spirit'. Though rather a poor form of literature, 'the need of doing something made me spend a week over this masterpiece of madness, the product of a hyper-exalted brain'. And her fantasies, so far removed from Casanova's normal, waking, rational, cynical self, proved to be infectious. 'As soon as I went off to sleep', he reports with some dismay, 'I experienced the disease which Sister Mary of Agrada had communicated to my mind weakened by melancholy, want of proper nourishment and exercise, bad air, and the horrible uncertainty of my fate. The wildness of my dreams made me laugh when I recalled them in my waking moments. If I had possessed the necessary materials I would have written my visions down, and I might possibly have produced in my cell a still madder work than the one chosen with such insight by Cavalli.'

His intellect could remain powerful and critical only so long as it remained part of a free life. 'The book of the Spanish nun has all the properties necessary to make a man crack-brained', he admitted, but 'for the poison to take effect he must be isolated, put under the Leads, and deprived of all other employments.' And a little later on confesses 'thus, in the depths of my soul I began to grow mad'.

He retained, however, for a considerable period the hope of arbitrary release. He calculated, with a nicety later noticed among psychotics, that he would be released, at the latest, by October when the new Inquisitor took office. 'All this appeared to me unanswerable, because it seemed natural, but it was fallacious under the Leads, where nothing is done after the natural order.' Confinement he discovers to be outside of that 'perfect unity' of man and nature which had formed the central tenet of his philosophical conception of life. But now 'I saw I was in a place where, if the false appeared true, the truth might appear false, where understanding was beareaved of all its prerogatives, where the imagination becoming affected, would either make

the reason a victim of empty hope or to dark despair.'
This inversion of the natural order and consequent loss of a proper sense of reality is highlighted, by Casanova, and becomes terrified by the touch of his own hand, turned bloodless and cold as if part of his own body had become detached and transformed into some dreadful other body.

Casanova declares that the loneliness of confinement 'must be learned by experience to be understood' but he would not wish such an experience on his enemies – and this, remember, from a man who held that the wish to destroy (in simply physical terms) one's enemies was a natural, instinctive function. Indeed he regarded it as an 'appetite' of the same order of generality as hunger or sexuality; forming with them the core of human nature.

Casanova tells us much that recurs throughout the 'literature of confinement'. His catalogue of horrors is not complete, but certain essential elements are there. The shock, the disorientation, the reversion of what we take to be a natural order of things, the smell, a fairly complete dislocation in time and space, the elementary problem posed by your own body and its needs. One gets a sense of the primitiveness of the experience.

It is worth noticing, also, the weakness of Casanova's account. Although he reconstructs his time in prison as honestly and accurately as he can he proceeds, as it were, from the outside–in rather than the inside–out. It is a memoir, a recollection, in which he cannot suppress the overall pattern of his life. So we find a resurgence of his naive optimism and rationalism; his overwhelming desire to explain, to render an account and thus domesticate his prison experience by incorporating it into a larger and more pleasing scheme of things. One gets a rather different impression on reading only those sections composed from his prison experience, than one does from reading his Memoir as a whole, in which his imprisonment appears as only an interlude between adventures. More than that he cannot resist making of it just one more adventure in an adventurous life. It turns after all into a dramatic escape story which fits well between his seduction of the nun (one reason, perhaps, why he was so affected by Sister Mary's book?) and his trip to Paris. He fails to take account, in a more formal sense, of the radical dissociation between his prison experience and his life in freedom. In writing of it as an adventure he contradicts its essential nature and misrepresents the quality of its difference from ordinary life. He cannot, in fact, quite succeed in thus incorporating its negativism into the rest of his life and his prose style, despite his best efforts, is forced to take some account of this. The recollection of his imprisonment is somewhat less exuberant and florid that his other memoirs, somewhat less given to philosophising in general or in passing the time of day with the reader. We can sense the relief with which he passes on to more familiar territory.

Casanova may serve as our prototype. He does not directly answer our question – how does it feel to be locked-up? – but reading his account of his own imprisonment makes us aware at once of the profound transformation confinement brings about in our normal subjectivity. How can this transformation be represented more fully? What alterations in our own experience can best suggest to us its wholly alien quality? Casanova speaks of it as a curious inversion; we can look at this inversion more closely by describing in turn the transformation it effects in our experience of space, of time, and of our own bodies.

2 The Appearance of Nothing

Many writers have represented confinement in a series of disturbing reversals. In a general sense this can be understood as an inversion in the 'normal' relationship we assume obtains between 'thought' and 'experience'. In confinement we come to experience the world directly in a manner we reserve more normally for reflective thought alone. Its space is as perfectly abstract as its time, and the bodies of its victims are aspects only of its universal substance.

SPACE

A French poet, Henri Michaux, puts the matter for us very well; he writes, 'Space, but you cannot even conceive the horrible inside-outside that real space is'.

The difficulty is a very general one, but no more readily solved because of that. While we are trying to describe the manner in which confinement constructs its world, we do not even know the space and time of our own everyday lives. Certainly our personal experience of space is distinct from our concept of space; just as the world of confinement is hardly hinted at by the concepts through which we only talk about it.

If asked about space we do not find it problematic. We can answer readily enough that space is extension; pure extension, symmetrical and limitless. Its difficulty, as a concept, has to do only with this boundless quality, which we intuitively demand of it, despite finding in it an equally impossible idea. Space itself does not appear interesting; it is the objects that fill it out that attract our attention. We think of objects rather than the space that we deduce must be there to contain and separate them. Space is reduced, usually, to the emptiness among our points of attention, which, however narrowed, never reaches a continuous solid substance underlying such appearances. We have no organ of space perception: its apprehension is a higher-order intellectual function, absent from the first innocence of our sensory awakening. Space remains necessary for us because of the plentitude of subjects which we see and touch, everything which we can differentiate and which our life forces upon our attention.

We do not, however, experience space in this way, not in the real world. The pure, extended quality of space, its symmetry, boundless and formless qualities are all denied by the human agent that perceives and organises such perfect emptiness through a variety of arbitrary devices. Distinctions of left and right, forward and back, gradations of nearness and farness all bear the mark of human ingenuity and carry a meaning, which is absent in the mathematician's or logician's category. This introduction of qualitative distinctions into what is held, abstractly as an ideal continuum could readily lead us into a complex ethnography. It is not, however, necessary to be seduced by such formal complexity. To describe the space of confinement it is sufficient to invert only one of its normal human qualities; that quality which has been illuminated by Bachelard in his intriguing and original book, The Poetics of Space.

Bachelard describes what he terms intimate, or, 'eulogised space'. His interest lies in the quality of space that is seized upon and defended by the imagination. This quality, he contends, does not adhere to any empirical distinctions that can be detected in spatial categories, but lies wholly within our own subjective judgment. The image of such 'eulogised space', the forms in which such images appear and the affective relationships through which we recognise them, are all qualities of the subjective life which flow into the exterior topography and transform it.

In talking of the space we love, the space capable of receiving our impressions and throwing them back to be stored as memories, as nostalgia, Bachelard notes that the 'house holds a privileged position'. The house remains 'our corner of the world' and 'all really inhabited space', he assures us, 'bears the essence of the notion of home'. The house is the place made safe by and for our reveries and dreams. Such transformation of a place into a home operates wherever man settles himself, as a natural psychological extension of his presence; his imagination 'works in this direction', he assures us, 'whenever the human being has found the slightest shelter'. It 'allows one to dream in peace'. Indeed it has the function of integrating thought, dream and memory into a composite image of the place which contains our life. This is not the space of pure extension, it does not seek extension, so much as condensation. It 'would like above all still to be possessed'. It need not reflect one particular abode, but contains a whole series of separate physical identities which merge into our own, unique, intimate space. It is in this sense that 'space contains compressed time' as our intimate recollection plays, as in a dream, with the separations of the natural world.

Bachelard cites many descriptions, mainly from modern French poetry, of such intimate space. Others could be added. We can note, for example, the care with which Anaïs Nin portrays throughout her Journals, the intimate space of her life - her house at Louveciennes, houseboat in Paris, flat in New York, house in Acapulco, hotels and cafes associated, in her memory, with particular moods and periods of her life. The colours and textures, merging as the Journal develops into the kind of condensed image which so fascinates Bachelard.

Intimate space is as varied as the subjectivity that flows into it. Bachelard points out the house is internally organised, from cellar to garret, and each floor and room occupies a definite location in our consciousness. Anaïs Nin, again, tells us of her house at Louveciennes in which 'Every room is painted a different colour. As if there were one room for every separate mood; Lacquer red for vehemence, pale turquoise for reveries, peach colour for gentleness, green for repose, grey for work at the typewriter.' A variety recalling the more splendidly decadent work of Huysmans whose A Rebours overwhelms the reader with the aesthetics of intimate space.

Franz Kafka in a delightfully clever story, The Burrow, in a paradoxical fashion brilliantly evokes this human, subjective quality of intimate space. Paradoxical because it is written in the first person but refers to some burrowing creature of indeterminate species. The burrow protects, encircles and replicates, through the labyrinthine character of its many passages and galleries, the complex inner life of its builder. Burrow and creature are perfectly at home with each other, so that one is hard pressed to say which is the more perfectly human. 'Sometimes', declares the little creature in an ecstasy over his creation, 'I lie and roll about the passage with pure joy.' And echoes Nin and Huysmans in his appreciation of the variety of his cellars and passages, 'emitting their variegated and mingled smells, each of which delights me in its own fasion, and every one of which I can distinguish even at a distance, as far as the very remotest passages'.

This labyrinthine and variegated quality extends beyond the intimacy of the house to encompass neighbourhoods, districts or entire towns in the warmth of personal recollection, just as Anaïs Nin remembered Fez as a kind of miraculous projection of the pattern she felt animated her subjective life. Or, even more remarkably, her friend, Henry Miller, appropriated, through detailed roadmaps, half of Paris for his 'eulogised space' before he even visited that city.

Eulogised space is not boundless, however extended: it is always personally localised. It has a liking, also, to be enclosed. Do not children spontaneously seek out such enclosed spaces for themselves – dens, cupboards, narrow spaces, tents, boxes, nests? To be alone with their view of the world, and share it with someone similarly sane. This desire never leaves us; we continually give way to it, in homes, in rooms, in beds, in clothes; reducing the scale of our immediate environment to more manageable proportions and endowing it with the quality of ourselves. We impose boundaries around this immediate space only as screens capable of accepting the images we project upon them, allowing us to expand, to fill out the whole of these shifting, bounded spaces with the potentialities of the self.

It is not such personal enclosure, whose boundary remains permeable, that we fear. We continually seek a snugger niche, a more perfectly individualised space in which we can deny, in making it part of our sensuous activity, the abstracted, mathematical quality of 'pure' space.

But we do fear confinement, whose peculiar intimacy cannot be avoided, although it is opposed at every point to the special humanness of Bachelard's 'eulogised space'.

The most obvious attribute of such space is its separateness. It is a place set aside for its particular purpose. Often set apart by the necessity of a long, usually terrifying journey. But even where it is housed within the midst of normal life it retains its special identity. They are not places we may freely enter or leave, the boundaries around its space are impenetrable in either direction. Prison walls are not simply physically thick, they create a kind of mythical boundary, to mark off its special enclosure. Dostoevsky, for example, feigns astonishment at the 'notes' of the ex-convict which he claims to have found and from which he compiled his House of the Dead. 'They revealed a quite new world', he says, 'unknown till then' – but a world that once entered becomes all embracing and out of which it becomes equally difficult to imagine the place to which you once belonged. 'Beyond the palisade one thought of the marvellous world, fantastic as a fairy tale', a place that is, that can hardly exist for the adult imagination. 'It was not the same on our side', he goes on to remark, most profoundly, 'Here there was no resemblance to anything.' A judgment echoed by some of his modern compatriots, among them Nadezhda Mandelstam, whose husband Osip was a poliical prisoner in Gulag, and who talks in her beautiful book Hope Against Hope of crossing this boundary, to the space of confinement, as entering 'something beyond the looking glass'. To a space defined by 'different concepts, different ways of measuring and reckoning'.

The physical boundary itself is always too dense, too high, too strong; more than can be required by the necessity of rendering its space 'secure'. Chekhov notes an example of this in his Ward Number Six, a neglected ward of a provincial hospital, which houses the few helpless lunatics who 'threaten' the town. There 'windows were disfigured by an iron grille on the inside', bars as unnecessary as the welded lock, but the pervasive feature of the bounded space of confinement.

Bars and locks, in recent times, have replaced the chains of an earlier period in their power to transform the space of confinement into a hostile space. They are again a manifestation of the 'purity' with which confinement seeks to establish itself. The prisoner 'never will get completely over the memory of the bars', declares Malcolm X in his Autobiography. They enclose the victim in an ever tighter circle of hostility. Not that chains which retain the advantage of being felt have been entirely abandoned. They remain too useful for that. Jean Genet points out that Harcamone, the godlike hero of his The Miracle of the Roses, had his chains 'riveted on', a privilege due him as a condemned man, as someone to be more closely confined, to have his space entirely pervaded by hostility, as part of his punishment, and not because he might otherwise escape, or commit suicide. And Wole Soyinka, incarcerated during the Nigerian Civil War, speaks eloquently of this spatial hostility, which seemed to flow through him, when he was chained. 'I sensed a vivid contradiction', he reports – one that allowed him, briefly, to sense his real being in a more direct, if negative way. 'I defined myself as a being for whom chains are not; as, finally, a human being. In so far as one may say that the human essence does at times possess a tangible quality, I may say that I tasted and felt this essence within the contradiction of that amount.'

Such restricted, hostile space can be fabricated, in a moment. Hugh Lewin, who recounts his prison experiences in South African jails in his book, Bandeit, tells us of a method of interrogation which creates, for as long as necessary, a hostile space within which the victim soon loses his hold on any reality with which to resist. His interrogator Swanepoal (a mark of historical 'progress' this, prisoners now know the name, and develop a personal relationship with their interrogator rather than their jailer) drew a chalk line on the floor around Lewin, who was forced to stand upright within this space, while his interrogators shouted at him, abused and physically threatened him.

This constriction, hostility, immobility created a space that was no longer space as we experience it: 'The room wasn't a room any more, not a room with chairs and desks and a couple of windows. It was a world with four faces, sometimes six, a world that was a void, moving around and around, swimming with faces and sheafs of paper, a talking, pressing world'.

The boundary, then, marks a more than physical separation. It confirms the edge of another world. Movement across such a boundary in either direction must be highly ritualised. The boundary closes off, in a decisive fashion, any connections between the worlds that lie to either side.

Such a boundary marks the categorical division between the experience of life and of confinement. Life itself knows no such severe, impenetrable, wall. This is where, I think, we have to be especially careful. It is tempting to go back to Bachelard's investigation of intimate space and see analogies within its normal topography to the space of confinement. A partial correspondence at least is suggested by the cellar of a house. But although the cellar is invested with an image of a 'dark entity', and can house as Bachelard describes 'buried madness walled in tragedy'; it remains a space appropriated by the subject and lacks therefore the pure spirit of confinement; its terror belongs to the world of life - it is a fear of what might be there, a fear which, however tenuously, holds on to a rational appraisal and, even where it claims the power of an image alone, represents some significant human predicament. And it is still saved by the umbilical cord of stairways and ladders to the light above. The prison cell admittedly, wherever it is situated, is inhabited as a place underground, but its connection with the cellar of our private nightmare is superficial. The horror of the cellar is of a different, still human kind. Edgar Allan Poe realised that in one of his most terrifying stories, The Cask of Amontillado. Its supposed author has determined to be avenged on Fortunato, and persuades his victim to descend with him to the cellar to inspect some new sherry recently arrived in the vaults below. But this turns out to be no ordinary cellar. It is much too large for that. They move deeper into the interior, each gallery more ancient than the last, more removed from the scent and sound of domestic life. Finally, having traversed an impossible distance, he gains his revenge. Amid the bones within an old crypt he chains his victim to the wall of a tiny alcove. He proceeds to block up the entrance. As the final stone is laid in place the victim's screams of terror, which had already turned to hysterical laughter, cease completely and the entombment is perfected in silence. The perpetrator of the deed remains anonymous. It is, in the reverse direction, like Dostoevsky's release, 'an unspeakable moment'; nameless, silent, totally apart from the world above with which it has severed all connections.

This quality of hostility which pervades the interior of confined places seems more central to its nature than does its simple physical dimensions. Of course we think of confinement as being enclosure within a small space. But this need not be the case; it can be an entire hospital as well as a single bed; a labour camp complex as well as a solitary cell. But at some point within confinement you run against a solid wall which has, as one of its first effects, a shrinking of the space it contains.

Simple lack of space often enough presents, however, a striking and immediate threat. Casanova, remember, could not walk upright in his cell. We learn from one of the letters from prisoners in San Quentin collected by Eve Pell in her book Maximum Security that some of the solitary confinement cells there the 'pit' and 'strip cells', were smaller than the cage capacity stipulated by California State Regulations as the minimum requirement to house a gorilla. Bao Rua-Wang in his memoir Prisoner of Mao experienced something very similar in solitary in his Chinese jail, a cell into which you had to half slide as its opening was so small. Victor Serge in his unique and uncompromising book Men in Prison points out that 'before the end of the first hour, the prisoner discovers that expedient: walking', and measures his world exactly in the twelve steps it takes to circumscribe his cell'. Memoirs abound with precise measurements, the simple fact of their presence, of being so obviously central to the prisoner's recollection, testifies to the force with which this shrinkage in space gripped them.

Smallness as such, however, remains an aspect of the more pervasive quality of hostility. A quality expressed even more forcibly through its lack of internal differentiation and variety. Hugh Lewin, again, says 'Walking into prison is like walking into a butcher's fridge, empty. It is cold – no curtains, no carpets, no heaters, nothing decorative, nothing unnecessary, just this long dull corridor like a sleazy passenger liner, with heavy blind doors.' A point made clear, also, in many fictional works. In David Karp's modern fable One, his hero Burden finds himself in the Security Headquarters of the State to which he believes himself dedicated (his opposition lies so deeply hidden he must, ultimately, be turned into another person to be 'reformed'). He is awakened in the middle of the night, ostensibly for a 'medical examination', and escorted along a featureless corridor at the very end of which a woman is washing the floor. 'But then Burden thought there was no end to the corridor. It circled back upon itself and for all he knew the figure progressed completely about the circle during the night and repeated the trip night after night.'

Even Nabokov, the most playfully human of writers, remains faithful to this empty interior. In his Invitation to a Beheading, which is a 'study' of impending but still indeterminate death, rather than of confinement, he described this change in space. His condemned hero Cincinnatus C (reminiscent of Constantine Constantius, pseudonymous author of Repetition) finds his jail 'bare, redoubtable and cold', though he admits its prison-like character was muted 'by the neutrality of a waiting room'. However, the passage of time alters this, the inscriptions adorning the walls of his cell become mysteriously erased, the list of regulations pinned to his door disappear, the water pitcher vanishes and his cell is reduced to an empty space, a uniform environment.

Of course divisions exist within this space; its lack of internal differentiation is something that strikes the visitor or the long-termer more than the inmate still struggling to domesticate his surroundings. These divisions, however, are made with mathematical, not human, precision. It is divided according to some principle, or abstract geometry, to produce equal, identical sub-units. Divisions which refuse to be seized by the imagination and remain aloof, as it were, from the advances of subjectivity. Anatoly Marchenko, whose account of his years of imprisonment and confinement in labour camps, My Testimony, is one of the most compelling memoirs of Gulag, describes his prison in the following terms: 'All the cells in Vladimir jail were so alike that if you blindfolded a con, led him into the wrong cell and uncovered his eyes, he would automatically go to his usual place without even noticing where he was.' A principle of identity that was generously extended to the 'exercise yard'. This yard, bounded by walls identical to the walls of the internal cells, and of precisely the same dimension as these cells, made its one concession in an absent roof to allow prisoners to pace to and fro for half an hour and stare blankly at a rectangle of sky.

And Wole Soyinka, incarcerated in something approaching a concrete honeycomb, gazed from his cell at the low prison buildings opposite, exact replicas of the one he occupied, and observed, 'These man-made hives seemed feeble pock-marks on the authentic face of emptiness'. The emptiness that encloses all prisoners is the same space. The 'cube of air' that is the universal cage of confined space.

This final phrase of Soyinka's, from his prison memoir The Man Died, strikes a note of profound despair. Space, emptied of its subjective content, the only content it knows, becomes transformed into a reality that realises exclusively, and more precisely, its logical form. In other words the confined are forced to experience space as a pure category. They experience its undiluted abstractness and must live in a world which we, thankfully, can only think. They have to exist in the 'impossible' abstract-concrete substance of 'real' space, as if its abstract idea had come to life and rejected any merely human interference in its perfection.

This sounds rather strange, a fanciful formulation at best. But it is not a formulation 'deduced' from the evidence of other writers, it is, in plain terms, a repetition of what they have said. Different writers, of course, express it within the idiom of their own tradition: and some come very close, in fact, to the quasi-philosophical form we, still at liberty, find natural.

A most brilliant example can be found in Andrey Sinyavsky's book A Voice from the Chorus. Sinyavsky was sentenced, with the poet Yuli Daniel, in a celebrated Moscow trial in 1966. He spent the following six years in prisons and labour camps. The recreation of this experience, in his book, is a most original and subtle contribution to the 'literature of confinement'. His work is less a 'realistic' record than a collection of apparently disparate essays, portions of letter, reflections and notes; the whole interspersed with the 'chorus' of his fellow prisoners' voices. Prison lore, other prisoners' letters, remarks, advice, disconnected and disjointed, are continually intruding and throwing into relief the half-finished character of Sinyavsky's own thoughts. His method then, is the direct antithesis of Casanova's. There is less attention to everyday 'empirical' detail, and much of the work comprises reflections on Literature, the theory of art and the like; but the form itself works marvellously to convey the sense of restriction, mental dislocation, and sensuous fragmentation which belong in confinement. The abrupt shifts, juxtaposition of heterogeneous elements, creates a more lasting impression than the content of even his most luminous and diverting essays. He makes clear, in fact, that prison is no place for literary experiment, or original thought; it is 'snugness and warmth that give birth to new ideas', and there was little enough of either in Dubrovlag. His originality, we feel, must have been stored up in advance, to inform his perfect construction.

'A man unconfined in space', he says, 'constantly aspires to go forward into the distance', nearness and distance belong naturally to it. But in the space of confinement even although you try to move, and may even appear to succeed, 'you seem to be walking through it, only to come upon your illusion and discover yourself rooted to the same spot'. And he continues, later, 'I resemble a cockroach – not when it runs, but when it sits, rooted motionless in one spot, vacant and aloof, staring fixedly at one inscrutable spot'.

This emptying out of the subjective qualities in space affects distant objects as well as the immediate confines of a cell. All objects lose their appearance of reality, of being part of the natural world at all, even though, as distant hills, or a forest the landscape glimpsed, often, at oblique angles, lies beyond the conventional boundary that restricts the subject to his place. Sinyavsky, after a couple of years noticed this draining away of the qualities of objects, as if their sensuous attributes were being sucked out by the void surrounding them. 'The landscape is gradually beginning to look like stage scenery to me', he records, and adds that this is not an aspect of his sensitivity alone; but affects everyone. He had even been warned to expect it. It would take time, but was, he was assured, inevitable. None could withstand the idealisation of the space they inhabited. Thus, later, some prisoners could plaster their cell walls with picture postcards and imagine themselves transported from the narrow restriction of the prison – but to no avail. The fact that they were allowed to do so is indication enough of its purely ironic significance. They were already living in a 'picture-book' world and could not, that easily, escape. There developed a falsification of space made transparent in his beautiful remark, 'Look: the moon in the window – how life-like it is'. Outside and inside had become indistinguishable, the space from which the prisoner came was no longer a meaningful part of his subjective life. Hugh Lewin makes a similar remark, 'It was like being in a prison movie'.

Finally, Sinyavsky is driven to say, 'To all intents and purposes space no longer exists here'. Space in the sense, that is, in which we experience it. The space of confinement, which is hardly space at all, is nevertheless absolute within its own domain. 'One is engulfed by the environment', Sinyavsky continues, 'because of something not subject to normal explanation, to logic; a feeling of growing isolation and detachment.' A world, to repeat Nadezhda Mandelstam, 'of different concepts, different ways of measuring and reckoning'.

The isolation and special quality of hostility, the absence of internal difference or quality, its abstractness, or its impossibly concrete abstractness, makes it difficult, as has already been noted, to credit the existence of any other place. Its world is complete, absolute, as demanding of its inmates' unqualified assent as our own is to us. People on the outside, Sinyavsky says, 'I can only liken to spectres or phantoms . . . People pay little attention to them, though fearing them, do not believe in the reality of their existence.' They belong to the 'fairy-tale' world beyond the prison boundary.

We can see now this boundary does not simply divide and separate, but, at the point where it becomes truly impregnable, works to annihilate what lies on either side. It becomes a boundary that encloses a universal system of co-ordinates. What does it matter to the normal person, on either side of the divide, that another, different system of co-ordinates might exist somewhere else? They remain mutually incomprehensible, expressible to each other only as logical paradoxes. The space which we first see as defined by its restriction, by being a bounded part of our space, turns out, on closer inspection, to be bounded separateness from our space, and this space, once we are inside it, oddly re-extends itself to the limits of the sensuous world and becomes no longer a division within the infinite but a self-sufficient universe of its own. It becomes the new measure against which any other existence can have an only imaginary appearance. Space on the inside becomes more and more the only space there is, a first-hand experience of the space of the logician; equal, symmetrical, boundless. The severe restriction of the boundary dissolves into nothing as it becomes instead merely the outer limits of the real world. While Sinyavsky says that on the inside space is absent, he might as easily say its space is infinite; an infinity created by the wire fence or brick wall, or picture postcard landscape.

Other writers, also, have a clear intuition of this 'pure' space. David Karp, in a powerful passage of his novel, One, has Burden confined to a solitary cell. But it is no ordinary 'cube of air' faced with solid visible walls. Its walls curve away, so that the outer limits of the cell are never completely visible. The lighting and colour heighten the effect, dissolving the solidity of the barrier that, nevertheless, leaves him no hope of escape. He is entirely hemmed in, but the boundary of his space tends to dissolve in a mysterious fashion. He cannot get his bearings in such a place, his normal spatial sense is totally decomposed by the invasion of his senses by pure

extension. He is confined in infinite space.
This same kind of metaphysical abyss permeates the central chapters of William Golding's Free Fall. As in some other fictional works (like Karp's One or Poe's The Pit and the Pendulum) the central character finds himself suddenly confined in total darkness. He has to feel his way, explore his new environment by touch alone. Golding's character 'lay on the concrete, having discovered that the place was a cell; examined dully the view of total defeat'. The cell was too small to allow him to stretch out except across the line of the diagonal. But to stretch out in this fashion, in the dark of a cell never seen, is a terrifying manoeuvre. 'But who could sleep', he asks, 'with only the level floor as contact? What dreams and phantoms might visit one unprotected at his back and not rolled up in cloth?', emphasising an essential contrast between the intimate space of a bedroom and hostile space of a cell. The difference between curling snugly and being crushed into an impossible position. He withdraws from contact with emptiness. He huddles in the universal gesture of confinement, 'knees up to the chin, hand over the eyes to ward off the visible thing that never appears'.

Golding's character, however, has not quite completed the transformation to this new space of infinite, infinitely enclosed, extension. He looks towards the centre of his cell; as if pure space could have a centre, and seeks in his imagination for the object, secreted there, which is terrifying him. But the centre is empty, and he has only placed his terror there in obstinate disregard of the new and freer geometry of his existence.

Jean Genet puts it more directly, and accurately, in talking of the Mettray Reformatory in the Miracle of the Roses, he says, 'its centre was everywhere'. That is to say nowhere. Such expressions have been recognised since Nicholas of Cusa as the paradox at the core of the notion of space as pure extension.

Let us say, in short, the space of confinement is a hostile space; at once infinitely constricted and infinitely extended, present and absent, concrete and abstract, its only quality the emptying out of all qualities. A human imposition of the non-human. Something, we begin to realise, of a philosophical masterpiece. Perhaps its victims have discovered the 'horrible inside-outside that real space is'.

TIME

It is difficult to isolate the peculiar character of space without linking it to the transformation that affects, in the same moment, the sense of time. The centrality of time, as well as of space, in the organisation of our sensory impressions and in the construction of our sense of reality, has been noticed often enough by philosophers and psychologists. And as with space we commonly experience time in the subtle variety of a human, conventional system of classification.

It is again only as a concept that we can tolerate the pure duration of time. Even where we measure by the regulated death of seconds, minutes, hours, days, we cannot live through their exact passing unaffected by the varying and less precise tempos of our interests and preoccupations. No hour is of precisely the same length as its predecessor. 'Leisure time' is qualitatively distinct from 'worktime'. Boredom, distraction, concentration, excitement, grief, jealousy — any subjective 'state' — bears a particular relation to time, each distinguishing for itself its own colouring, its own distinctive melody of duration.

Not only is the immediate experience of time highly differentiated and conventionalised, longer periods are equally subject to human qualification. Our own time, biographical memory, is distinct from historical time and both from the arbitrary definition of generations. Childhood is distinguished from adolescence as well as maturity or old age, each time of life defined as well by its 'appropriate' activities and concerns.

Confined time, however, does not, any more than confined space, contain human difference. Time, like space, becomes pure, abstract, infinite, uniform.

The captive can lose all 'sense' of time almost in an instant, its uniformity does not even allow him to be bored. Victor Serge in his Men in Prison, puts it clearly. 'Minutes, hours, days slip away with terrifying insubstantiality. Months will pass away like this, and years. Life! The problem of time is everything. Nothing distinguishes one hour from the next: the minutes and hours fall slowly, tortuously. Once past they vanish into near nothingness. The present minute is infinite.'

His statement is quite complete in itself, but brief and we avoid too much that is disturbing by brevity here. Consider then, another statement, this time from Arthur Koestler's Darkness at Noon. Rubashov has just been arrested, awaiting interrogation he discovers, like Serge, the expedient of walking. 'Soon, or what he thought was soon, he felt dizzy from the motion. He looked at his watch: a quarter to twelve: he had been walking to and fro in his cell for nearly four hours on end.' Then he recalled a 'younger comrade' who 'in his second and worst year of solitary confinement, had dreamed for seven hours on end with his eyes open: in doing so he had walked twenty-eight kilometres, in a cell five paces long, and had blistered his feet without noticing it'. A little later, we are not told how long (we must become lost in time as well), he is able to reflect on how completely the transition has been effected. 'Strange, thought Rubashov, how quickly one grows used to the intense environment; he felt as if he had been breathing the air of this corridor for years, as if the stale atmosphere of all the prisons he had known had been stored away there.'

Often, however, this transition to the 'new time' on the inside itself takes a little time to be completed. Dostoevsky reports a period of initial clarity and retention of a 'normal' temporal sense. He puts this down, in fact, to the shock of new impressions. 'The first three days were certainly the most unpleasant in the whole term of imprisonment' and he can recall their every detail. 'The first few weeks, and indeed all the early part of my imprisonment, made a deep impression on my imagination. The following years, on the other hand, are all mixed up together, and leave but a confused recollection.' These later impressions merge into a generality. 'I remember life as the same – always painful, monotonous and stifling.' Dostoevsky's description is rather similar to the temporal telescoping effect achieved by Thomas Mann in his great novel The Magic Mountain. Mann treats the reader to an exceptionally detailed and sophisticated description of, among much else, the transformation of temporal experience that results from withdrawing to a luxurious sanatorium in the Swiss Alps. Hans Castorp's first day at the sanatorium takes us over a hundred pages into the novel. The narrative continues, one feels still at ease, can follow early events without difficulty. But with great subtlety the author allows this clarity to dissolve within us. Time falls away, and plays no part as a determining factor in events and seems hardly any longer even to contain them. As we go deeper into the characters isolated in their resplendent hotel we suddenly realise we have to measure the distance from the beginning in years rather than weeks or months. We have lost track of 'real time' despite following so carefully the brilliant conversation which has deluded us into thinking we have retained contact with the world of events going on below. But The Magic Mountain is a positive counter-image, a refuge from the troubled world rather than a prison. The experience of confinement more normal to such a condition of prolonged illness, is made clear enough in A. E. Ellis's distressing book The Rack.

Prisoners, patients, inmates, with apparent good sense often go to incredibly laborious lengths to 'keep track' of the passage of days. Dostoevsky tells us of prisoners who counted off the pointed stakes that made up their encircling pallisade: each one representing a day in their confinement. Genet, somewhere, mentions a similar device using the bricks of the cell wall. Dolgun in his chilling memoir Dolgun tells us how he manufactured a calendar from pieces of masticated bread dough shaped into numbers and left to dry and harden. Some know, instantly at any moment you care to ask, the exact number of days and hours before their release. Nor is it only where a fixed point of release lies in the future that such elaborate time-keeping occurs. Victor Serge describes some of the fantastic games with time into which all prisoners are drawn. 'How many steps, how many times around before the next check by the man on duty . . . Thirty-eight trips . . . Lost, lost! Right, thirty-eight. The captive comes to a halt with a great silent laugh'; one of those laughs of solitary man that the psychiatrist recognises so well. There are analogies from our own life. Pain is an obvious example. Toothache is genuinely endless, as we experience it we cannot recall the point when it began, certainly we cannot accept that it will end. But when it is over our recollection is capable of localising the whole episode within a single 'timeless' moment, almost as if it had become a spatial category so much has its quality of persistence been anaesthetised.

The reckoning of time, the fabrication of human measuring devices appears to be a remnant of life to which the confined hang on, as a lifeline. But Serge's remarks go further. It ends in a solitary and pointless gesture. And both Dostoevsky and Genet are similarly disparaging about such devices which seem to them not only 'artificial' but, more seriously, incapable of holding off one moment of the eternity which time in confinement becomes. Such manufactured accounts do not even measure off the units within the pure duration that confinement actually is. They remain no more than mental diversions, like card games, crosswords and coded messages which lose, quickly enough, whatever power of distraction they initially possess. Such methods lack the power to close off some portion of duration and domesticate its awful immeasurable persistence. Even as a diversion it fails; leading inevitably to fantasy and further dissociation. It ends by losing the victim even more completely in time. The minutest calculation serves only to hasten the ultimate annihilation of all lived time.

The point is that time on the inside can only be measured, it cannot be lived. The units into which it becomes divided have only an abstract, mathematical significance. Maria, the heroine of Mary Wollstonecraft's unfinished novel, Maria or The Wrongs of Woman, observes that 'day after day rolled away'. She seemed to be 'sailing on the vast ocean of life, without seeing any landmark to indicate the progress of time'. Such is the absence of landmarks that time seems to fill up a present endless moment, obliterating past and future in an infinitely extended present. 'And tedious as the present moment appeared' continues Maria, 'They passed in such an unvaried tenor' that she was 'surprised to find that she had already been six weeks buried alive'. Tedium and boredom are the wrong words, they belong to the living, but time in the House of the Dead does not possess even those humanly unlikeable qualities.

Many others have talked of this emptied out time. Hugh Lewin in Bandeit calls his prison in a telling phrase 'a twenty-four-hour-a-day-world'. It is not just the completeness and unalterability of the routine, but the fact that it is imposed, and even those occasional deviations from its settled plan predictable, repeated, merging with the routine itself into a void. 'Always the same,' he complains, 'the same regular interruptions.' And the sanatorium can be as rigorous in this as the prison. In The Rack, Ellis has his central character complain 'whatever the time of day it seemed as if it was always that time of day'.

The hostility of time matches the hostility of its internal space; and timeless time that has no texture is incapable of being felt. It is this time, belonging more to logic than the world of human personalities that Andrey Sinyavsky writes about with such composure. He is surprised, on his first acquaintance with the Gulag Archipelago, by the apparent youthfulness of its prisoners. 'In the labour camps', he says, 'people are literally preserved', their inmates no longer distinguishable according to the normal flow of time. 'Earth's time', he continues 'no more applies here than it does on Mars.' But this is noticeable paradoxically only after a period of 'adjusting' to its own peculiar nothingness. During his first year of confinement Sinyavsky suggests 'the forward movement of time creates the illusion that an otherwise empty existence is being filled and made meaningful'. But the feeling of a 'forward motion' did not survive the next year. There is no longer any point in talking of 'meaning'. 'The notion of eternity', he remarks, 'is an inescapable empty continuum of everlasting duration, yet passed within restricted spatial limits: this is the eternity where there is no time, only infinite confinement.' Later still these spatial limits dissolve and his senses float in a void. A world where 'all of a sudden you realise with a start that another year has passed' only to suffer in the same glimpse that announces this discovery, its loss once again, 'never being sure where we are' in time. No wonder he says 'coming out of prison is like making a posthumous appearance in the world!', or that he finds the rediscovery of time, its 'change of gear', the most difficult task of his release.

These phrases are echoed again by Soyinka. 'Time vanished. I turned to stone', he declares, like Sinyavksy metamorphosed into a cockroach. And Nadezhda Mandelstam: 'I also felt that time, as such, had come to an end', and suggests the multitude of 'confessions' extracted from victims of Stalinist prisons 'was only possible at a "moment of truth" during the madness which afflicted people when it looked as though time had stopped, the world had come to an end and everything was lost for ever'.

Time emptied of its human content lacks even the quality of duration, and is reduced to the nothingness of its space. Svidrigaylov's cry in Crime and Punishment, 'eternity in a yard of space', expresses exactly this emptiness. Life in a 'cube of air'.

Confined time, then, can be suggested in this abstract concept of 'pure' time. We cannot experience such time, that is to say it offends our language and logic to say such a thing. It remains, none the less, the simplest and most direct description of the experience of time within confinement.

Space and time operate together, they form a grid through which more normally our senses make sense of the world. But what can the senses make of eternity or infinity? Soyinka despairs; Mandelstam is more precise – 'I had lost everything, even despair'.

This, of course, is only a formula of words. We can say the confined experience a world apart, a world of abstract-concretions, where the distinctions between thought and experience dissolve and merge, where despite its being the most concrete and particular existence imaginable, there is nothing to pit against its awful abstraction. But this formula of words is merely a way of putting the matter for our world of thought, hence its perversion of logic. That is as much as can be done by direct description. If a doubt remains, a doubt that shares in the tenacity of our formal education and its dislike of paradox, it might be dispelled by looking at this man perched on his pole on Solovetsky Island. But he is dead. Try it yourself, perch on a bannister for a time. How long? Try to guess ten minutes, half an hour, three hours? Better still have someone else, without telling you, decide how long you must keep your balance. Then see if you glimpse an existence beneath despair.

CORPOREALITY

What, then, can the senses, deprived of their proper media, make of confinement? This is another way of asking what confinement does to the senses. What is characteristic in the content rather than the form of such experience. Our experience is normally centred upon the body and the body, a complex socio-psychological entity, so undergoes its own metamorphosis with this transformation of time and space.

Here the little formula used to describe the emptying out of space and time, that the confined experience these dimensions in a manner we can only think about them, requires some modification. Literally speaking it can still provide a good description, but it can become somewhat misleading. We too easily identify experience as 'concrete' and thought as 'abstract', but the corporeality of the human body confounds such a distinction. The experience we normally have of our own body is not a simple, concrete or material reality but a highly complex 'construction' of sensory images. It is only as a concept that we allow our body to be objectified as a purely material substance. It is only as an idea that the body exists as an assemblage of anatomical structures and physiological functions. Only biologists consider bodies in these terms, and then, of course, only other people's bodies. They remain fully alive to their own bodies which exist for them, as ours exist for us, in immediately present sensuous experience. The body of bones, flesh, lungs, skin, etc., belongs in the textbook, not walking the street. 'Pure' corporeality is an abstraction, distinguished from other substances through its particular type of 'reactiveness' or 'sensitivity'. Immediate sensuous experience 'subjectivises' this material substance, making it our body and, as such, the centre of our world.

Immediate sensuous experience, of course, just like our immediate apprehension of space and time, always appears more 'natural' and necessary than in fact it is. The experience of our body is subject, just as much as our apprehension of space and time, to the conventional distinctions we bring to bear upon it. Time and space are measured and enter differently into experience in different societies; so, too, does the body. Our bodies, for example, depend heavily upon the Christian Tradition, especially upon its modern ascetic imperatives and the secular 'theories' of self-control which have developed from it, which conditions sensuous experience and defines for us the meaning and function of various bodily states.

The confined body is liberated from these conventional definitions of its own experience, just as it is released from the arbitrary classification of space and time; and is left, similarly, with nothing. The confined body becomes La Mettrie's L'Homme Machine, the scientist's ideal human object. These new phenomena have to do particularly with the nature of the boundary we normally maintain between our body and the rest of the world and which in confinement is systematically undermined. Two basic ideas seem essential to its definition. The first has been explored particularly by Mary Douglas in her book Purity and Danger. There she draws attention to the anxiety which surrounds any physical movement over this boundary. Intrusions into the body and excretions from it are always regarded as liable to 'pollute', and correct ritual procedures are invoked in avoidance. Substances coming from the body are generally regarded as 'dirty' in a comprehensively moral and aesthetic sense. Innumerable taboos regulate our everyday behaviour in regard to the maintenance of our bodily boundary; and rituals of cleansing, preparation of food, elimination and physical contact are practised in all societies. These prevent the boundary of the body from becoming as physically ambiguous as might otherwise be the case, making as sharp a distinction as possible between what material constitutes our body and what does not.

Norman O. Brown, however, has shown in his Love's Body that this boundary as an image is constructed and continually reconstructed from the material that passes through it. Relying heavily on pyschoanalytical literature he points out the body is immediately present to us as a kind of sediment of 'introjections' and 'projections'; that is, with the symbolic content of our relationship with other people. this results in a shifting boundary, one that cannot be finalised or defined precisely because love's body can never localise its own needs within itself, nor gratify itself without venturing into the realm beyond its apparent physical limits. Its precise individuality and determination is a construction which depends upon continuous symbolic movements.

The body, then, plays a central part in our sense of individuality, and, more surprisingly perhaps, becomes individualised through a kind of symbolic dissolution of its own distinctiveness. It is a boundary that exists only by virtue of those functions that transcend it. The quality, we have already seen, of the boundary of confinement is its impenetrability which leads in consequence (we are tempted to say by 'logical' necessity) to its ultimate disappearance. It becomes, instead, the rim of existence, the outer limit, rather than a division within, experience.

Confinement, true to its logic of inversion and reversal, reduces the body to a merely physical substance by insisting, on the one hand, upon its symbolic isolation and, on the other, by ignoring its physical identity. This reversal empties the body of its human qualities.

The descriptions we have of the body as it enters confinement, however, always begin with a 'filling up' rather than 'emptying out'. This is meant quite literally: Casanova tells us, 'I had been in this hell-on-earth for fifteen days without any secretion from the bowels.' The body is overwhelmed with the power of its own needs and the intensity with which its senses are stimulated. The body becomes immediately present, cannot be forgotten or taken for granted. The first experience of confinement is of some urgent bodily need; a need which it is no longer in your power to satisfy.

The senses become stimulated in uncontrolled and unwanted ways, and undergo in the process a complete reorganisation. Where sight tends to dominate our sensory organisation and provides us with our most compelling sense of reality, in confinement the other senses come into a new prominence.

The smell of confinement, for example, is overwhelming and unforgettable. It is all-pervasive and, like its space and time, hostile. We have all walked into a hospital and been sickened by the smell; it becomes much worse than that. The smell was the first thing Edward Buca noticed about his prison cell, the odour of the barrel half-full of urine nearly choked him. Still he tried to overcome it: 'I didn't pay much attention to it', he claims, though he could hardly ignore it and admits, 'but I should have . . . it was to be part of my life for the next fourteen years'. And throughout his book Vorkuta Buca rightly places the *parasha* at the centre of his world; it ranks with the cockroaches that infested their slightly warmed wooden hut, and the tents in Arctic conditions to which they were driven finally as a refuge from the cockroaches, as symbols of an alien way of life. Buca is not alone; Marchenko talks of the 'prisoners' inseparable companion, the 'sloptank', and again of the 'inevitable sloptank by the door: without this object prison wouldn't be prison'. A judgment not restricted to the Russian labour camps. The solitary cells at San Quentin, we can learn from some of the too brief letters collected by Eve Pell, were adorned with human excrement. Everywhere the morning ritual of 'slopping out' is the most important in the daily routine. There is no relief from the smell: the odour of rotting vegetation being cooked, mingles with other decaying excrescences and gives rise to a composite sickly-stale atmosphere. Marchenko, not surprisingly, 'went cold at the thought of having to eat and sleep there'. And Hugh Lewin recalls, 'Above all, I can still smell — still feel almost — the overwhelming smell of Local . . . the sweet sick smell of shit'. He had no need to add the cautious 'almost', for the prison smell is quite palpable; his senses intertwine, he gains a privileged access to that kinesthetic borderland whose possession, by young children and great artists, we so greatly envy.

The noise, often, is as bad. 'We seem fated to

live amid noise and shouting', observes Andrey Sinyavsky. And George Jackson, though he is generous enough to attempt its 'explanation', complains bitterly of the incessant din of prison. His fellow prisoners 'have no past, no future, no goal other than the next meal. They're afraid, confused and confounded by a world they know that they did not make, that they feel they cannot change, so they make these loud noises so they won't hear what their mind is telling them.' Later he plugged his ears and made sure he remained locked in his solitary cell.

Hysterical laughter, shouting, swearing, sounds of fighting and screams form the chorus of the captive's life, or what remains of his life: Sinyavsky's chorus out of which his own voice emerges still with something, amazingly, of its own quality, and out of which George Jackson's letter, 'written in bedlam', preserve, cocoon-like, his individuality. Bedlam, indeed, is the place of confinement before all others and is recognised by its noise; raucous, loud, incomprehensible. The confined live amidst this 'horrid noise' that Mary Wollstonecraft's Maria could not tolerate, 'the dismal shrieks of demoniac rage . . . the uproar of the passions', she complains. And it is still the same for Hugh Lewin, complaining of the always shouted orders, the always slammed doors. Dostoevsky cries out, 'Oh, what a Babel this place is!'

The noise and smell overwhelm, by their hostile, meaningless intensity. There is nothing in them upon which the senses can seize and fashion into meaningful signs, into the substance, in other words, of a human world. These sensations refer to nothing, they are disembodied, the smell is a smell of decay, of decay in general, of universal putrefaction that inhabits the whole of confinement's undifferentiated space. The noise similarly belongs to no one, has no meaning, carries within it no weight of purpose or intention.

The same can be said, horrifying though it is to say so, of touch or, if we want to be more agreeable, of tactile stimulation in general. Confinement hurts; it is physically painful for a long time. Arthur Koestler provides two very powerful images of this in his Darkness at Noon. Rubashov, we must not forget, suffered throughout his imprisonment from toothache. As if that was not sufficient, to prepare himself for the 'physical means' that might be used against him he stubbed out a cigarette on the back of his hand, believing that it is only the unknown limit of pain that might puncture his will to resist. To a mind still conditioned by its own freedom such an 'action' seems to be almost rational, almost comprehensible; a move in a game of terror, a device to keep one jump ahead of the enemy. But if instead you give way to the 'squeamishness' that cold thought tries to transcend, then you see it as a move that can only lead further into confinement. The 'cunning of confinement' is always to use the captive's resistance against himself. Rubashov's self-mutilation is just one of the manoeuvres through which confinement gains a hold, perverts normal logic and reverses the normal order of things. It is the same 'logic' discovered in the intricate measuring of time and space; a mechanism of resistance that serves only to lead the victim deeper into the empty centre of confinement.

The initial physical assault has been mentioned by many of its survivors. The transit camp, the interrogation cell, the transport train have, in the writings of Solzhenitsyn in particular, gained a palpable reality for those of us thankfully spared their closer acquaintance. Even in less barbarous forms, the stripping, prodding, searching is universal. Allowed to shiver, flesh turning blue with cold, cramped in one position, some part of the body aching and sore. Each writer reports his own version.

Dostoevsky devotes a good deal of attention to the physical punishment that formed so large a part of prison life in his time. Interestingly enough the other physical conditions of his confinement appear almost shamelessly lenient compared to the genius of more modern practice. Solzhenitsyn has exhaustively catalogued the spectacular progress in hardship and physical suffering in the second volume of his *Gulag Archipelago*. Superior food, better clothing, protection against the elements, even a sense of freedom, are characteristic of *The House of the Dead* compared to its sequel. The 'hard labour' of those days is a joke compared to Vorkuta, or Kolyma or Mordavia. Yet Solzhenitsyn avoids the picture of some poor wretch being tied to a rifle-butt and dragged slowly down an avenue of soldiers armed with flexible green rods: the prisoner might be condemned to two, three, even five hundred strokes; a thousand was not unknown. Not a few died, despite the presence of the doctor (blessed doctor) to ensure the proceedings stopped short of this final release. Physical horror in one form or another is part of the world of confinement. And not just in the prison or labour camp the 'treatment' for T.B. so vividly described by Ellis in *The Rack* is not the least distressing item of its ample pornography.

Dostoevsky, however, is more bewildered by the chains and shackles than by the rods, which he insists (wrongly) on trying to comprehend as a 'rational' punishment. The chains, for him, present the bleak face of confinement face-on. He was horrified to see 'men fastened to the wall at the bedside by a chain about two yards long'. And even more horrified by the sight of an old, withered dying prisoner still shackled though his wrists and ankles had become so skinny they might easily, had their remaining strength not been entirely drained away, have slipped their hold. He cannot comprehend such 'useless precautions', which were not removed until the old man expired.

Both the rods and the chains, however, belong to confinement itself rather than to any 'rational' device within it; both form part of that physical assault in which confinement introduced itself to its victim. Disordered physical sensation is never absent and threatens at every moment to engulf the body in some unbearable torment. This pain is often difficult to localise, shifts elusively and refuses 'treatment'. This too is meaningless; like sound and smell reduced to pure, disorganised intensity. Wole Soyinka, Alexander Dolgun, Anatoly Marchenko, Edward Buca, George Jackson, Casanova, Hugh Lewin, Jimmy Boyle – the list is endless – continually seek relief from, at best the annoyance and worst the intolerable pain, that made their bodies continually present to them in a new, horrifying way.

It would be quite misleading, then, to construe those ingeniously cruel experiments in 'sensory deprivation' as analogies of confinement. The very reverse is as plausible. The confined cannot escape for one moment the unwanted, painful stimulation of the senses.

Confinement, in beginning with such an intense sensory assault, succeeds in establishing its presence, depersonalising the body it assaults and transforming it into a simple mechanical contrivance. The victim discovers in this initial attack that his senses have been deprived of any responsiveness to his will, and that his bodily needs and functions, likewise, must answer to imperatives beyond his own control. The body becomes 'objectivised', a thing which, along with every other object of confinement, confronts its victim as an obstacle. Your body is no longer your own and refuses to submit to your own inclinations or wishes.

The confined are deprived from that elementary

care of the body to which we all, unconsciously, devote so much time. Anatoly Marchenko complains again and again of being denied, or outrageously hurried over, care of his body. You cannot clean your teeth, at least never properly, or wash, or relieve yourself. A tiny morsel of soap and one issue of water to last an entire day-and-night – for everything. And the perpetual 'Hurry, hurry; that's enough, you're not at home now, back to your cell'. And George Jackson makes a similar observation, 'each morning if I can find or beg a piece of soap I wash myself. This is indeed counted as good fortune' – of the same order, one might conjecture, as Ivan Denisovich's second bowl of porridge. And Osip Mandelstam realised his cell-mate was, in fact, a stool-pigeon because his finger nails were clean. There is no way of escaping the filth, or the lice that so loved Casanova and were still there for Edward Buca and his friends to squeeze so precisely between the dirty nails of their thumb and forefinger. The bathhouse is no help – a trickle of barely warm water, previously used for cooking and washing dishes. Then stand in the freezing cold for the count to be taken again. At Vorkuta some failed to survive their first 'bath'.

And Rubashov's toothache, that perfectly describes the confined body. We know about toothache, no matter how bad it may become we realize it will become even worse (a more profound insight than his gesture of burning his hand to learn how best to 'resist'). Rubashov lacks the strength to allow the doctor to extract the rotting fragment in his gum. It would take thirty minutes and there was no anaesthetic. It is not a question of strength, no one could give himself to such an operation in confinement. This objective lump the body becomes is like a toothache. Never leaving you alone, never properly part of yourselves even though it brings such anguish; even in blessed moments of partial relief you sit in dread of the inevitable resumption of the torment. In confinement your body is against you. Ellis describes the feelings of his central character in just the terms we have chosen: 'His existence was purely physical; an agglomeration of aching, burning flesh, he felt himself to be no more than the sum of its functions and sensations'.

We can seek some relief in a brief formula. The body in confinement is defined as the meeting place of two opposed movements. Of an over-stimulation of the sense from the outside and of unfulfilled needs from the inside. Such a body knows properly speaking neither appetite nor satisfaction nor desire but only pain and discomfort. This is just another way of saying the body has become an assemblage of sensitised parts and organs, reduced to its form as pure corporeal substance.

The measure of this, while it is still in its 'early stage', is glimpsed by Sinyavsky when he says 'My cares are simple, my pleasures unsophisticated: yesterday for instance, I cut my toe-nails'. Soon such simple pleasures, themselves signs of the purely physical prominence of the body, were a faint, troublesome memory of happier times.

The body becomes burdensome. It is left to get dirty, denied food, surrounded by its own smell, reduced to a simple physical presence. Its properties are not part of our bodies, but physical properties of a hitherto unknown object. Wole Soyinka noted, 'My body becomes of new absorbing interest to me, a new occupation to while away the hours. I have not till now taken much notice of the physical fact of the body, only of its sensations. Now it has become a strange terrain where flakes come off every part merely by rubbing.' An object apparently with a structure and form of which we know nothing.

The confined body is experienced, then, as a pure corporeal object, not as a living body. It is experienced directly in a manner that can be described as the way in which we think about the body. This is achieved through a 'filling-up' of the body with unwanted stimulation, engulfing it in sensations from without and the pangs of unfulfilled needs from within. It appears from this as if the body, though becoming a burdensome object, nevertheless maintains a certain, though painful, identity. It emerges at the meeting-point, so to speak, of those two streams of sensation, and the surface of the body, its boundary, might be defined in this conjunction. However, the reversal of confinement is more complete than to allow such physical identity a more than imaginary presence.

First of all the ritual demarcation of the boundary is abolished. There are many signs of this. Dirt is the main one. Filfth adheres to the skin and is never removed, attaching the physical surroundings to the body, extending it over the boundary we try to insist upon. Being forced to stay within sight and smell of the body's wastes abolishes the boundary in the opposite direction, preventing the complete separation from what once constituted part of the body. And not just part of your own body. Victor

Serge tells us that often he could not bring himself to take his time in the exercise yard. The yard became covered in cigarette ends and spit. 'I have often resisted the temptation of those twenty minutes of fresh air, so great was the nervous repulsion I felt for that "slimy mucous".' It becomes difficult to localise sensations; they begin to extend themselves into the void that surrounds and penetrates the inmate. Then other bodies become identical; they appear the same, the same clothes, the same dispirited expressions, the same hunger, the same stoop and shuffling walk, you talk to yourself and don't realise it, you think other people's voices are your own.

If the physical boundary that we maintain so conscientiously is broken down, the one that we symbolically cross and re-cross, the social dimension of our identity, becomes impervious to our own desire, locking us, psychologically, inside ourselves. That shifting line marked out by progressive 'incorporation' and 'projection' becomes a rigid opaque shell. This boundary is never established within confinement because the processes through which it is defined — free symbolic exchange with other people — is excluded. This process of emotional identification of the body belongs only to the living and has been rigorously excluded from The House of the Dead.

Confinement begins by imposing the 'sensitised' body upon this living body. The body of pure corporeality. But as we go deeper into nothingness the familiar 'emptying-out' of human qualities reasserts itself. The body becomes not simply an object, but a dead object, a mechanical contrivance rather than a sensitive substance.

Marchenko tells us that he 'went cold' at the sight and smell of his cell, the thought of eating and sleeping there apalled him. But eating and sleeping proved more powerful than the memory of conventional behaviour and after a relatively short time he admits, 'I could greedily swallow my sprat in the midst of blood and vomit and it seemed to me there was nothing in the world tastier than that sprat of mine'. And once these things become possible the taste itself soon loses all distinctiveness. Soyinka tells us that food became for him 'a mere chore. I permit it no taste, no pleasure or disgust, no contact physical or sensual, neither intimacy with my body nor recognition by the mind.' And this soon applied to Marchenko as well; once disgust is overcome, pleasure cannot sustain itself. We must be careful again of the 'I permit' that Soyinka claims for himself. It may appear to be a deliberate strategy on his part to outwit confinement, to retain some hold upon himself and preserve some corner of the world with which to exercise his own will, or over which he could retain some measure of control. But what control. To talk to nothing. The displaced cunning of confinement has trapped him and he acts upon himself destructively, incessantly, in accord with the confinement's own imperative. In confinement all choices are choices for confinement; all choices the wrong choice. To actively resist or passively submit are both part of the same negative dialectic of self-destruction.

The most dramatic 'symptom' of this 'desensitising' of the body is the self-mutilation to which Marchenko in particular has drawn his attention. He introduced this gruesome aspect of confinement with the almost casual sentence, 'When a con slits his veins, or swallows barbed wire, or sprinkles ground glass in his eyes, his cell mates don't usually intervene'. Still a newcomer, Marchenko, on first witnessing such actions, was both horrified and puzzled. At first he thought it might be a desparate means of gaining some temporary respite from forced labour. But this is hardly credible as Marchenko points out it involves a too difficult calculation. To inflict an injury sufficient to gain a 'rest' in hospital means coming very close to death. Otherwise you will be forced to carry on working, despite being unable to fulfill the norms. Your rations will, in consequence, be reduced, you will be further weakened and almost certainly die within a short time. Even if the wound is serious enough to avoid forced labour you might not receive medical attention. Solzhenitsyn even tells us of places where the 'punishment' for self-inflicted wounds is a period in solitary, at the end of which the dead body is dragged out and buried. Even if there is medical attention you will be forced back to work too quickly; weakened, unable to meet the norms and you have lost again. The ingenuity of, for example, Alexander Dolgun who was able to avoid being transported to a camp with a particularly bad reputation among prisoners, by infecting his arm, seems rare. He received in fact 'expert' help from a doctor friend.

Self-mutilation can hardly be 'explained' in such terms. It constitutes, however, a 'symbolic wound' and might even be viewed as the final remnant of meaning left in confinement before even its possibility is denied its victims.

Tattoos are the most common form of such mutilation. No easy matter with only a sharpened rusty nail, urine and melted rubber for equipment. Tattoos are most frequently in the form of political slogans. Marchenko mentions 'Khruschev's slaves' and 'Slave of the USSR' as popular, inscribed always on the forehead. Not, however, for long. They were removed - surgically - simply sliced away and the edges of the skin sewn together. This, of course, stretched the skin and left a nasty scar. Incredibly many cons repeated the trick - more than once. Marchenko tells us of a prisoner who after three 'operations' to remove tattoos had the skin so tightly stretched he could no longer close his eyes. 'We called him "the stare"', he concludes without comment.

More common even than those were operations to remove 'objects' that had been swallowed. Again, unbelievably some cons had been opened two or even three times to have knives, spoons, lumps of glass, nails and any other solid object removed.

Nor is that all. One fellow, Scherbakov, tattooed his ear with the words 'a gift to the 22nd Congress of the CPSU' then cut it off and hurled it in the faces of the guards.

Still there is more. Marchenko tells us, again in his calm matter-of-fact way, about Sergei K. Sergei came by a piece of wire. He manufactured a sharpened hook from it and attached it to home-made twine. He had also acquired a couple of nails. He hammered the smaller nail into the flap on the cell door and tied the twine with the hook to the nail. Sergei undressed, sat on a bench at the table and swallowed his hook. If the warders came in they would drag him across the cell floor like a hooked fish. Then he took the longer nail and hammered it through his scrotum to the bench on which he was seated.

What is the meaning of such disfigurement? this is a question we can hardly avoid, despite warning against such academic curiosity. Marchenko, in fact, concurs in this warning - 'I too caught myself thinking', he confesses, 'my God, if only I could do something - hurl a piece of my body into the face of my torturers! Why? At such moments the question doesn't arise.' Indeed it would not; it is only from this safe side of the divide that such questions can arise.

When the body becomes a burden there is a sense in which it makes sense to do things to it: to cast lumps of it aside, turn it into something else over

which you can still exercise some control: or force
into it bits of dead matter or sharp instruments
to awaken its deadened interior and accomplish
some ultimate 'incorporation'. The mad, of course,
have a history of such self-mutilation; ironically,
one of the 'rational arguments' adduced to justify
their confinement. Still, we need not suppose it
has a single meaning. We can simply say it is a
characteristic of an intensified condition of confinement.
there may be self-mutilation which is the last stage
of conscious revolt against confinement. Still to
dispose of the body as one wishes, to do something
to it which surpasses even your captors' torments.
There may also be the form which is deep in unconscious
acceptance of the way of confinement. The body
once it has become completely desensitised is available
for 'experiments'. We can leave bits of it about
or take foreign objects into it because it has ceased
to have any distinctive existence, any sense of
itself. It is only physical and the necessity of extending
ourselves psychologically in space and time is taken
up into an insane, physical allegory. The body
becomes indistinguishable from other objects; and
its mutilation might be regarded as a desperate
effort to create an object within an objectless world.
But time and space are void and the body a dead
object, assimilated to other objects, part of an
undifferentiated substance out of which nothing can
be made to emerge.

Whether those form two independent 'types' of
self-mutilation is hardly important. The first leads,
by the cunning of confinement, to the second, as
a kind of practice for its 'emptier' form, in which
life is almost completely extinguished, the struggle
more attenuated, more desperate; and instinctive
flicker before it is extinguished for ever. Self-
mutilation is an act of withdrawal, whether defiant
or uncomprehending; a sign of isolation; carved
on this other impersonal body with which the captive
is afflicted. In the inverted world of confinement
it is its own peculiar ceremony of initiation. Performed,
despite resistance upon the victim by the victim
itself and marking the end of his apprenticeship,
his entry completely into its perverse world, the
joining of his substance with the unusual substance
of confinement, a physical union accomplished by
the gradual weakening and final 'transcendence'
of his individuality, the annihilation of his personality.

It is this alienation of the body which presents
the victim with the sternest face of confinement.
It is in this the real torment of confinement first

takes hold, and leads the victim by its own twisted logic towards self-destruction. The only 'solution' to the burden of raw sensation, intensified beyond endurance, is to go deeper into confinement and seek out its calm, untroubled, anaesthetised centre.

METAMORPHOSIS

Soyinka has remarked that 'The act of being a prisoner is in itself not even a process of, but an instant, metamorphosis.' This does not contradict the previous descriptions which refer to the 'realisation' of this metamorphosis. Soyinka's remark is quite correct and reinforces the undifferentiated nature of this transformation. We can isolate space, time and corporeality for 'analytical' purposes, but all the illustrations that have been cited under any one of these headings could be used, just as well, under any of the other two. In confinement, and for once it does not negate the living world in this, space, time and corporeality coalesce in immediate experience which refers to its own total world and not to any of its 'individuated dimensions'. Separated from one another they may not appear to alter in any fundamental way this world of experience; but when they have all been transformed, and transformed in their relationships to one another, then this world can no longer be sustained and the abyss of confinement is opened up within the subject.

Franz Kafka has succeeded more completely than any other writer in conveying a sense of the completeness of this transformation. His brilliant story Metamorphosis remains the purest, most compelling evocation of the world of confinement. He goes further than Sinyavsky in abandoning a 'realistic' mode of presentation, but creates in the reader an overwhelming sense of otherness which we have seen is the hallmark of confinement. His fantasy, in fact, trusts the reader's own psychological powers and plays on them for its effect. Yet there is nothing vague about his, and our, intuition – his story is written with precise physical detail. Its images are perfectly concrete, have the quality of being felt. In this Kafka has accomplished a seemingly impossible task. He is faithful to the peculiar, emptied-out subjectivity of the world of confinement, yet remains all too comprehensible to us. His story should be swallowed up in madness, but although its effect is mysterious it grips us as powerfully as confinement grips its victim. We know it is a fantasy yet cannot evade the compulsion that seems to lie within it. It has an oppressive effect that weighs on our memory. We notice that same, inexplicable physical response that followed on reading George Jackson's letter. We cannot 'discharge' its horror by 'explaining' it away. He has created a physical world so precise, so tactile, that it should be devoid of all meaning.

He succeeds nonetheless in this double impossibility. He evokes within us the alien presence of confinement and 'projects' us outwards, into an impossibly concrete physical reality. Kafka has discovered for us the human story of confinement and succeeds in matching the form and content of his work; and in its human subject matter, as in everything else, confinement proves to be a perverse inversion of normal life, its metamorphosis.

Kafka announces the presence of this other world with dramatic directness, in the instant metamorphosis which Soyinka mentions. 'As Gregor Samsa awoke one morning from uneasy dreams', he begins, 'he found himself transformed in his bed into a gigantic insect.' This takes us to the heart of the matter at once. He awoke to his new, alien, horrifying body. Not only that but 'he found himself transformed', not just 'was transformed', or 'thought himself transformed', but 'found himself transformed'. This locates the world of confinement directly in experience, which he will describe, rather than an 'objective' circumstance which he might analyse or explain. Nor does he mention any particular insect, indeed it is not a 'natural' insect at all but the insect Gregor Samsa would be if he were an insect and not a person. It is a 'gigantic', oversize, impossible insect. A universal horror. We might imagine it to be a huge cockroach. 'He was lying on his hard, as it were armour-plated back and when he lifted his head a little he could see his dome-like belly divided into stiff arched segments.' Such insects belong in the House of the Dead. Perhaps Sinyavsky was thinking of Kafka's story when he said 'I am a cockroach'. And it was cockroaches that tormented prisoners in San Quentin, as well as the lost souls of Vorkuta. All but one, alas, who writes fondly (in one of Eve Pell's collection) of his 'pet' cockroach – a possibility more chilling than having to kill whole armies of them with naked feet.

This powerful image of confinement creates a sensation of dreadful physical constriction. The armour-plated back and stiff, segmented belly perfectly reduce Gregor to a state of physical helplessness, almost, at first, to a state of immobility. This new body is not one for which he would have wished; it has been created for him, and impressed upon him in an unpredictable moment. It is just there, it does not belong to him, it is not even a human body but an insect's. A lower scuttling form of life; the kind that excites those passions among children for experimentation with penknife and matches. There is in its debasement something to arouse our most unacknowledged negativism and cruelty.

Gregor's new body is impossible to control. After waking he could not so much as turn over in bed and go back to sleep; the sleep in which he might recover his true form. It was not just his lack of strength in relation to his new physical structure. The new structure itself was quite strange to him. 'He saw no way of bringing any order into this arbitrary confusion.' It is only gradually that he is able to acquaint himself with the rules that seem to govern his new physiognomy.

This is not, either, the insensitive body, as we might imagine fitting to such a low level of life. Later, when the reaction of his family begins to mount in the intensity of its bewilderment and anger, his father throws an apple which breaks through Gregor's hard shell and lodges in the softer substance of his back. It stays there until it rots, causing him dreadful pain. No one, of course, is concerned to remove it. Nor, for that matter, to wash him now that he cannot do so for himself. The apple, lodged in his back, has the same kind of decisiveness as Rubashov's toothache. It is impossible to conceive of confinement without this persistent bodily distress.

The transformation is total. It does not stop with a transmuted body. Thus, though Gregor remains lucid to himself he cannot any longer make sense to anyone else. It is as a privileged reader that we, unknown to Gregor, share in his lucidity. To his family, and to his superior who calls at the house to escort him to work, his existence remains opaque. When Gregor tries to speak to them to 'reason' with them (a wonderfully ironic situation) he cannot make them understand. His inward clarity becomes perverted in some way. 'The words he uttered were no longer understandable, apparently, although they seemed clear enough to him, even clearer than before, perhaps because his ear had grown accustomed to the sound of them.'

His family cannot become used to his new appearance. Even after a month Gregor has to hide himself away when anyone enters his room. A curtain has been provided for this purpose. Not that many do visit

THE APPEARANCE OF NOTHING 45

his room, which remains locked most of the time. His sister was his only real visitor: like Lawrence visiting Casanova once a day with food. The food, of course, was no longer the same as that consumed by the other members of the family. He, less fortunate than Casanova, had to make do with their left-overs.

His room, to which he is permanently confined, became increasingly more cell-like. He noticed from the beginning that it seemed 'rather too small'. Then his mother and sister decide to empty it of furniture; ostensibly to allow him more room to move about (there is never any shortage of such good excuses to advance confinement's hold over its victim). His mother, however, has a momentary doubt: 'Doesn't it look as if we were showing him,' she wonders aloud, 'by taking away his furniture, that we have given up hope of his ever getting better and are just leaving him coldly to himself?' Gregor agrees; and the emptying of his intimate space was too much to bear; he rushed from his hiding place to frighten them off. But he could not prevent a more fundamental re-orientation in space. He finds that he can crawl up the walls, or across the ceiling; normal spatial distinctions have lost all meaning.

These formal elements do not, however, stand on their own. They are given a 'human' content by Kafka. At first sight this seems to complicate matters in introducing an additional theme to his story. This second theme could be described as a study in family relationships, and might be termed a reversal of the Oedipal situation.

Prior to his metamorphosis, we are given to understand, Gregor's parents and sister depended heavily upon his efforts as a breadwinner. In fact they took these efforts for granted and lost all initiative in worldly matters. His sudden transfiguration into an insect appears at first to be a disaster in more ways than one. After the shock of his appearance comes the shock of his loss, which necessitated a complete alteration in their domestic arrangements. Gregor's sister and mother are forced to take up the responsibilities of looking after the house and cooking all the meals. (They were afraid Gregor could not be concealed from the domestic 'help'.) His father, significantly, had to turn back to his failed business ventures, the reason, in the first instance, for Gregor assuming the responsibilities of the head of the household. Gregor heard his father shuffling through his old business papers and the sound contained 'the first cheerful information Gregor had heard since his imprisonment' (Kafka openly calls it 'imprisonment' now). The sound signifying as it does the beginning of his father's rehabilitation.

It is in his father's attitude that we first begin to suspect there is more than shock, or bewilderment, or annoyance at Gregor's metamorphosis. His mother and sister retain some sympathy for Gregor, but his father cannot come to terms with it. It was his father who first drove the gigantic insect back into its cage-like room 'hissing and crying "shoo" like a savage'. It was his father who hurled the apple that was left to rot in Gregor's back. And it was his father who finally realised they had to leave Gregor, or whatever the thing was in Gregor's room, alone to die.

Gregor co-operates in everything, his only thought is to save his family embarrassment and difficulty. He maintains a 'childlike' credulity and innocence in his wish to 'exercise patience and the utmost consideration, help the family to bear the inconvenience he was bound to cause in his present condition'.

Gregor's metamorphosis is also the metamorphosis within these domestic relations. At first it appears as an inexplicable accident of some kind to which the family must come to terms, only later do we realise it is an opportunity through which the father can regain his rightful place as the head of the household. Finally we see it is the means by which his father has freed himself from the torpor and lethargy of his dependence on his son. Kafka, in other words, has reversed the roles within the Oedipal struggle which Freud had unearthed as the basis of psychological development. In Freud's view the son, dependent firstly on his mother, forms a necessary emotional attachment to her. He becomes sexually jealous of his father and, symbolically and mythically, must kill him in order to release himself from the dependence of his earlier years. In Kafka's story the father has become dependent on the son and is jealous of his wife's and daughter's affection for him. To overcome his resentment and re-establish his own identity he has to destroy Gregor. The father is entirely successful in this. The whole situation appears to be neatly resolved in the death of Gregor. The family set off for a new life in a new town. Their spirit of solidarity and intimacy rekindled. They are optimistic, confident of finding a happy and deservedly fulfilling future. The parents are turning their attention to finding some suitable man for their daughter. 'And it was like a confirmation of their new dreams and excellent intentions that at the end of their journey their daughter sprang to her feet first and stretched her young body.'

It is not simply that they are 'recovering' from the unfortunate demise of their son; they are being released from what seems to have been his hold over them. They do not even need to forget their ordeal, it was as if he had never been born, never existed at all. This feeling evoked in the final passages of the story is important. They have not just killed Gregor, nor allowed him to wither away, they have annihilated his existence. Gregor dies not at the end of his life, but at the close of his confinement, which is a different matter. It is this which allows his family to establish a position and set of relationships which take no account of him, not even of his memory. They have overcome his existence entirely, and rid themselves of his participation in their own lives. In being thrust into confinement Gregor is being thrust back in time as well. He becomes increasingly childlike, trusting and naive, physically dependent, and loses the power of speech. His 'regression' deepens as the intensity of his father's hostility mounts. He is reduced to the status of an unwanted infant, then, miraculously, one step beyond that to the nothingness that was there before he was born. It is not his death, but a kind of regression out of life that we witness.

The intense power and remarkable economy of Kafka's story derives from the condensation of these themes in the image of metamorphosis. The theme of confinement and the psychological content of domestic conflict are explored through the single basic transformation of Gregor into an insect. The only way the father can reassert his identity is by engineering a state of affairs in which Gregor had never been born. The only way to do this is by confining him and allowing the nothingness of confinement to dissolve his existence. One is reminded of the thrilling official formula in Mandelstam's case, 'isolate but preserve'. Yes, you have to take care to 'preserve' the victim who would otherwise wither away completely.

Metamorphosis is as perfectly condensed as a good dream and illuminates every aspect of an alien existence. Kafka does not explain the metamorphosis. He begins with it, he looks at it; he is never curious as to its cause, nor, interestingly, are the members of his family. It remains inexplicable because from Gregor's point of view, a point of view that takes place wholly on the inside, it is not an act of any kind. It is deprived of all intention or will, and forces itself upon him as a kind of brute condition, an alien power. Even if such an alien power turned, ultimately, on some deeply recessed mechanism within himself, this will remain hidden and could never be discovered, by him at least; and no 'explanation' could relieve the intensity of the world it creates for its victim.

Kafka has recapitulated for us the description of confinement. He begins with the transformation of the body, then elaborates the framework of space and time that surrounds this new existence. There is no necessity in an ordering of this description, any point is as good a starting point as any other. It is a synthesis, so that any description tends to bring about an artificial decomposition.

Confinement is the imposition of an absolute. Its boundary is imperceptible, puts itself around the edge of existence and denies the possibility of a world beyond. The impenetrability of the division between confinement and life, its absoluteness, is intolerant of any other division within its world. It progressively sucks out the substance of human attributes and qualities. Such qualities are always recognised by their conventional nature, their participation in and expression of a human culture. Confinement reduces such distinctions to nothing. Its space becomes an infinitely pure extension; its time the pure duration of eternity; its corporeality pure physical substance. Confinement imposes abstract categories as real substances. In this sense it is a 'concretion'. The extensions of space and time which exist for us as the emptiness which we fill up with our actions become, ultimately, transformed by it into the extension of physical substance, a continuous substratum whose perfect physicality, its absolute condensation of matter, is a something that we cannot experience. It is the experience of nothing.

Kafka, however, has described this impossible experience for us. He has given it, in addition, a human meaning. This is important because the 'literature of confinement' becomes more diverse and fragmented at this point. The unity which we have so far maintained, the ease of referring to any of its major or minor works to provide some descriptive detail gives way to diverse interpretations of its meaning. In particular the fate of the 'self' in confinement has become a matter of dispute.

3 Self-Destruction

What happens to the 'self' in Confinement?
The 'framework' of experience allowed within confinement could be described in Andrey Sinyavsky's observation that 'A person in prison corresponds most closely to the concept of man'. Our experience however is only contained within such a framework, and should not be mistaken for the framework itself. The centre of our world is the self rather than the body. It is difficult, of course, to separate the two; the body/self constitutes for us (just as space and time do as its precondition) an indissoluble unity that remains the primary psychological reality.

Many writers express, in their different idioms, the dissolution of this unity that confinement brings about. A fatal separation between self and body occurs; either with dramatic suddenness through intense 'physical means', or more insidiously through the gradual falsification of our normal assumptions about reality. A wedge is driven through our natural selfhood. The body, in becoming purely physical substance, can no longer 'house' that psychological reality we recognise as ourselves, our own individuality and identity. The nature of the self which has been thus dissolved is subject to opposing judgments.

Eldridge Cleaver, for example, in his Soul on Ice, declares, not surprisingly, 'It is very easy for someone in prison to lose his sense of self'. Soyinka concurs, 'I believe I have even annihilated my being as I have the environment – a vague floating feeling is all that remains'. Or Nadezhda Mandelstam: 'Having entered a realm of non-being, I had lost the sense of death'. There is nothing left but to lie, half-curled, face to the wall, or huddle like Golding's captive 'knees up to the chin, hand over the eyes to ward off the visible thing that never appears'.

Against such testimony we can place other, more defiant, statements. Sinyavsky, normally so reliable, for example, says 'Driven into a cage the mind is forced to break out into the wider open spaces of the universe through the back door'. Finding a sense of freedom, still, despite his being 'forced' to seek such a fantastic liberty. And soon after

49

his imprisonment he can say, with a certainty we feel draining away in the succeeding pages. 'We are not outcasts or prisoners, but reservoirs. Not men, but deep pools of meaning.' Or, in another metaphor, 'We melt away in sleep and, free of all burdens, easily swim over to the other shore'. The insistence on an inner sense of freedom of the self never really deserts him, despite the hardship, illness, constraint; despite, in other words, being in confinement. Nor is Sinyavsky alone in this. Genet proclaims that only in a cell do you become 'master of time and of your own thinking'.

The self both expands and retreats. It begins by receding inwards more deeply into its body and, when there is finally no niche allowed it there, is driven out to find that it has been freed at last from the physical constraint of its normal existence. Is it conceivable that confinement in some way allows us the freedom to transcend our bodies and realise at last a spiritual existence more fitting to our real, purely human, nature? Free at last to form 'authentic' relationships with other selves similarly untrammelled?

This would be an odd result. Yet there is a hint of this in Solzhenitsyn's First Circle. One wonders if, in Mavrino, the prisoners have not played a great trick on the world from which they have been excluded: creating in their confined state a community of equal, equally free, spirits in imitation of the Ancients' wisdom. And Golding ultimately rescues his hero left there huddling 'knees up to chin' in total darkness. 'Was loss of freedom,' he asks pointedly, 'the price exacted, a necessary preliminary to the new mode of being?'

The notion is highly attractive. It gives to human nature an incorruptible, indestructible core. That the self cannot be destroyed in the way in which the body can be reduced to simple substance. In his notorious novel Justine, de Sade has one of his characters argue that 'In reality, man does not have the capacity to destroy; he has, at best, the power to alter the form of a thing'.

Yet this seems contradicted by the annihilation of Gregor Samsa in Metamorphosis. The question, clearly, is crucial and made the more difficult because the 'literature of confinement' appears to confirm in its very existence, an inextinguishable spiritual freedom. These works in themselves, expansive, original, often beautiful, always uncompromising, seem to testify to a positive self-expansion as a constitutive element within confinement, and Jimmy

Boyle would seem to be quite accurate in calling his memoir A Sense of Freedom. It would appear altogether arbitrary to deny such an obvious fact. It would be just as arbitrary, however, to abandon the intuition which has brought us to this point. At an intuitive level we cannot accept its otherness as in some way limited by the human material with which it has contact; as if, in some aspect, it retained an affection for life and freedom which is nowhere evident in its other aspects. In pursuing its fundamental negativism into the human realm it is doubly important to retain a firm hold on such an intuition, and with it the moral sense to oppose it with the absoluteness with which it advances its own case. Confinement is a world apart, an absolute with its own negative power and its own negative synthesis.

The apparent contradiction – that in confinement the self is both lost and found, enclosed and freed – cannot be resolved by a logical trick because, as we have seen, confinement is constituted by such contradictions. But we can interpret it symptomatically as alternative expressions of the dissociation confinement effects between the self and its body. If the body is reduced to pure substance, the self, dislodged from its physical hiding place, both 'loses' its normal home and 'finds' itself in a realm of absolute, abstract freedom.

THE SELF

'What is the self?' asks Kierkegaard, as Anti-Climacus author of The Sickness Unto Death and answers 'a synthesis'; a synthesis of the finite and the infinite, of freedom and necessity, of the temporal and the eternal. A synthesis that relates itself to itself, that is to say, is 'self-developing' and self-subsistent, determined by its own activities and by the seriousness of its own choices. It is, in addition, a synthesis whose validity is conditioned by its relation to a transcending reality, by its repetition in the ultimate choice of faith.

That, ideally, is what the self might become, it is not, of course, the self of our everyday experience. The everyday self is a partial synthesis, inwardly imbalanced, imperfectly developed, afraid of determining itself more fully in the irrational leap. The self of our normal experience is despair, which is The Sickness Unto Death, the special malady the possibility of which 'is man's advantage over the beasts'.

It is Kierkegaard's meticulous examination of despair, in all its forms, that makes him the first really convincing secular psychologist of the modern era. Yet he was always, and always regarded himself as a fundamentally Christian writer, whose task was to awaken his reader to the life of faith. By Christianity he meant a particular form of existence, defined inwardly and individually, rather than external conformity to a community of believers, or a reflective acknowledgment of doctrinal truths. Christianity was primarily a subjective religion, and through it the subject gained the highest 'potentiation' of his own individuality and might triumph over despair by becoming, through a hidden, secret, personal relationship with God that 'single one' to which we all unconsciously strive.

In the self as conceived by Kierkegaard, Christianity and the market economy are perfectly merged. Religion, having already withdrawn from the physical universe to an infinitely remote point in time and space, was buried so deeply within the subject's potential individuality, that it left no outward trace. It would be difficult, and irrelevant, to decide whether Kierkegaard was the last great religious writer transforming traditional conceptions of religiosity in line with the individuality new to civil society, or the first secular psychologist to 'discover' the self as an object of investigation, but unable, quite, to transcend its traditional forms of representation. In any event his unique writings expressed most consistently and powerfully the ideology of selfhood which had its roots in the Christian tradition and has been established in a secular form within our society. He makes clear not simply the notion that each individual has a 'personality' which ought to be regarded as a 'sacred' entity, but that individuality is something which has to be achieved through a continuous struggle; that our fundamental duty, as Christians or simply as persons, is to 'realise' the self that lies concealed within the multiplicity and diversity of our actions. Despair is his term, simply, for failing in this task and is, thus, the 'universal sickness'.

As he was concerned above all with the self, rather than with theology or philosophy, he resorted to a method of 'indirect communication'. It was not possible to demonstrate, by some kind of scientific proof or philosophical analysis the possibility and validity of religious selfhood. Even worse Kierkegaard himself could not write from a fixed position because he could not himself make the final 'repetition' into faith. He had continually to write about his own existence in a disguised form, to assume a shifting 'incognito' from which to describe existence in ways he already knew to be false, not to refute them but to trace some particular species of despair to the point where it might undergo a repetition into a 'higher' form. But this repetition cannot be made except by the self and his writing, what he called his 'maieutic art', aimed at arousing the self to make such a repetition on its own behalf.

His first major work, Either/Or, places before the self the decisive choice between the aesthetic and the ethical spheres of existence. The book appears anonymously; Kierkegaard, like Dostoevsky in The House of the Dead, concealing himself as the editor into whose hands the manuscript has fallen. The Either is supposedly written by a 'Young Man' and the Or consists of long letters in reply to him by one Judge William.

The young author of Either has produced a work of extraordinary brilliance, but one that lacks real seriousness. Judge William complains that the diverse and unco-ordinated fragments (literary reviews, a beautiful essay on Mozart, aphorisms, psychological studies) are a direct reflection of the young man's continually changing moods and interests. They lack any central concern because the young man himself exists only in a multiplicity of immediate activities. The meaning of such activities is defined only by their ephemeral pleasure. He oscillates wildly, therefore, between the highest flights of reflective ecstasy, and the deepest melancholy. He suffers from boredom, it is the only abiding characteristic of his subjectivity, and it is to escape boredom that he flings himself into first one and then another passing enthusiasm. But he cannot escape; boredom accompanies his most energetic efforts to evade its grasp because it exists in immediacy, in the search for pleasure as an end and in the most extravagant efforts to be relieved of its burden.

Kierkegaard is at pains to present the aesthetic at its most seductive. The young man is a reflective genius, he lacks nothing in self-consciousness, he has been marvellously educated to the appreciation of the higher culture. But still he is bored. Indeed he knows he suffers from boredom and this is an 'advance' over the casual conformity of most people's everyday lives in which boredom, though its only principle, lies perfectly concealed. The 'young man' is not saved by his intellectual virtuosity. By remaining trapped within the aesthetic sphere of existence his intellect is made subservient to his continual search for pleasure. He loves thought, abstraction, but nothing can retain his interest for long. He has no determined selfhood, as an individual he exists in a whole series of succeeding possibilities none of which are fully realised; and is 'volatilised' as a result out of existence by his brilliant theoretical projects. The self within the aesthetic sphere, in other words, has not yet coalesced into a genuine syntheisis and remains subject to whim and accident. 'You are constantly hovering over yourself', complains Judge William. 'Your life resolves itself completely into interesting particulars.'

The Or diagnosis the source of the 'young man's' unhappiness, but how is he to escape the tyranny of immediacy and condense himself into a more substantial personality? Judge William's answer is basically very simple, 'If you have, or rather if you will to have the required energy, you can win what is the chief thing in life, win yourself, acquire your own self.' It is entirely a matter of will, or as the Judge expresses it a matter of 'choosing' a notion which is central to the ideological development of individualism throughout the Nineteenth Century.

It is through choice that the personality 'immerses itself' in the chosen object. Choice is the paramount activity of the self, it is in choosing that the self comes into existence. As such it is a quite irrational activity. 'the inner drift of the personality leaves us no time for thought experiments', says the Judge and the 'young man' has refused to make such choices, allows himself only 'aesthetic' choices in which the self is never at 'risk' because the self never becomes part of the choice. The 'young man' plays with theoretical possibilities without ever attaching himself, passionately, to one rather than another. He thus remains aloof, detached, ironic, an observer of the choices he posits for himself without ever, in fact, choosing among them.

The ethical sphere of existence depends entirely upon such moments of 'serious' choosing. What makes the choice so decisive is the 'danger that in the next instant it may not be equally in my power to choose'. One cannot choose and then return to the situation before the choice, each choice carries with it a new Either/Or, a new set of circumstances including, most significantly, a new set of inner determinants, a more 'developed' and stable selfhood, which realises itself in a process of continuous free choices.

The decisive choice is not between good and evil, but between a form of existence which recognises and lives within such a distinction and one that does not. The choice is between aesthetic immediacy which is determined by pleasure and pain and the ethical which exists in good and evil. The crucial element linking the two, which allows the personality to be lifted from immediate incoherence to ethical determination is 'not deliberation but the baptism of the will'.

The young man is in despair, trapped in the aesthetic because he cannot make this irrational movement of the self. He cannot go beyond a splendid transience. The 'solution' to his despair lies in despair itself. He must despair, more 'seriously' develop his talent for despair so that it will 'devour everything till he finds himself'. Despair, in fact, is the beginning of the self, where doubt is the beginning of philosophy. And though doubt is natural to thought 'one cannot despair without choosing' and in despairing the young man has already made a choice which goes beyond reflective consciousness. Despair, the Judge remarks 'is a kind of doubt of the personality'.

Despair then opens up the possibility of serious choice, the choice for despair and not the despairing choice. In this everything is changed, but changed inwardly. The self comes into existence in a new, more coherent and determined form, but without losing the particular characteristics it developed within the aesthetic. 'The self contains a rich concretion', he tells the young man, 'a manifold variety of determinants and characteristics, being the whole aesthetical self which is chosen ethically.' thus by despair 'nothing is destroyed'.

It is this 'repetition' into the ethical that concerns Judge William. His prototype of the ethical life is marriage, which he is at pains to argue, is not a 'cold, uncomely, unerotic, unpoetic, state' and allows, in fact, a more secure enjoyment of the sensuous immediacy which the young man, in seeking too directly, destroys by boredom.

Later pseudonyms take up the transition, more difficult and demanding, from the ethical to the religious sphere. It was one of Kierkegaard's unique insights to insist upon the categorical separation of the religious sphere. Religious existence was determined by the distinction between faith and sin. The self could no more be led by reason or science to faith than he could be persuaded by them to the ethical life. Religious life demanded the leap of faith, a second repetition of subjectivity, and was as distinct from the moral life as the ethical was separate from aesthetic immediacy.

The leap, however, does not deny ethics any more than the first repetition destroyed the aesthetic. It is again an inward transformation. The self is now chosen 'infinitely' in its 'infinite relation to God'. And just as the despair of boredom is the spur to self-development within the aesthetic, driving the self to the point of a more coherent crystallisation; so guilt within the ethical sphere drives the self to a still more inwardly perfect structure. The leap restores the self, free from the guilt of the ethical. Kierkegaard, as Johannes de Silentio of Fear and Trembling, was fond of recounting the story of Abraham, ready to slay his son as an act of faith and achieving in this, not simply a new self, but the restoration also of his son. Religion, then, goes beyond but does not destroy the ethical, it preserves it in its proper place.

What is essential in Kierkegaard's description of the self is firstly the notion of a self-determining synthesis. It is this characteristic of selfhood which we recognise as fundamentally irrational: it cannot be 'explained' by relating it, logically or empirically, to some other anterior state or condition. Secondly the idea that the self exists in a number of different discontinuous forms related progressively as the Stages on Life's Way, the aesthetic, the ethical and the religious defined by their own essential opposition; pleasure/pain; good/evil; faith/sin. Repetition is the inexplicable transition between these spheres. Thirdly there is the description of selfhood as despair. Only the religious, and ultimately the acceptance of the 'offence' of Christianity overcomes despair, that is to say establishes the self at the highest point of its potentiation. This particular impossibility means that our experience can always be described as a form of despair, a self which is not fully itself. Fourthly Kierkegaard, in The Sickness unto Death, came to make a final important distinction which cuts across the 'developmental' sequence of the Stages. Despair is of two rather different kinds; the despair of weakness is the more common, it is the despair of not willing to be oneself, the despair of passive acceptance,[1] of boredom, of guilt. But there is also the despair of defiance, which rather than seeking to overcome its own suffering, glorifies it and develops a demonic, compulsive love of boredom, of guilt or of religious suffering. This attachment to the self's negative image is the most subtle and dangerous of traps because it is as demanding of commitment and strength as the self's 'proper' development. Finally there is the conception which runs through the entire authorship, pseudonymous and direct, reaching its climax in his masterpiece Training in Christianity, of the self as engaged in a continuous struggle to 'realise' its full potential and to come completely into existence.

In propounding such an extreme individualism Kierkegaard gave the finest expression to a cultural mythology which became, and continues to be, a real force conditioning our experience. We have not escaped completely from it. Boredom, guilt, the aesthetic flight from 'reality', the demands of 'self-realisation', are closer to us than most would care to admit. And if we allow ourselves a brief, indulgent smile of congratulation at having at least rid ourselves of the 'spiritual trials' of the religious sphere it fades quickly enough when we find ourselves, without it, in a more extreme solipsistic trap than before. Abandoning the religious sphere removes the conditioning element, the telos of self-development and internalises the ultimate standard of self-development. The self then becomes its own measuring device as well as its own source of energy. We are left, like Dostoevsky's Underground Man with the compulsion to self-realisation, and sometimes the requisite energy, but without an imminent sense of direction. The argument between the Either and Or is then re-opened and cannot be resolved. The despair of defiance, which is an open denial of the self's telos, has thus become more common since Kierkegaard wrote.

THE CONFINED SELF

Kierkegaard described the many variations in the experience of the self, but he did not describe the confined self, that is a 'category' which lies outside of the Stages in Life's Way, a form of the self, as Mandelstam says, which is 'beyond despair'. Confinement, however, goes beneath, rather than beyond despair. As a 'cure' for despair it succeeds by abolishing rather than transcending the selfhood of our normal experience. It is in going 'beyond' despair that confinement has laid itself open to opposed judgments. It is possible to regard this alteration in our normal unhappiness as either a privileged access to the 'true' self freed at last from its own weakness and irresolution or, alternatively, as an absolute loss.

We cannot jump too quickly, however, to the other side of despair. Kierkegaard's astonishingly rich language provides us with descriptive terms through which some of the most characteristic transformations of inwardness brought about in confinement, can be described. It is as if confinement sets up its own, parallel and exclusive dimension of existence, with its own Stages towards self-annihilation, its own peculiar, inverted form of repetition, its own negative dialectic of choice and its own final resolution of suffering.

The confined self can, then, be described in rather different ways, assumes a number of different disguises and presents its victims with its own Either/Or. Just as in 'real' life, confinement contains an aesthetic and an ethical 'sphere' - and even the possibility of their 'religious' transcendence.

Andrey Sinyavsky's A Voice from the Chorus, we might say, is the Either of confinement, its aesthetic face; Alexander Solzhenitsyn's Gulag Archipelago is its Or, its ethical conscience. We might add, anticipating somewhat, that the novels of Jean Genet are its Training in Christianity.

The aesthetic 'solution' to the problem of confinement is expressed perfectly in Sinyavsky's beautiful book, which has provided us already with so many fine illustrations. The form of his work, slightly puzzling at first despite its authentic 'feel', from the reader's point of view, depicts, through its hectic variety the contradictory structure of the aesthetic self. The interpolation of his 'voice' amidst the clamouring 'chorus', the diversity of its content - reflections on Russian Literature, on fairy stories, descriptions of his own sensations - and its tone of rather bewildered curiosity are so effective because they replicate in a literary medium a new condition of selfhood. The form, and even the subject matter, of his book bear a striking resemblance to the Either, written just over a century before by the bored 'young man'. The 'Chorus' in Sinyavsky's somewhat slighter work, indeed, plays a similar role to the melancholic aphorisms - the 'Diapsalmata' - that are a feature of the latter.

Sinyavsky's book is as much an expression of himself as it is a description of the world he inhabits. The point being, of course, that confinement makes such a distinction difficult to draw. In setting down the fragments through which his consciousness is allowed its apparent freedom he describes for us also, and more clearly than any more direct method might, one way in which confinement decomposes the personality.

Sinyavsky in 'escaping through the back door' has 'volatilised' himself in a series of poetic experiments. The self suddenly discovers a new liberty by escaping from the constraints, the meticulous unchanging rhythm, to which his body is subject. Yet this hardly conceals the despair in his voice. 'What is a poet?' asks the 'young man' in the opening sentence of Either and answers at once, 'An unhappy man who in his heart harbours a deep anguish, but whose lips are so fashioned that the moans and cries which pass over them are transformed into ravishing music'. Sinyavsky is a considerable poet and we can even allow ourselves to read his book with pleasure. But everything we have said of the literary experiments of the 'young man' apply also to him. This 'inner freedom' of the self is a poor substitute for an existence in the real world. There is an excess of infinitude, an unchecked imagination; unchecked because there is no longer anything to resist its wishes. In confinement the world disintegrates into a formless extension capable of reflecting any image which the self cares to project upon it. It can present itself according to any whim, it no longer even requires a powerful imagination to subordinate 'objectivity' to its latest fantasy because objectivity, in becoming a perfectly concrete substance, cannot 'contain' the self which in consequence evaporates into an unreal, empty dimension. The self escapes all concrete determinants and appropriates to itself the terrifying freedom of a void. It can represent itself, to itself - there is no Other - as anything; Anything, that is, but a person. It is akin to the aesthetic self which Kierkegaard has described for us, but here the self is in despair neither through weakness nor defiance, but because it has been forced out of its synthesis as a condition of its most attenuated survival. The self is a fugitive from existence because confinement is, quite literally, non-existence, and cannot therefore provide it with a medium.

Confinement, then, is the negative synthesis to that constituted through freedom, by the self. The self becomes multiple, fragmented, diverse and has a purely ideal existence. Just as the 'young man' pursued himself through innumerable experiments in living we can trace Sinyavsky's vanishing self through the decomposition of his book. 'I notice', he remarks in a suggestive phrase, 'that my shadow walked beside me, but moved independently from me.'

Sinyavsky's 'aesthetic' existence preserves a sense of his own identity, no doubt, a little longer than might seem possible amidst overwhelming hostility. It is as cultivated, as 'rarified' as the 'young man's' but is moving, so to speak, in the reverse direction. The problem with the young man was to bring him to the point of decisive choice, but Sinyavsky has been plunged beneath such a point. He cannot any longer make a choice, even the simplest – when to eat, when to sleep, when to relieve himself – now belong to others. The choices that appear to be open to him are not real choices at all but wholly inward fantasies. Even resistance is not available as a choice because, as we have seen, the 'negative dialectic' of confinement ensures that even this choice leads towards nothing, towards self-destruction. All choices implicate the chooser more deeply in confinement; and while for the 'young man' there is nothing to lose in a 'repetition' into higher categories of existence, for the confined self everything is lost and the more decisively he chooses the more rapidly he moves towards the empty centre of the prison cell.

Koestler has described a similar decomposition. Rubashov after his initial staunch refusal to cooperate is left to 'himself', in solitary confinement. The continuous internal monologue in which he debates with himself the proper course of action becomes dramatically transformed into a genuine dialogue. He appears to himself as two people, yet neither voice properly belongs to him, they seem to converse on their own terms and Rubashov, or what is left of him, is relegated to the role of dreamlike spectator. 'Rubashov' we are told 'gradually became convinced that there was a thoroughly tangible component in this first person singular, which had remained silent through all these years and now had started to speak.' He called this a 'grammatical fiction' but could never catch it at rest and examine its content; it 'seemed to begin just where the thinking to a conclusion ended. It was obviously an essential part of its being to remain out of the reach of logical thought, and then to take one unawares.' Confinement forces this suppressed aspect of the self out into the open, decomposes and disintegrates the self into such 'component elements'. It is as if a higher synthesis were falling apart, bits keep falling away from it like the pieces of Soyinka's flaking body.

The self is left with a purely imaginary coherence, one that can be sustained only so long as the captive's memory functions normally. But in confinement the memory, like everything else, works against the self's natural desire to survive.

Because time has ceased to exist, or exists only in a 'pure' unusable form, the memory is dissipated in a chaos of recollection. Many writers attest to the large amount of time and energy the prisoner or patient devotes to personal recollection. It is what 'keeps most people going'. George Jackson, for example, during the early stages of his imprisonment, admitted, 'I think about my personal past quite often'. And Eldridge Cleaver tells us that it was only on being incarcerated that he began to review his life for the first time 'taking a long look at myself'. Dostoevsky reports too that 'every one of us in that prison has his own peculiar, interior, strictly personal life', one that dwelt in the past. While Jean Genet's writing is filled with his own lyrical reminiscing.

The self, seeking to reinforce its structure, has to use these materials from the past; memory after all is the only non-hostile aspect of the environment. The prisoner begins to live in the past rather than simply off it, his personality absorbed in a world no longer present to him. This appears to be a more daringly imaginative escape than that accomplished by the most sophisticated cultural flights of the 'young man'. Yet in confinement it is no great trick to live entirely in the past, no imaginative leap is necessary because time, on the inside, has been abolished and the distinction, in consequence, between memory and experience, becomes trivially semantic. The prisoner lives in past time, the time stored within him, and can even give way to the illusion that it is 'time regained'.

Whether self-consciously 'projecting' itself into aesthetic categories, or unconsciously seeking itself through its own recollection it could be said that the self in confinement is forced into despair. That is to say the self is not permitted to assume the synthesis natural to it. This appears to be a paradox. Kierkegaard was at pains to point out that despair is a fundamentally self-inflicted condition. How then can one be forced into despair? Yet in confinement such compulsion, however much it offends our logic, is all too real. The captive is first forced to despair, and afterwards, as if that were not sufficient, is forced beyond despair.

Kierkegaard describes as the 'unhappiest man' a type of recollection of the self which is peculiarly prevalent in the initial stages of confinement. The self which cannot live in the present may either live in hope or in memory. Within confinement, hope is very quickly extinguished; remember that it infected Casanova for only a short time. Recollection, however, takes on a new, inflated significance and becomes the predominant form of consciousness for the confined. Kierkegaard points out there is one way of combining hope and recollection and that is to wish the past had been different. This type of hopeful recollection is one of the confined self's trademarks. The self begins to hallucinate its own past as a kind of fantastic exercise of its freedom. But this invented history leads to nothing.

The 'unhappiest man' is not yet, however, confined. He is a dreamer who, from time to time, must come to terms with his existence in the real world and recognise his fantasies for what they are. But for the confined recollection ceases to be discreet psychological function; the self can be driven ever further into the past without suffering any self-conscious dislocation from the present. Present and past have little meaning, how can they when the framework of time has been purified of its normal markings? The self cannot be 'discovered' in recollection because the memory, like other dimensions of normal existence, is denied its proper medium.

The young man chooses to live 'theoretically', and despairs; the confined man can live only theoretically and is pushed beyond despair. The 'young man' chooses to live in immediacy and lacks the consistency of a self whose identity is extended through time; the confined man in being forced to live in unvarying immediacy apparently 'escapes' through recollection into an imaginative existence. But it proves an impotent fantasy that leads, as all roads in confinement lead, to 'eternity in a yard of space'. If the aesthetic self is sunk in its own boredom, the confined self is trapped within its own madness.

The confined self, nonetheless, appears to have a structure and can take on more than one guise. As well as its aesthetic, fantastic form, it can present to the world - on the outside at least - and ethical phase. This, at first less plausible representation is, in practice, the preferred model of the 'survivor' discoursing on his life on the inside. This ethical self within confinement is as abstract as its aesthetic alternative, indeed, as it is a purely theoretical accommodation to the same decomposing situation is really only a subspecies rather than a separate type in its own right. It has assumed a certain importance however in recent years, most especially through the writings of Solzhenitsyn and merits, as a result, separate treatment.

The typical strategy of the ethical self is to seek confirmation of its identity, not in escape, but in the story of its own and other people's oppression.

Unlike the more directly aesthetic self, it ceases to regard itself in isolation but attempts to join with the society of other, confined souls. The transition from the aesthetic disintegration of George Jackson's prison letters in Soledad Brother, to his historical/political self in Blood in my Eye, is indicative of such a 'development'. He progressively thinks away his personal past and begins to study historical works to furnish himself with a more comprehensive, more robust and more valid selfhood. 'I cannot think of myself as an individual,' he declares in his later book, reaching beyond the constraints of personal letters to a more encompassing historical consciousness. Naturally this is not to deny the relevance of his own bitter experience to his historical reflection, far from it; but the reverse movement is less happy still. History cannot furnish him with a new self or a new identity, even if he thinks it might. The crucial point is that he remains locked away from the world of social life and politics; he can only think historically because he has ceased to exist historically. He has been excluded from the historically activated public realm, condemned to an atemporal world where history has no other meaning than the recollection of a vanished world. In avoiding aesthetic personal fantasies he must indulge in historical studies which take him just as far away from his existence as a living individual.

In his books he recounts the costs of acquiring an 'historical consciousness' in prison. His relationships with other prisoners deteriorated; he needed privacy, he needed silence; he needed above all the silence of solitary confinement. the cunning of confinement laid for him an irresistible trap. He embarked upon an ambitious programme of self-education the better to equip himself to deal with the conditions of confinement; and soon began to crave the solitary life. His heroic attempt to ward off personal decay and madness drove him just as certainly, by another route, into the centre of the confined world – the solitary locked cell. He could escape the worst horror of imprisonment only by provoking a more intimate acquaintance with confinement. The benefits of such a course, however, proved no more real than the pleasures he sacrificed to accomplish it. In 'progressing' from personal recollection to historical consciousness his selfhood has apparently gained a wider contact with the world; but it remains a purely formal, theoretical exercise. He has 'progressed' from the unreflective immediacy of his youth, to a more mature, reflective immediacy. But he must remain below the point at which the 'baptism of will' can provoke a real subjectivity to emerge. That possibility is denied him; that is the meaning of the loss of freedom deemed the 'logical' punishment in all advanced societies.

Despite the obvious seriousness of his writing this is not the 'seriousness' of life about which Judge William spoke with such measured passion. the only possibilities allowed him are unreal, fantastic projections. Such possibilities draw out the infinity of the self without ever making it concrete; prefers the eternal to the temporal – indeed no longer recognises such a distinction – and miraculously transforms the real conditions of uncompromising necessity into a realm of absolute freedom.

George Jackson, we might say attempts to excavate a portion of human history to receive the imprint of his fugitive self. Solzhenitsyn, on the other hand, attempts to survive by incorporating the history of an entire epoch into his still existing, powerful personality. It is not here a case of 'historical consciousness' offering a false way out for the beleaguered personal self, but a vast projection of an inner hostile world onto the stage of history to expose the corruption, folly and barbarity of a civilisation.

The diversity of Solzhenitsyn's work suggests, as it does in the case of Kierkegaard's prodigiously varied literary production, that some particular aspect of the author's selfhood is, in turn, being crystallised. Solzhenitsyn's oeuvre becomes both a reflection of himself and a history of modern Russia; it is sufficiently comprehensive and well articulated to represent everything in that history, both private and public. But while Kierkegaard's variety remains promiscuous and teasing, never allowing us to leap over its intricate particularity to grasp a single culminating statement of his truth, Solzhenitsyn finds his authentic voice in The Gulag

Archipelago. In it he explores the nature of confinement through his own confinement, and his own confinement through the history of other people's confinement. There ceases to be – and in this he enters deeply into the consciousness of confined selfhood – any fundamental distinction between the 'self' of personal recollection and the 'subject' of history.

The Gulag Archipelago, is thus unlike conventional history or conventional autobiography. It expresses in some of its immediate characteristics, as well as in its deeper structure, the world of experience created for the confined. It is extremely long, it is repetitious, one quickly loses oneself in it. Wherever we care to begin we know the 'story' will deteriorate rapidly towards some fresh barbarity and end in annihilation. It is massively 'objective', hardly assimilable to the 'historical consciousness' trained in the conceptual trickery of scientific method. It is indigestible, it is ultimately, it must be admitted, boring. It is peopled by an endlessly extending list of victims. Names are named, seemingly without limit in a complication beyond any immediate comprehension; soon they merge into a composite picture of the captive; hungry, depressed, without hope, cold, dirty, worn down by the struggle, daily more desperate to survive and stave off nothingness for a little longer. It is noticeably difficult to quote from it, as we have from Sinyavsky or Soyinka, lucid shorthand descriptions of decomposing minds and bodies. Solzhenitsyn works in a different way; he recreates for us the pure physicality of confinement, its massiveness and impenetrability, its twisted logic, its despair. It is neither a fascinating story nor a work of explanation as historians pretend to, but an attempt to describe a world so minutely that we can enter into it and are, indeed, forced into it, against our will. It is as opaque as a real prison, we begin reading, lose ourselves in its limitless extension, and when we put it down escape back into our own world, unable to remember much of what we have been reading but retaining still that slight sensation of nausea that signalled our crossing, however briefly and safely, into its dense, meaningless emptiness.

Such work cannot, however imposing, provide a home for the ethical self. In confinement the self and the subject of history may coalesce; this indeed, is one of its properties. But this is another success for confinement and not a means of survival for the self. The effort of preventing the self's 'escape' into private fantasy is heroic, we feel the enormous passion of the attempt; but the attempt fails at the outset because it begins with a 'meditation' between self and history in which the self is lost. History and the self can absorb each other only on the plane of reflection; this, in fact, was a major focus of Kierkegaard's critique of Hegel's philosophy. Now, however, the philosophical dispute is carried on with the earnestness of a life-and-death struggle. However detailed and complete his documentation of confinement becomes, however much it faces up to the stark reality that contains him, he cannot succeed in providing himself with the personality's sustenance - freedom. The peculiarity of Solzhenitsyn's 'fantasised' self is that it does not seek to escape the world in which it finds itself by denial and flight, but attempts to maintain itself by portraying as accurate and complete a picture as possible of this enclosed space. But in confinement there is no such refined escape; stoic acceptance, historical understanding or personal fantasy impose, each in their different ways, the negative, self-destructive properties of confinement on its victim.

Solzhenitsyn, no more than Sinyavsky is left any real choice and resorts, just as George Jackson, to a gross, cold, impersonal consciousness. By not trying to escape in imagination, rooting himself in the reality of confinement he is just as surely destroyed because he has to force himself to depict a world in which he cannot live.

Solzhenitsyn implicitly realises this and attempts to exercise a real ethical self in the here and now of confinement. He insists, even at the end of The Gulag Archipelago, that moral judgments can still be made, indeed must be made, on the inside. He insists Ivan Denisovich could only have been a zec rather than a trusty or blatnoy. He does even allow his own past to escape his ethical censure, and even criticises others for their lack of scrupulousness in this regard.

His criticisms, however, never reach their target. In confinement the preconditions of the ethical life are taken away; there is no choice, no possibility, no freedom. His complaints become a kind of rhetorical moralising rather than ethical judgments. He can retain the ethical in a theoretical sense alone, as an aesthetic version of the ethical.

Others have also attempted to retain one foot in the ethical. Marchenko, for example, regarded one of his cell mates with repugnance. This fellow, Ivan Mordvin, had sunk so low as to steal from one of his fellow prisoners. Worse, he carried out his theft in an insidious manner, stealthily, over a period of several nights he lifted someone else's sugar from its hiding place. He was discovered and called out at once for the guard, knowing well enough the others would attack him. He was transferred to another cell where he 'confessed' in order, apparently, to arouse some obscure current of sympathy. But Marchenko has no sympathy for such a coward and they eventually fought.

It is easy for us, on the outside, to admire Marchenko's 'strength of character', or Solzhenitsyn's steadfastness and dignity. But we are applying standards to their behaviour, as they are themselves, which belong only to our, relatively much freer, social life. We can admire too Ivan Mordvin's grovelling weakness, love his humanness, his pathetic, half-hearted introverted selfhood. Mordvin, after all, did not subordinate himself under concepts which no longer had a meaning for him – he already knew survival to be the only morality. He realised his true condition and behaved accordingly. Moral posing has no place in confinement, it strikes an anomalous note. That man on his pole, on Solovetsky Island, could he have lived, could he be expected to live, under ethical determinants? Would the austere Judge William urge upon him the 'baptism of the will' and insist he despair more seriously? Hardly; he can only sit and observe his own disintegration in pain and fantasy.

Insisting upon the superiority of the ethical self within confinement is not itself an ethical viewpoint, but a form of aestheticism that remains blind to its own limitations. This is doubtless a harsh judgment. In the labour camps, for example, the dead souls must be preserved, must be harnessed as useful labour. A certain minimal attention to physical needs must, therefore, be secured and in consequence a primitive form of social organisation places a thin screen between the prisoner and the void of pure confinement. In these circumstances certain real choices may still appear – whether to steal, to make friends, tell lies – and beyond such particular choices a fundamental question; exploitation or death?

Unbelievably the memoirists from The House of the Dead debate such issues and invite others to reflect with them on the relative merits of different forms of behaving as a captive. This not only imposes false standards on lives deprived of the means to conform to any standard, it draws us away from the real subject matter. It is confinement, not the labour camps, or prisons, or asylums, that concern us. But confinement nowhere exists in its 'pure' state, we can glimpse an aspect here, another aspect there and piece together the otherness that lies within all its forms. Each manifestation falls short of its own standard of perfection and leaves in consequence a smaller or larger space in which the human can once again take root. But this is only a glimmer of real life allowed as a practical necessity to confinement's advancement.

Beyond any particular self-defeating 'tactic' of survival confinement appears to present its victim with an either/or as vital as that confronting the free subject – it can be simply stated; acquiescence or resistance? Resistance manifests itself in all those devices through which the captive attempts to 'hang on' to himself. But ultimately to no avail, he is lost to the world and in the peculiar negative logic of the inside resistance and acquiescence join forces to drive the captive beyond hope and despair. Confinement is ruled by equifinality, all roads lead to the same ending; but its cunning is to pretend its inmates are still at liberty to choose, are still faced with the seriousness of a genuine either/or.

Confinement, we might say, is a repetition, but a curious inverse repetition; a repetition in the wrong direction. It forces its subject beneath the point of choice; it is an existence outside of possibility. Confinement escapes altogether the discontinuities – those 'leaps' through which the self emerges in freedom – and, like Hegel's speculative philosophy consists in a series of fluid transitions and 'mediations'. In confinement everything goes smoothly, its 'development' is continuous, unidirectional and driven by inner necessity. The prisoner need not exercise his will to succeed in becoming a more perfect captive. To realise the selfhood imminent in confinement he need do nothing, or alternatively he can struggle against his own disintegration, soon it makes no difference, both paths lead to a more or less rapid erosion of the personality.

The confined self attempts to save itself for a time by deserting its synthesis in favour of reflective and imaginative 'categories'. The 'aesthetic' version provides an 'escape route' through personal recollection and fantasy. The 'ethical' version buttresses itself with moral concepts that belong, as surely as personal fantasies, to another world. These tactics of the fugitive self might be linked to what Kierkegaard termed the despair of weakness. They wish, quite rightly, not to be the self of their present existence. It is an effort to deny the real consequences of being locked up, to insist, despite everything, that you are still the same person. They are, in consequence, constantly in flight from their immediate life, but in flying from it end, as if they had never made the attempt, in nothingness.

We can find examples also, rarer and even more disturbing, of what could be called confinement's version of the despair of defiance. Even among prisoners and captives there are those who do not simply acquiesce but choose, with demonic energy, life as it is; welcome confinement's negative synthesis, and fall in love with its inversions. they do not seek rebellion or escape but the celebration of confinement as the crucible of human nature. In confinement all pretension, ideology, conventional morality and deception fall away to reveal the human in all its naked power and beauty. Confinement releases the human from its normal constraints and frees man from the ordered, settled, unbearably constricting life on the 'outside'. It is only by the imposition, around the self of an impenetrable barrier that these purely human powers and passions can become transparent.

Confinement, in purifying the human of all external and arbitrary limit becomes the subject of a lyrical, impassioned philosophy. Man alone, without preconditions, freed from the imposition of alien norms, stripped of the hypocrisy regulating 'free' lives, possesses once again the womb of existence. It is here, in confinement, that immediate sensuous experience, free of all guilt, becomes available in its full range and intensity.

This powerful conception is among the most challenging contained within the 'literature of confinement'. The Marquis de Sade inaugurated (and completed) this particular form of the genre. The most radical of genuinely modern writers, de Sade, like Hegel, sets out to describe the infinity of the human subject. He refuses to accept any dialectical limit, any measure of validity or judgment. He thus goes beyond the Enlightenment philosophy in a quite dramatic and self-conscious manner. The contrast to Casanova is quite profound and revealing. Where Casanova failed ultimately to give confinement its due, de Sade, who wrote almost all his works inside a prison of one kind or another (he spent twenty-seven years incarcerated in eleven different institutions) finds within the cell the secret of a unique human nature. Casanova was unable completely to grasp the otherness of confinement, but de Sade has so surely grasped this other world that he disappears completely within it. This, curiously enough, is his revolutionary method of discovery. It is a kind of practical research in observing the human appetites and passions which appear to govern man even in the absence of social life and which, therefore, have a certain independence from educative and progressive devices. His celebration of confinement, and of the passions it seems to intensify, is founded on a conception of the world emptied of everything but the 'absolute ego' of the human subject. Confinement's impenetrable boundary creates just such an emptied-out world. Casanova, who cannot help but see Nature and Reason as conjoined in harmony within the human subject, is horrified by his separation from the constraints of normal life with its laws and regulations. 'The natural order is reversed', he complains. But de Sade goes farther than this; confinement, and only confinement, allows the subject the absolute freedom – which is its basic right – to create the world to suit itself. Confinement forces its victim into that odd condition of suspended, but infinite, possibility which is the theoretical starting point for all modern conceptions of human nature. It forces him back into that pre-conceptual void out of which he can allow his real nature to emerge. It is, thus, only in the prison cell that he can discover and experience directly that absolute freedom the intuition of which animates all varieties of modern revolutionary politics. It is, indeed, the only method of attaining the ultimate ideal of total freedom. It is by being locked away from nature and society that the subject can become cleansed and purified, and the world made perfectly plastic to the desires that spring spontaneously within him.

Confinement, in tracing its way back to that undifferentiated state of non-being, re-opens for the subject willing to inhabit its centre all those questions and possibilities which have already been resolved (in the wrong way) for us left at liberty. Nor can there be, in confinement, the shock of disillusionment which every human action brings in its wake – because confinement in removing everything, removes the possibility of action. The subject remains poised, as it were, on the edge of existence, where he is privileged to remain, as a 'concept of a man' and can never fall from this pinnacle of theoretical perfection because all possibilities remain, for him, intact. In never 'realising' any particular existence, he never suffers that sense of loss at some pleasure forgotten, or resentment at having his 'real nature' perverted by some choice that turns out for the worse. The absolute freedom of confinement comes uncomfortably close, as we shall see, to the playworld of an ideal childhood.

The notion, then, that de Sade is in a simple way exploiting the erotic undertones in the idea of confinement is at best a superficial characterisation of his writing. True, confinement carries its own weight of eroticism. There can be, even now, a good deal of passive voluptuousness in the notion of 'languishing' in prison. And the paraphernalia of constraint, when taken out of confinement and transposed, piece by piece, into our world, can be accorded a purely sexual meaning.

A much more profound description of confinement's eroticism is provided, however, by de Sade. His scenes of cruelty and debasement are an essential ingredient of the 'absolute ego's' attempt to recreate its condition of primitive universality. It is not sexuality – the erotic relationship – that interests de Sade, but the possibility of eroticising experience in general when the subject is plunged back to the point of his own origin. There is nothing foreign to him, any and all possibilities of human activity can be eroticised because there is no 'natural' limit to such appetites and it is only through living in the false world of social relationships that we have come to think there is. It is in confinement that we rediscover the 'polymorph perversity' of our appetites.

Despite the most strenuous efforts, however, the self remains isolated in these manoeuvres; its freedom is absolute but fantastic, existing solely in its own theoretical projects.

The eroticism of confinement turns out to be an 'advanced' form of the aesthetic consciousness, a kind of conceptual narcissism. This is because the otherness of confinement exhausts its content of objects and leaves the subject alone with its own fantasies. Its eroticism is perfectly introverted; the self can be linked with an image of another self, which can only be another image of itself. There can be no 'object relations' because there are no objects. In the end, de Sade would have to agree with Jean Genet when he writes 'My solitude in prison was total'.

As much as does the Gulag Archipelago, de Sade offers us the world of confinement as a concrete reality. His writing is long, indigestible, objective and physical and in this – again in contrast to Casanova – he incorporates the features of confinement into the form of his books. Jean Genet, however, who with de Sade is the most accomplished lyricist of confinement, is a more dangerously seductive writer. He offers us a little breathing space, moves us along in a series of barely discernible transitions so that when we finally find ourselves in the midst of confinement we are liable to think we are still free.

Genet began his career on the inside of the Mettray Reformatory which he remembers in his *Miracle of the Roses* with the kind of horror we would 'naturally' expect. 'I suffered then,' he says. 'I felt the cruel shame of having my head shaved, of being dressed in unspeakable clothes, of being confined in that vile place.' And we recognise his reaction. He tells us, 'In order to weather my desolation I withdrew more deeply into myself', a process described as well by Soyinka, among others, in similar terms. 'I recognise', we read in *The Man Died*, 'and welcome the beginning of the withdrawal process, an accentuation of the imposed isolation by an instinctive self-isolation'. This withdrawal seems an imperative of confinement; and it can only be a matter of words whether we call it the self's effort to survive, or confinement's power to expel the self from its natural domain. Genet describes it perfectly, 'I know how to withdraw into myself. Since my quintessence has taken refuge in the deepest and most secret retreat . . . I no longer fear anything, I am rash enough to think that my body is free of all distinguishing signs, that it looks empty, impossible to identify, since everything about me quite abandoned my image.'

This withdrawal, however, is not a stable solution. We have already seen the self cannot withdraw into the 'safety' of the body because the body itself is not safe, becoming transformed into a mechanical contrivance incapable of housing a self. The self is thus 'forced' to escape from its own body. Genet escaped by expanding himself into the nothingness that surrounded him and making it his own. He found he could look at the world of confinement, and his own precious life with a new eye and a new emotional meaning; he could adopt confinement's own point of view of himself, not despairingly, but ecstatically, 'And it staggered me to know', he confesses, 'that I was composed of impurities.' His prison had indeed become 'the closed area, the confined, the measured universe in which I ought to live permanently'. He will

seek to 'act and think only in terms of prison'.
His spirit, liberated from the constraints of conventional morality by prison life, was able to participate in the free but previously forbidden universe 'of criminality and confinement'. By 'repudiating the virtues of your world', he is free to live in confinement and write in praise of its humanness. There he becomes 'master of time'. Confinement is his 'garden of saintliness' whose central characters possess a beauty and purity those at liberty cannot recognise. It is confinement, in fact, that has released in him such lyrical powers as a writer. 'My talent will be,' he tells us, 'the love I feel for that which constitutes the world of prisons.

Genet presents, however, something less theoretically complete than de Sade. Confinement, for Genet, becomes a mechanism through which a 'transvaluation of values' takes place. He presents it as an inverted world rather than a world of infinite possibility, and in this sense is less radical, and less profound, than de Sade. The advantage of his superficiality, however, is in the precision with which he can then describe the world of prisons (rather than of confinement as an absolute) in which he lives. The pimps, big-shots, homosexuals come to life in his books, just as, in Edward Buca's Vorkuta or Marchenko's My Testimony, the social structure of the labour camp is preserved. They each describe one particular form of confinement, but confinement – unfortunately privileged in this respect – can be grasped 'in itself' as an absolute. Genet's reversals and inversions are suggestive signs in this regard. They both describe an existing world – the social life allowed to survive within enclosed prisons – and at the same time represents at a more general level the otherness of which confinement is composed. In learning to love the remnant of life left him on the inside, and reducing everything to that possibility alone, he creates in us the same kind of shudder we felt on reading of the prisoner who came to love a cockroach as his only companion.

Confinement breaks what we feel in our life to be an indissoluble link between the body and the self. The body is 'objectified', reduced to pure corporeality, and the self is 'volatised', forced free of its physical embodiment and left to its own devices within the void. This 'split' between body and self is one of the most obvious and impressive conditions of confinement.

The self, once 'released' from its normal moorings, may present itself, for a time at least, in a number of different forms. Kierkegaard's description of despair and its 'potentiation' through ethical and religious categories can serve as a first approximation in delimiting these forms. Confinement, however, reverses the development of the self and takes away from it the power of repetition. In confinement there is no genuine either/or, it remains intolerant of all radical distinctions.

There is a sense in which the 'defiant self' realises the true form of confinement and confronts squarely the external reality which conditions its existence. In 'choosing' confinement it chooses itself, it chooses nothingness, chooses the infinite possibility of nothingness. The confined self comes into contact, in other words, with the absolute otherness of confinement and adopts it as its own image. This absolute otherness of confinement, its radical heterogeneity from life on the outside makes it possible to apply Kierkegaard's descriptive categories. We could say of de Sade that he chose the infinite relation to the infinite; that his is a religion of confinement, aesthetic and the ethical 'choices' are not on the inside real choices because they have at best a reflective, abstract relevance, the 'defiant self' too becomes a form of consciousness rather than a mode of existence.

The result of this 'abstractedness' of the self is ultimately its evaporation into fantasy. All choices lead back to a more positive conditions of selfhood because the self has been excluded from participating in its own determination.

Lack of freedom sets up a hostile 'logic' of its own. Where, for Judge William, the crucial point is simply to choose so that all choices result in a deepening of the self; in confinement there are no real choices and all apparent actions lead away from the self and projects it farther and farther into the void. One is reminded again of the melancholic 'young man' of the Either who declares, 'choose to do it and you will regret it; choose not to do it and you will regret it'. But the similarity does not go deep enough. The young man's regret is over his inability to choose in the right way; in confinement one is forced to choose the wrong way; and cannot even regret it.

This reflects a fundamental reversal in the relation of the self to the dialectic that conditions the validity of its choices. Kierkegaard's question, throughout the immense variety of his works, remains fundamentally the same – how to become a Christian, how can the subject appropriate for itself a Christian existence? The self has to struggle upwards towards its religious synthesis and finally make the leap into faith. In confinement the relation is reversed. The self strives to defend itself against the encroachment of the absolute and tries to maintain a human corner where it can resist the 'transcendental' power of confinement. But it cannot succeed; it is forced to compromise, to co-operate, to resist and in the end to capitulate to its negative synthesis. The self is penetrated by an alien substance but with such cunning that at the very point where it is about to decompose the last remnant of the human it can appear in all the seductive glory and spirituality of life's ultimate secret.

4 The End of the World

Confinement has so far been described as if it were a consequence of being locked-up; an experience predicated upon physical constraint in one form or another. Confinement, it is true, does follow necessarily upon such physical measures. The captive subjected to restraint cannot, in the end, resist its advances. But there is no simple chain of causation here. Confinement is a metamorphosis into another, alien, world which should not be mistaken for its visible, varied appearance as a prison, a hospital, a labour camp or an asylum. Once on the inside the transformation is total. Confinement's inverted repetition constitutes a new experience and brings into existence within its victims a new negative subjectivity.

There is no necessity, in fact, in finding confinement in one place rather than another. The temptation is always to provide confinement with an empirical substance that, more properly speaking, does not belong to it – it after all is nothing. Succumbing to the temptation leads only to semi-rational arguments and excuses; in short to an 'aesthetic' theory of confinement that avoids its strenuous, committed rejection. As an experience, however, confinement does not depend simply upon the presence of locked doors, chains, bars and straitjackets. We can find confinement also among those still 'at liberty', though they are often enough locked-up when this is discovered.

It is a commonplace (and like most truisms it is never taken seriously) to say that the confined are driven mad by being enclosed. But it might equally be claimed that the mad suffer from confinement, whether or not they are physically constrained. There is no fundamental difference, in other words (from the viewpoint of the subject), between the confined self and the self-confined self. The experience of confinement is everywhere the same – that is to say the manner in which they experience their world constitutes a common language – and is only loosely related to those physical antecedents that fill up its emptiness, for us, with the rationality of a cause.

The correspondence between madness and confinement

has been made by many of the authors whose testimony has already been quoted. Dostoevsky, for example, explicitly represents confinement as a species of madness. His descriptions of some of his fellow-prisoners, indeed, read like extracts from the textbook cases of the following generation's academic psychiatry.

This gives to The House of the Dead the appearance, at first, of somewhat unsympathetic and harsh judgments. He claims many of those who shared his prison lacked any moral sense. They showed 'not the least sign of shame or repentence', they lacked, apparently, any redeeming characteristics. 'Intrigues, calumny, scandal of all kinds, envy and hatred reigned above all else', he tells us. Later judgments as he became more involved with particular characters and 'causes' are less sweeping and condemnatory. He becomes amazed, for example, at the diligence and calculative skill displayed by some prisoners in the accumulation of small sums of money (we are back in the days when such things were still possible). He was even more surprised by the manner in which such sums were spent; in the purchase of fancy clothes or in immediate debauchery (even that was still possible). Dostoevsky remarks that 'Their pleasure in feeling themselves well dressed amounted to childishness; indeed in many things convicts are only children'. This theme of childishness recurs frequently throughout his book, recurs, in fact, throughout confinement. Old people, for example, once they have been 'institutionalised' become 'merely' children. And Gregor Samsa was thrust back into childhood, before being driven finally beyond childhood into non-existence. Psychiatrists have even seized upon the phenomenon and dignified it as a 'theory' of regression. Dostoevsky notices too his fellow convicts' unpredictability - another sign of their 'madness'. Many prisoners appeared perfectly calm and quiescent, but 'Suddenly one prisoner to the astonishment of his superiors becomes mutinous, plays the very devil, and even ventures upon some capital crime.' Such outbursts, Dostoevsky regards as hardly surprising;

> it is simply the convulsive manifestations of his personality, an instinctive melancholia, an uncontrollable desire for self-assertion which obscures his reason. It is a sort of epileptic fit, a spasm. Even so must a man who is buried alive and suddenly wakes up strike against the lid of his coffin. He tries to rise, to push it from him, though reason must convince him that his efforts are useless.

Life asserts itself for the last time – and loses. the convicts then, were 'either in a perpetual smouldering agitation, or else in deep depression'. They suffered hopes 'so ill founded that they were more like the illusions of approaching insanity than anything else'. And 'everyone moved in a sort of waking dream . . . all seemed to suffer from a remote hypersensitivity . . . nearly all were taciturn and irascible'.

Spanning the years, Sinyavsky agrees that to understand confinement 'is to go mad'. Others have made similar remarks. Eldridge Cleaver admits to the prisoners' 'paranoia as thick as the prison walls'. And Jean Genet speaks of his prison as a 'house of illusion'. Or Soyinka, eloquently describing the madness that gripped him in solitary confinement. 'In a moment of enforced calm I moved out of the echoes of voices in the streets, of voices in the markets, out of whispers in corridors, glances in gatherings, out of the rain of spittle and contempt, moved out of the target, from the target of pointed fingers, the giggles in the dark, out from the wise nods of the geriatric consciences, out of the mockery, the assuaged envy and jubilation of the self-deluded.' And Osip Mandelstam also suffered from voices that became 'like a composite quotation of everything I heard', and pursued him for months after his 'release' from Lubianka.

The world of confinement to put it simply is a madhouse. It is not drawing an analogy to equate the two, it is, rather simply a matter of detecting within each a common, emptied-out, core.

In addition to this direct equation their inner identity can be drawn through their common likeness to an intermediate form – the dreamworld. Dostoevsky, quite early in his book declares the whole prison is 'like a dream'. And Genet links together the world of prisons and dreams in 'anxieties, falls, fevers, apparitions, inexplicable noises, singing, suspected presences'. Or again Soyinka draws them together when he hopes that 'It is not possible to have the same dream dawn after dawn' – only to discover in his prison life that it is only too possible. The dream image is instructive. We all know the dreamworld as a world apart, where logic and time do not apply. We know it suspends our sanity and self-possession. Dreams in modern times have often been regarded as temporary bouts of insanity, necessary in fact to maintain the reason and sense of the waking self. But the correspondence goes deeper. We know that dreams are constructed from wishes, more than that, from wishes that cannot be openly acknowledged. The distorted representation of such wishes in dreams makes oneiric images, in Freud's famous expression, 'a highroad to the unconscious'. The unconscious itself can be described only in terms of the wishes through which it seeks entry into consciousness.

The dreamworld becomes possible, then, only because of the withdrawal of our waking sensory self that keeps reality constantly before us and provides, normally, an insurmountable obstacle to the free realisation of the unconscious. The removal of this reality – the destruction of the ego – allows an absolute freedom to construct the world in conformity with our hidden desires. It is just such a 'regression' to dreamlike possibilities that informs de Sade's erotic vision of confinement.

As well as recognising confinement as a form of madness we can draw upon another branch of the 'literature of confinement' – reports of mental 'breakdowns', psychiatric investigations, memoirs from asylums – to find descriptions of madness as a species of confinement.

To replicate the description of confinement from these other sources, which all begin at least with experience unconstrained by any visible physical boundary, helps overcome our reluctance to conceive of confinement as being anything other than a particular place.

It has been necessary also to introduce a certain sequential orderliness into this description, to move according to an apparently 'logical' plan from a prototypical example, through changes in the a priori framework of space, time and corporeality to a synthetic metamorphosis and a new selfhood. There is no suggestion, however, of any underlying causal or logical order to such a description. To emphasise the immediacy, totality and absoluteness of confinement we can organise this additional description, using the alternative sources from the madhouse, in the reverse order. Now that we are intimate with the ways of confinement we can make our own inverted repetition and describe in abbreviated form all its characteristic devices from this new material. We can begin again with the self-confined self and discover again the terrifying dislodgment of the self from its body, then find a synthetic statement of its own peculiar metamorphosis in Chekhov's story Ward Number Six, before tracing the decomposition of corporeality, time and space that leads to a prototypical example; the 'case' of Daniel Paul Schreber.

THE SELF-CONFINED SELF

Antonin Artaud, during his second stay in an asylum wrote in an essay 'Fragments from a Diary in Hell' of having been 'abandoned by my body'. He no longer belonged inside his own skin but floated about himself observing his body as a horribly sensitive contrivance over which he no longer had proper control.
   The self, given this extraordinary liberty from its normal physical embodiment, has to construct a fantastic content for itself. The self-confined self, just as much as the confined self, is both lost and found in the same moment. Forced from its natural synthesis the self escapes into thin air, into nothingness, continuing to fashion a life for itself as if it still existed and resorts to the most extravagant fantasy. It is quite characteristic of the mad to believe in their delusional system, their whole selfhood depends upon it, hence its extraordinary resistance to 'treatment'. We are much less likely, however, to believe them. Their fantasised selfhood is not 'authentic' has no substance or reality to it and we are quite content to call it delusional. We remain less gullible, for some reason more certain of ourselves, when confronted by the extravagant claims of the mad that they have 'found themselves' in their illness; than we are when confronted with the equally extravagant morality of The Miracle of the Roses.
   The mad, too, as they are in confinement, have been forced to make the negative repetition and are subject to the negative dialectic, that we have seen dissolves the selfhood of captives of all kinds. As Freud recognised, the psychotic suffers from his efforts to get well, his resistance, his grasping with all the strength of desperation to a phantasm of himself. His 'symptoms' are not direct expressions of the 'illness' itself, but efforts, logical within their own terms, to defeat confinement. But, as we have seen, in confinement resistance is converted into a diabolical complicity, into symptoms and the visible forms of madness.
   Artaud remarks again, in another essay 'A Description of a Physical State', that this flight of the self from its natural synthesis renders the real world unrecognisable. This 'disembodiment of reality' consists

especially in a 'sort of break . . . between objects and the feelings they exercise on our mind' a crumbling of our normal ability to organise our sensory impressions. A breakdown in the 'instantaneous classification of objects . . . in their own sensed emotional order'.

Artaud's intense personal reconstructions are codified and ordered by psychiatrists in terms such as psychosis and schizophrenia. They give confinement another name, as if it were not already overendowed with disguises. The academic literature can also be nevertheless a rich source of description. Eugene Bleuler's classic text Dementia Praecox or the Group of Schizophrenias has remained a standard work of reference largely because of its powerful and comprehensive descriptions of psychotic 'symptomology'. His case material always outweighs his 'theoretical' analyses and this has given the book an appeal beyond the narrow confines of the history of psychiatric thought. It is astonishing how often, in fact, he describes experiences in terms which were to be repeated almost word for word by Nadezhda Mandelstam, Andrey Sinyavsky and Wole Soyinka.

Bleuler notices for example the wild oscillation between lethargy and torpor on the one hand and demonic rage on the other, recalling Dostoevsky's description of his fellow prisoners. Their selfhood has been driven away, they no longer care to have an 'interest' in their bodies; hence

> they sit about the institutions in which they are confined with expressionless faces, hunched up, the image of indifference. They permit themselves to be dressed and undressed like automatons, to be led from their customary place of inactivity to the messhall and back again without expressing any sign of satisfaction or dissatisfaction. They do not even seem to react to injuries inflicted on them by other patients.

At other times, however, the same patient may be subject to the most violent and unendurable sensitivity.

Extremes may be present within the same patient simultaneously. Bleuler describes this as a condition of 'ambivalence'. The patient might experience a powerful desire to eat and, at the same time, be overwhelmingly disgusted by the sight of food. He might declare himself to be, and at the same time not to be, a person. This 'ambivalence' whatever its meaning might be in particular cases, certainly expresses or represents the removal of distinctions and differentiations which is common to the experience of confinement. Confinement, like the unconscious, knows no contradictions. The absolute freedom it allows the self cannot be confounded by any limit. You may become anything and nothing at the same time, escaping all the limitations normal to existence at the cost of losing the content, the material, from which the self is really composed.

The 'inner-life' of the schizophrenic, despite its erosion, assumes, for the patient, as it does for the prisoner, an overwhelming significance. An 'inner-life' is, after all, all they are left. Bleuler concurs with de Sade in describing this inner-world before it, too, is annihilated, in terms of wishes and desires. Schizophrenic patients, he writes, 'have encased themselves with their desires and wishes', referring to the condition as 'autism'. A withdrawal to the level of elemental, undirected desire. This 'regression' often creates for itself a physical constraint more severe than even an asylum can impose. Bleuler reports that one of his patients 'had built a wall around herself so closely confining that she often felt as if she were actually in a chimney'.

The schizophrenic may, for relatively extended periods, retain his intelligence and intellectual powers. They have however become detached from reality and he lives entirely within his own fantasy world. The schizophrenic experiences, along with Golding's prisoner in Free Fall, the metaphysical abyss which is the prelude to a 'new type of knowledge' and becomes along with Genet 'master of his own thinking'. This subjective self-absorption intensifies and becomes elaborated into a complex delusional 'system' barely comprehensible to anyone on the 'outside'.

The self-contained self, more obviously than the vanishing identity of the prisoner is beyond despair, has been caught by some kind of inverted subjectivity against which its best efforts become self-defeating. The self within confinement, whatever external form such confinement may take, has nowhere to go, has nothing to weigh against its awful immediacy, its imposition of its own reality and its own logic without regard to the modest need for freedom.

The powerful negative synthesis effected by confinement, and its capacity to drive life beyond despair is vividly described in Anton Chekhov's dramatic story Ward Number Six.

The setting is typical of Chekhov; a provincial town cut off from the flow of great events. The town is isolated, the hospital stands outside the town itself and Ward Six itself is a forgotten corner of the hospital. There are only five patients, it would hardly seem worth a second glance, it rarely attracted a first glance.

The patients were 'looked after' for the most part by Nikita, a retired soldier, who saw his duty as that of a guard and whose basic conviction was that 'they have to be beaten'. The major protagonists of the piece, however, are one of the patients, Gromov, a kindly, sensitive and well educated man of noble birth who suffers from 'persecution mania'; and a doctor, Ragin, who is new to the town. Ragin throws himself into his new work with passionate, but shortsighted, idealism. He begins with the highest expectations of his own efforts, and the greatest contempt for his superior who has allowed neglect and complacency to ruin the hospital.

Gromov is 'always in a state of agitation and excitement', 'always under the strain of some vague undefined expectation'. He spends most of his time lying on his bed or 'discourses on human baseness, on violence vanquishing truth, on the glorious life that will one day appear on earth, on the iron grilles on the windows which constantly remind him of the stupidity and cruelty of the oppressors'. Years before Gromov had witnessed prisoners walking in the streets, in chains. His reaction was uncontrollable and much more intense, we imagine, than our slight nausea on reading George Jackson's letter. 'For some reason', Chekhov writes, without suggesting the nature of the reason, 'he felt that he too would be clapped in irons and led this same way through the mud to prison.' He became convinced that he was about to be arrested, his every movement became laden with dread; he could not shake off the powerful impression of impending doom and, giving way completely, 'abandoned himself to terror and despair'. He avoided other people and preferred instead, to remain in solitude. He hid in the cellar of his house – finally he was sent to the hospital.

The new doctor, much to everyone's surprise, visited the patients in Ward Six. He became fascinated by Gromov's conversation and recognised in him a kindred spirit. He returned again and again to enjoy the intellectual stimulation afforded by his new companion.

Ragin soon came to realise that although the hospital

was totally inadequate and the conditions under which the patients were 'held' were abhorrent, there was really nothing he could do about it. The task was beyond him and, in addition, he quickly found better 'reasons' for leaving well alone. 'So long as there are prisons and asylums', he tells Gromov, 'someone must be put into them' – an excuse he later admits to be rather feeble. He revises his argument in favour of a more radical defense of suffering. The patients, had they been spared their illnesses, would be left even worse off; 'their insipid lives would be as empty as an amoeba's', he declares. Their suffering imparts a meaning to their otherwise vacant lives, it heightens their self-awareness and enhances their subjective vitality. In this he confuses confinement and despair. Even a philosophy of personal suffering, indeed especially such a philosophy, ought absolutely to reject confinement which leaves no possibility, no freedom and in consequence no spiritual trial.

Gromov responds to the argument by accusing the doctor of attempting, rather inadequately, to rationalise his growing indolence and complacency.

His recurrent visits and animated discussions with Gromov excite considerable comment among his colleagues. Ragin was summoned to appear before a committee. Some excuse was offered, but in effect it was an examination of his sanity (the same trick is still used: Zhores Medvedev tells us in A Question of Madness that he was called to his local school to discuss his son's progress, and found himself committed to an asylum).

Ragin was persuaded to accompany a friend on a convalescent trip abroad. But he has already withdrawn into 'his own' world; the world he shared, with Gromov. A world shared not by virtue of forming with him a genuine social relationship, but as a result of their both 'belonging' separately and individually, to the world of confinement which, as a void intolerant of all social distinctions, reduces experience to a common form. He found he could not raise his friend's thoughts 'to a serious, elevated plane', no more could his companion interest Ragin in any diversion or frivolity – 'He lay with his face to the wall and suffered agonies while his friend tried to divert him with talk, and found rest only in his absence'.

When he returned to the hospital Ragin found his position had been usurped by his assistant, and he had to find new lodgings. His withdrawal

continued. He gave up reading and could enjoy only
'dull' mechanical chores. He resisted any further
visits from his friends. He 'lay down on his sofa,
turned his back, and listened with clenched teeth;
he felt layers of scum forming on the surface of
his soul, and after their visits the scum seemed
to rise higher, as if it were going to choke him'.
Finally, he threw a 'tantrum' and evicted his friends,
answering their advice that he go into the hospital
as a patient with the declaration that there was
nothing wrong other than that, 'in the course of
twenty years I have found only one intelligent man
and he is mad'.

But in the end he does agree to go into the hospital;
into Ward Six. In a brief moment of lucidity he
tries to escape and is beaten by Nikita. But it is
all over by then, he has realised his true condition,
his confinement which began as a purely mental
phenomenon has been given a substantial, physical
form, and the following day he dies. Both Gromov
and Ragin, interestingly enough, find themselves
locked away only after their subjective worlds have
undergone irreversible changes, changes which themselves
anticipate the consequences of being incarcerated.
Confinement, as a metamorphosis in experience, can
begin anywhere.

The important distinction between confinement and
despair can be made in the contrast between Chekhov's
Ward Number Six - which is a description of confinement
- and his A Dull Story - which describes despair.
The central character of the latter piece, having
discovered fairly late in life that his whole existence
has been a pointless, meaningless waste of time,
is condemned to live on, in guilt, for years. In
this we might add Chekhov's 'solution' to his story
is more successful than say Tolstoy's Death of Ivan
Ilych or even Thomas Mann's Death in Venice, both
of which similarly bring their central characters
to the point of realising their own despair - and
then allow them the ultimate release of death. But,
as Kierkegaard often repeats, despair is the sickness
unto death, a sickness which never kills, which
offers no physical release. Judge William might see
the conclusion to A Dull Story as optimistic; its
hero has begun to despair 'seriously', he has become
conscious of the triviality of his secular career
and is left sufficient time to persevere in his inward
journey.

Ward Number Six, however, must end in death
because confinement, in the end, annihilates its

victims. It does so only after a prolonged, one-sided 'struggle' in which everything human is sucked out of the captive, forcing him to resist, and in resisting forcing from him a more deeply destructive acquiescence, an insane co-operation in the task of self-destruction.

Perhaps the end comes too quickly for Ragin who is not drawn out of existence with quite the finality of Gregor Samsa's metamorphosis but he suffers, none the less, the same decomposition and personal disintegration.

Chekhov describes the whole world of confinement in his Ward Number Six. The transformation in the experience of the body is less marked than in Metamorphosis, but is none the less clear. Ragin could feel at times 'layers of scum' forming on his soul and we should not doubt he felt this as a physical process. Others have reported similarly alien physical experiences in which they seem to be turned inside out, and their internal organs gain a maddening sensitivity. Artaud, for example, feels the erosion in his sense of reality 'in the limbs and blood', and can sense like Ragin his 'gastric functions flapping like a flag'. This inner sensitivity becomes so strange that it lies, as Artaud says, 'beneath what speech may express'. Speech serves still to suggest, however, a good deal about his other bodily changes. He had the feeling continually of 'dragging one's body about', it never seemed properly to belong to him. Yet it worried him continually with inexplicable and painful sensations. He felt, 'A sharp, burning sensation in my limbs, muscles knotted, as if raw, feeling like glass, brittle, fear, cringing at movement or noise'. Even when he gained some relief from the torment he was afflicted by 'a sort of dead tiredness' his body oscillating from frightful hyper-sensitivity to a dead weight which refused to respond to his will. His movements like Gregor Samsa's 'have to be reorganised'. He cannot localise in space and time even the sensations that distress him, he cannot remember how his body works. A burning sensation, for example, is 'probably localised in the skin, but feeling like the radical removal of a limb and offering the mind nothing but tenuous woolly pictures of limbs, pictures of distant limbs out of place'.

Others too have felt their bodies to be taken up into the operation of some diabolical mechanical device. Anna Kavan, for example, whose Asylum

Piece is one of the most sensitive and immediately comprehensible accounts of a 'breakdown' was afflicted by 'Machines in the Head'. Sleep was made virtually impossible by them. 'I am awake now for good, or rather, for bad', she writes, 'the wheels, my masters, are already vibrating with incipient motion; the whole mechanism is preparing to begin the monotonous, hateful functioning of which I am the dispirited slave.' There was nothing to be done but endure the torture, after all, 'What's the good of appealing to senseless machinery'. Its imposition, its frightful control is 'intolerable and inescapable at the same time'. The prospect of a lovely Spring day is a momentary pleasure, the view 'becomes phantasmal, transparent as the texture of dream plasma, banished by the monstrous mechanical outline of pulleys, wheels, shafts, which in their orderly, remorseless and too well known evolutions now with increasing insistence demand my attention'.

In confinement the body is no longer your own. Oscillating between intolerable sensitivity and intolerable insensitivity, it becomes transformed into a condition of pure corporeality. Eugene Bleuler in a torrential passage that can be quoted only in part from his Dementia Praecox, describes with Rabelaisian excess, reminiscent also of his great predecessor Robert Burton's Anatomy of Melancholy, some of the more characteristic bodily complaints.

> Any organ can be the seat of the most severe pain. The scalp can become so sensitive that the slightest touch of the hair may produce terrible pain. Every bone of the body may ache. The patients are beaten and burnt; they are pierced by red-hot needles, daggers or spears; their arms are being wrenched out; their heads are being bent backwards; their legs are being made smaller; their eyes are being pulled out so that in a mirror it looks like they are entirely out of their sockets, their head is being squeezed together; their bodies have become like accordions, being pulled out and then again pressed together. They have ice inside their heads; they have been put inside a refrigerator. Boiling oil is felt inside their bodies; their skin is full of stones . . . Any and every organ has been removed, cut-up, torn to pieces, inverted. One testicle is swollen. The nerves, the muscles, various organs are being tightened.

Hardly surprising that the self seeks to escape into fantasy; an escape which only heightens and accentuates the disruption in the normal sense of time and space. Anna Kavan remarks, for example, on the 'state of unreality' in which she had been living 'for some time. Perhaps it is not really so very long, perhaps not more than a month or so; one loses the sense of time as well as everything else in this wretched condition.' Or again she writes in bewilderment 'Last summer, or perhaps it was only the other day - I find it so difficult to keep count of time now'.

Lost in time the space in which she lives becomes menacing, hostile; the same house, on good days, 'looks like a harmless grey animal that would eat out of your hand' but on bad days, and especially at night 'the old house opens its stony, inward turning eyes and watches me with a hostility that can scarcely be borne'. The transformation leaves nothing of its former intimacy and warmth. 'The old walls drape themselves in transparent curtains of hate. Like a beast of prey the house lies in ambush for me.' Her space is as restricted and empty as a prison cell 'coiling itself around me, I know I cannot escape. Imprisoned in its very fabric I am like a small worm', or perhaps, we might guess, a cockroach.

THE OTHER SELF

The confined self and the self-confined self experience a common world. They have undergone the same metamorphosis. The experience of confinement is, because it consists in genuine nothingness, impossible to communicate directly. But the flattering self-consciousness of memoirs and reminiscences which make up so much of the 'literature of confinement' becomes a fullblown, hermetically sealed, theoretical system in the delusions of the psychotic.

Psychotics, as a general rule, do not write memoirs. Many are never released from the asylums which have become an integral part of their madness. There remains, however, on the margins of the comprehensible, the literary work which comes closer perhaps than any other to conveying the absolute negativism of confinement. Daniel Paul Schreber's Memoirs of My Nervous Illness has exercised its peculiar fascination over many readers without ever entirely giving up its secret. It is a message from someone on the other side; someone on the inside.

Schreber, who was an Austrian High Court Judge, recounts in his book the circumstances and nature of his two separate 'nervous' illnesses, and describes the two periods of his confinement in asylums. His first illness, a relatively short affair during 1884 and 1885 was accounted for in terms of overwork during his candidature for Parliament. The second dated from October 1893 and, he tells us in his book, 'continues still' (written in 1906). The second 'attack' was again attributed to overwork, in this instance as a consequence of his promotion to the duties of the High Court in Dresden. Though he recovered from his initial illness, the second attack, despite the most modern treatment of his psychiatrist, Dr Flechsig, proved intractable. He was deprived of sleep, no drugs were effective and after two nights at Flechsig's fashionable clinic he was isolated in a cell for dementia patients. He unsuccessfully attempted suicide.

His book was written while still a patient at the Sonnenstein Asylum and formed the basic 'evidence' in his pioneering legal battle to regain his liberty.

Confinement, it has been suggested, can be represented by reversals of one sort or another; the abstract becomes concrete and the concrete abstract, the transvaluation of values is accomplished within it. Schreber falls in with this convention. Much of his book is written in what he calls the 'basic language'. this comprises a quite complex vocabulary of terms which invert everyday meanings. 'Reward' in the basic language refers to punishment; 'unholy' means holy; 'juice' stands for venom; 'tested souls' are those awaiting purification, while those at various stages of such purification are referred to as 'Satans', 'Devils', 'Assistant Devils', 'Senior Devils' and 'Basic Devils'. Schreber himself disclaims all responsibility for such terms which, lying beyond the arbitrariness of human language, have been revealed to him directly, through voices that spoke to him. And, we might add, with which he could not converse – the confined are never allowed to answer back.

Schreber's 'theory', which describes his 'illness' is a complete cosmology, concerned with the nature of God and His relationship to the world. Schreber, though again it is no part of his own personal wishes, is a central character in this cosmology. He is, in fact, horrified at his own pre-eminence, at the special relationship to God which constitutes his illness, and which poses a threat to the stability of the natural order.

Schreber begins by telling us that 'the human soul is contained in the nerves of the body'. And we soon learn that 'God to start with is only nerve, not body, and akin therefore to the human soul'. God is a kind of infinitely extended, eternal person who has been 'volatilised' beyond all physical attributes. That is to say, Schreber's God is the experience of confinement as an absolute.

God, in the form of rays, has the capacity to enter into all created things. He, however, must be wary of direct contact with living human nerves, because they may trap Him in earthly matters. Living Souls have a powerful but dangerous attractiveness for Him. What God really seeks is dead bodies because death transforms the nerve substance into 'rays' which He can assimilate. He draws these deceased nerves or rays to Himself 'awakening them to a new heavenly life'. the purest of human nerves when extracted from corpses are reconstituted into 'souls' in the 'forecourts of heaven'. As 'souls', however, and in various stages of purification, they could be given a human appearance. These become the 'fleetingly-improvised-men' of Schreber's hallucinated experience. Those 'souls' who finally attain 'Blessedness' could retain, in their new form an impression of their past life, as memory but were unable to carry this forward, as it were, and lived in a timeless void without sensory impressions of any kind.

This, rather briefly, is the 'miraculous structure' of Schreber's cosmology. In a fairly direct manner it reconstructs for us much of the previous discussion of the 'literature of confinement'. If we simply remember that Schreber is suffering from confinement and assume his book is an effort to communicate this experience to us, then the correspondence between it and more familiar memoirists becomes apparent.

The otherness of confinement is represented (logically enough) by the otherness of God. This otherness, although it has an infinite superiority and power over the human is nevertheless dependent upon the human realm for its own form of life. Significantly God consumes dead souls, deals only with corpses and extracts from them the 'rays' which provide Him with energy. And through these reconstituted 'souls' He can influence those still living. Indeed God could, in the end, be destroyed by a too prolonged contact with the living. Confinement, in other words, is an otherness which exists by virtue of its power to destroy human freedom and feeds off the souls of its victims. It is a literal House of the Dead.

Schreber then goes on to describe how this otherness invaded him and began to reorganise every aspect of his experience. Schreber recognises it is possible for him to describe this only because he has, to some extent, benefited from a 'remission' in his illness and has recovered somewhat from its most serious phase.

The nerve language, the direct effect of the 'rays' upon Schreber, appears as 'silent voices'. They operate either directly upon him or through some intermediary, most importantly Dr Flechsig his psychiatrist, and aim at nothing less than the 'soul murder' of Schreber himself. The voices begin to direct and control him, 'contrary to the Order of the World and man's natural right to be master of his own nerves'. The voices at times extinguished his own will and sense of reality. Compulsive thinking was the result; the complete removal, in Bleuler's terms, of normal associative inhibitions. He thus heard, like Osip Mandelstam, the voices of hundreds 'if not thousands' of people at once; all invading him – an 'unholy turmoil in my head', he says, reminding us of so many other's initial reactions to imprisonment. The voices might talk coherently at first but their internal order broke down and trailed off into a meaningless repetition of 'pure' sounds.

The 'emptying out' of experience which is so characteristic of confinement had affected Schreber in particularly horrifying ways. His will had been overcome by an alien force; he had to submit and could not comprehend the new world into which he had been thrust.

As well as the bombardment of internal voices the 'rays' attacked him bodily, and attempted to 'unman' him. This 'unmanning' in fact was a necessary result of the collision between living human nerves and divine rays. Schreber was saved from a total bodily transformation by an admixture of his own and the detestable Flechsig's unpurified 'tested rays', which had the effect of polluting the channel between him and God. (And we might say kept confinement a little longer at bay by holding on to the most unsavoury of human attributes – remember Ivan Mordvin's partiality for sugar.) Even so, Schreber has discovered his body is no longer completely his own and is afflicted by a whole series of unpleasant changes. Leprosy and plague hover around his room and threaten him at every moment; they have already destroyed the rest of the world. He suffered from 'scorpions' in the head and tiny crab-like souls tried to destroy his brain. Worse than that, his body became the scene of countless terrible 'miracles'. 'Hardly a single limb or organ of my body escaped', he remarks, but those connected most directly to his 'unmanning' were the most terrifying. He suffered partial retraction of the sex organs, loss of hair from his moustache and beard, softening and 'dissolution' within the abdomen and loss of stature. Almost as bad was what he termed the 'compression-of-the-chest-miracle.'

His whole musculature was out of control and unresponsive to his most determined efforts at co-ordination. His stomach had been removed and food and drink disappeared into him by a miraculous absorption – one of Sinyavsky's fellow-prisoners similarly remarked that his food too disappeared before it reached his stomach. He suffered from the 'head-compression-machine'. His description becomes even more nightmarish than Metamorphosis, and more comprehensively grotesque than Bleuler's hectic observations; we are left wishing he had only turned into a cockroach.

The system of 'rays' that impinged on his body and the rays that emanated from him completely destroyed the normal physical limitations of space and allowed Schreber to experience directly the underlying substance extended throughout all created things in the cosmos. As a means of self-protection, Schreber began attracting some of the 'tested souls' to himself, absorbed them and destroyed them in his sleep. They, in turn, resisted, withdrawing to distant stars where, none the less, Schreber pursued them by simply extending his new nerve/ray substance into which his body was being transformed.

His body, in other terms, was being metamorphosed, through the horrifying device of 'miracles', into a primitive, undifferentiated substance without any specific identity that he could recognise as being or belonging to him. He was becoming, despite his strenuous resistance, at one with the underlying substance of the universe. And not as a temporary, reversible, mystic experience, but permanently and physically.

Yet some mystical charm still clung to this descent into nothingness. During the period of the most intense physical assault and the most bewildering confusion in the normal framework of his senses he experienced, he claims, the most 'holy' time of his life. It was 'when my soul was immensely inspired by supernatural things'. He too, it seems, experienced an extraordinary and unexpected sense of inner freedom at the heart of confinement. Schreber makes it clear that he was not, before his illness, a 'religious' person in the normal sense of the term, but looking back he sees his illness as the period of his 'holy time'. It was significantly during this time that he achieved the logical impossibility of 'direct communication' with the Divine. It was in this 'direct communication' that Schreber was warned of the approaching 'end of the world'. Indeed the end was not far off because Schreber regarded himself as the last survivor inhabiting the planet, all others were appearances only, no more than 'fleetingly-improvised' characters craftily stage-managed to deceive him into giving way and finally surrendering to God. What has occurred, he claims, involves a profound change in the relationship between God and the World. (Casanova, too, tells us that in confinement the natural order is inverted.) And this inversion may not appear in objective, visible effects but remains contained in an inward transformation. (Confinement, we might say, is a kind of repetition.)

Schreber's hallucinations mark a radical 'withdrawal' from the world of normal reality. 'I mainly sat,' he tells us, 'motionless the whole day on a chair at my table.' He considered this 'absolute passivity almost a religious duty' and a duty 'induced by the voices that talk to me'. This simulation of a corpse signals the near triumph of God over him; Schreber, indeed is enlisted at this point as one of God's chosen allies. This fantasy – that he has joined forces with God – completes the dominance of confinement over his resistance to it. In the end he is forced to acquiesce through his own stubborn insistence on the reality of his private, inner life. His extreme withdrawal as a means of escape, an attempt to find an area of freedom for himself in which his identity can be preserved, has the paradoxical result of requiring his complete immobility. The identity, within confinement, of resistance and capitulation is crystallised in Schreber's meaningless gesture.

The destruction of his world is almost complete, yet his delusional system succeeds in both positing the otherness of confinement and, somehow, communicating to us a sense of its real presence. Schreber begins with his own experience, we can sense time and space falling away within it, we can watch his body become changed into an instrument of some foreign agent. He describes for us the complexity of the self's flight from an unbearable reality. And in all this he allows us a glimpse, too, of the physical reality of his constraint. He reports, for example, as an incidental remark, that he was detained in a cell for dementia patients for two-and-a-half years; a cell that was emptied but for 'an iron bedstead, a bedpan and some bedding'. Its single window, like its companion in Ward Number Six, for the most part heavily shuttered.

The Schreber 'case' became the most celebrated psychosis within the psychiatric literature. Freud wrote a full length analysis based almost exclusively on the Memoirs; Bleuler too often quotes from Schreber's book and Jung (Bleuler's assistant in Zurich for a time) also wrote on the subject. A good deal of the subsequent discussion has been concerned, naturally enough, with conflicting aetiological accounts of Schreber's 'symptoms'. Jung claimed, for example, that Freud's 'explanation' - that the delusional system resulted from an inadequate effort to repress homosexual impulses - was weak and entirely ignored the 'religious' form of the delusional system, which was central to the whole 'case'. In Jung's view the religious 'archetypes' sprang directly from the unconscious 'unmediated' by the lower instinctual life.

The 'cause' of his illness is not, for us, the central issue. His symptoms doubtless refer both to a particular history of cause and effect and, what is critical for us, to his experience of the world at the time. That his delusions should have taken a religious form need not unduly surprise us. The peculiar pervasiveness of religious delusions within confinement has already been noted. Casanova himself noticed it. Soyinka's language becomes increasingly Biblical as the account of his imprisonment continues. Sinyavsky devotes several short essays in his book to religious themes. And Solzhenitsyn, in a slightly puzzled tone, declares that all 'religious' prisoners survive imprisonment intact. Schreber, in portraying the confined world through religious imagery is, apparently, in good company. Kierkegaard makes clear the basis of such a form of representation. He has pointed out (the first writer in modern times to do so), the radical separateness of the religious sphere from reflection (you cannot be led by rational argument to make the leap of faith), from sensuous experience (religiosity is not given directly in immediate experience), or from ethics (religion is not an alternative language of morality). The repetition into the religious sphere conserves the integrity of reflection, immediate experience and ethics, but places the individual in a new relation to them. It also precipitates a new relationship with God. It is in this restructuring of inward relationships that the self reaches its truth. Kierkegaard describes this relationship to God within the religious sphere as the 'single one'.

The experience of confinement, it has been suggested, is a kind of inversion of this protected repetition. It is forced, not voluntary, and in it there is everything to lose and nothing to gain. But it too results in a complete restructuring of inward relations, and involves a radically new form of subjectivity which leaves the individual in a state of isolation. This isolation, however, is at the opposite pole of 'self-development' from the 'religious experience' sought by the faithful and as an aid to which a temporary withdrawal from the world may be sought. The isolation of confinement is, rather, a simple negation of freedom. The 'solitary one' rather than the 'single one' who has been left with nothing more substantial than the memory of its own existence. This solitariness, indeed, sinks beneath any form of individuation; the captive does not sustain a private relationship to the world of confinement, he is like Schreber totally absorbed within it and cannot, in the end, distinguish himself from the cell which contains him.

Schreber's 'religious' delusions should not, then, be mistaken for 'genuine' mystical experience. His God absorbed him, his identity became confused and finally lost in the volatile substance of his fantasy. His delusional system was a protective device that destroyed him and within which he became hermetically sealed. But the 'idea' of the religious is an almost inescapable accompaniment to the notion of confinement. It provides, ready made, a rich language in which to express the helplessness, solitariness and irrationality of the subject, and a system of images which expresses for us the incommunicable nature of a nonhuman world.

Elias Canetti, in his book Crowds and Power, has also analysed Schreber's Memoirs. Schreber suffers, he claims, from a disease of power and interprets his book as a convincing phenomenology of power.

Canetti argues that the central 'symptoms' of Schreber's illness is the feeling of being at the centre of a hostile crowd. Schreber has the sensation of being in the midst of stars, or of small creatures or other objects. He feeds off these creatures, absorbs them into himself and draws strength from them. Schreber's whole book, he suggests, is a remarkably accurate account of political power in the modern world; the emergence of a powerful individual through the subordination of a crowd under him. Schreber's book is, in other words, an expression of the 'cult of the personality'; he is at the centre and expands in every direction as an omnipresent force. Schreber pictures God as an ultimate despot, and Canetti interprets the 'unmanning' process as Schreber's tactic of winning over, or seducing, Him. Schreber's aim in doing this is to gain complete ascendancy over the Order of the World. Canetti concludes that 'It is difficult to resist the suspicion that behind paranoia, as behind all power, lies the same profound urge; the desire to get other men out of the way so as to be the only one; or, in the milder, and indeed often admitted form to get others to help him become the only one'.

Canetti's view, however, is unconvincing at a formal level. It ignores, for example, the obvious fact that Schreber experienced his 'miracles' as an imposition. His only co-operative behaviour is a means to secure himself against an alien power, to regain his own body and banish his demons in a long and natural sleep. Schreber's aloneness is not the exalted status of the all-powerful; indeed quite the reverse; it is the solitariness of total subordination under an inhuman power. Schreber experiences the psychotic 'end of the world', not a conquest.

Canetti has in a sense offered a modern 'secular' translation of the Memoirs. A political version of otherness as total domination or total subordination. The religious form, however, despite the abandonment of the sacred within modern societies, remains the more powerful and convincing. The political, no matter how excessively authoritarian, remains a wholly human content. Repression, exploitation, totalitarianism and inequalities of all kinds have profound significance for the life of 'free' individuals in modern societies. But confinement belongs to a different dimension. If it is seen exclusively as a variety of political perversity then its absoluteness, its quality of radical distinctiveness from 'real life', is lost. Canetti's assimilation of Schreber's 'case' to a general theory of political power attempts to conjoin two very different kinds of horror.

Confinement and domination are, of course, related in a rather general and indirect way. Confinement must be imposed, it must be given its foothold in experience through the agency of existing human forms of life. Once established, however, it works through its own particular kind of negativism to pervert human agencies to its ultimate purpose. Its introduction is always, so to speak, on the back of oppression and political domination which has some limited and 'rational' end. But it outgrows these ends, and attains a life beyond its own instrumentality. It becomes an alien power. And it is as much an alien power for those who suffer a psychotic collapse while ostensibly at 'liberty' as it is for those cast into a solitary cell.

This transition from the instrumentality of confinement to its triumph as an alien force has been brilliantly documented in Schreber's case by Morton Schatzman in his fascinating book, Soul Murder. Schreber suffered confinement first as a child, at the hands of his father and the peculiar restraint to which he was subjected then re-emerged in later life as delusional ideas and hallucinated experiences. Schatzman describes the eccentric, though at the time not unpopular, ideas on child rearing held by Daniel Paul's father. Schreber senior, author of many pamphlets on mental and physical hygiene, it seems, was obsessively concerned with correct physical and moral development. To this end, he utilised a number of instruments to 'correct' the faults incipient in his son's growth and ensure his development into a perfectly 'upright' adult. The 'miracles' afflicting so many parts of Schreber's body in later years could be interpreted as 'images' of thos earlier forms of physical constraint. As a child he was forced to wear complex apparatus to 'correct' his posture. These included the use of metal shafts, tight harnesses and bindings so that he could not bend his back, or let his head drop or turn sharply.

Schatzman suggests that the fact these constraints were imposed by his father gave rise to intensely 'ambivalent' emotional reactions in the son. Schreber's later symptoms at one and the same time express his horror of such contraptions and his utter subordination to and love for his father who imposed them upon him. Schatzman's book is detailed and evidently plausible, but whatever the specific cause of Schreber's symptoms they provide, through a set of consistent and powerful images, a compelling first hand account of confinement. They tell us in a quite literal way, which is why it is so difficult to understand, how it feels to be locked-up.

The confined self and the self-confined self experience the world in the same way; they suffer the same split between the self and its body; they watch, bewildered, the destruction of space and time, they seek refuge, hopelessly, in fantasy; they may even cling to their impoverished existence as a revelatory truth. In confinement all things are rendered not simply equal but the same. The individual is absorbed into its universal substance, all those distinctions and differentiations of which existence is composed, all those dualities and contradictions which philosophical speculation attempts, again and again, to circumvent; miraculously coalesce and harmonise. Confinement is the wonderland in which difference is finally, and by no mere conceptual trickery, overcome. The metaphysical longing for unity, coherence and monism; that desire to discover beneath the flux of appearance an unchanging substance is at last satisfied as the captive is pushed over the precipice of despair into the void.

PART TWO
Childhood

'Somehow the sun does not seem to shine so brightly as it used; the trackless meadows of old time have shrunk and dwindled away to a few poor acres.'
Kenneth Grahame, *The Golden Age*

5 The Art of Recollection

Ford Maddox Ford begins his Memories and Impressions by noticing, quite suddenly, that he had grown up. The experience is not uncommon and another particularly fine example can be drawn from Richard Hughes's masterpiece, A High Wind in Jamaica; Emily was, we are told, 'thinking vaguely about some bees and a fairy queen, when it suddenly flashed into her mind that she was she'.

This profound change in the experience of ourselves is announced by a failure in memory. Maddox Ford realised he had changed because, he says, 'I was forgetting my own childhood'. And Emily, after an awestruck examination of her own body searched her memory unsuccessfully for some clue as to her origin, 'Wasn't she perhaps God, herself', she wondered. 'Was it that she was trying to remember?.'

Such a discontinuity in our personal history appears, of course, only in restrospect. We have no intuition of the leap we are about to make and do not notice the past slipping away from us until we awake one morning and find it no longer part of us, or, rather that we are no longer part of it. Despite the prodigious difficulties of growing-up we slip out of childhood, in the end, effortlessly and afterwards are bewildered and embarrassed at relics of ourselves - an old photograph, a forgotten playmate, an anecdote retold by a once favourite uncle - that are no longer recognisable. We are drawn by such curiosities, and even more by an insatiable desire for self-discovery, to play the game of 'earliest recollections'.

What can we recall of our own childhood? Very little it seems, though it is only recently that the phenomenon of childhood 'amnesia' has been widely noticed or appeared puzzling. G. Stanley Hall, one of the first 'scientific' students of childhood, for example, still found it worthwhile to warn against overdependence upon our own memory. In his introduction to the first American edition of Wilhelm Preyer's pioneering study of his own infant son, The Mind of the Child (published in 1881), he writes, 'many think they have all the knowledge of childhood they require from memory of their own childish years. This is wrong. Mental and moral growth necessarily involves increasing oblivion of everything of childhood save mere incidents.' Such oblivion can descend with remarkable suddenness and completeness, blotting out memories even of the games and pastimes which, only shortly before, formed such an important part of our lives. Iona and Peter Opie in their indispensable work, Children's Games in Street and Playground, remark that 'older children can be remarkably poor informants', quite suddenly drained of the information they were so willing to pass on at a younger age. They seem to cross a threshold into a world where such games no longer exist, and they forget apparently how they once played. They even become poor observers, failing to notice other, younger children continuing the traditions of play they become firmly convinced ended with their own 'generation'.

Our efforts to recall ever earlier incidents from our own childhood carries with it, however, a fascination that is intensified rather than diminished by the poverty of results. The 'mere incidents' of these recollections are in themselves often vivid and specific. From among them one quickly establishes a claim to temporal priority over the others – receiving a quite particular, favourite toy, the first appearance of a person to whom we were introduced (we were too young for him to be introduced to us) and who later became important to us, the shape of an upturned stool we once pushed around a smooth kitchen floor – in any event something quite specific. Such recollections, however vivid, remain oddly isolated and always resist accurate dating – making the indubitable precedence of the first an incomprehensible oddity. Equally odd, and puzzling is the triviality of such incidents, their obvious lack of connection with any of the great concerns of childhood. They stubbornly resist being drawn into a broader network of recollection.

Our memory in fact fails us. That peculiar capacity to recall at will something we wish to remember deserts us and we are left grasping at a few fragments as the only reminder of what must once have been a world saturated with sensations.

Occasionally, by piecing together the memories of others as well as our own, or projecting backwards in time memories which derive from a much later period, we can fill out the beginnings of our recollections with the semblance of a more complete record. Andre Gide, thus, provides a good but atypical 'earliest recollection' at the outset of his autobiography, If It Die;

the balcony, or rather the view from the balcony – the bird's eye view of the Place with its ornamental piece of water and fountain, or rather, to be still more exact, I remember the paper dragons which my father launched into the air from the balcony: I remember them floating in the wind over the fountain in the Place below and being carried away as far as the Luxembourg Gardens, where they used sometimes to catch in the top branches of the horse-chestnut trees.

With commendable honesty Gide catches himself in the act of filling out this earliest fragment with a complex of images which belong to a later period. He strips them away to leave the recollection, more accurately, bereft of contextual detail, picking out the flight of the paper dragon alone, carried in the wind and sometimes catching the topmost (in childhood always the topmost) branches of distant trees.

Once accredited as our 'earliest' recollection such images stay with us easily as more or less (usually less) useful pieces of information. We carry them around as part of our current stock of knowledge, retrievable, almost instantly, through the normal functioning of our adult memory. Once rescued from the threshold of oblivion this recollection at least will not share in the general vanishing of our childhood; we remain as confident of its presence, just beneath our consciousness, as we are certain of our ability (once mastered) to ride a bicycle or repeat the seven-times table. Little fragments of childhood escape from the general process of forgetting, in which the rest is lost, by being absorbed into our mature memory, and in the process we even avoid the fear, which might have been present at the time, that we might one day forget them. Once the chain of memory has been forged, however inaccurately, we become convinced of the illusion that our recollection stretches back through imperceptible gradations to this zero point in our personal history.

At other times we find, quite suddenly and unexpectedly, that we have not forgotten as completely as, in our less romantic moments, we had thought. A taste or smell seems magically to open a door on a world we had thought lost to our recollection. The perfume of rhododendron shrubs in bloom, or engine oil on a summer's day, or the note of a distant train caught at the right moment and without exerting our imagination we find ourselves once again seven-years-old, withdrawn into the deeply shaded safety of a bushy den, waiting for our friends to find us. We did not, at the time, notice the overpoweringly sweet aroma, or the waxy texture of the leaves, or the moist, resinous ground as we peered anxiously through arrow-slit windows for the approaching enemy. Then, years later, those very ignored qualities span the interval in time and allow us a privileged recollection.

This second kind of recollection might be called an impression rather than a memory. There is a difference in quality between the two; impressions are more complex, denser than our deliberative memory, they recapture for the moment an entire world of sensation. Where memory is specific and particular, recalling from our childhood some precise but isolated event, impressions condense a world of experience at a particular moment and then releases it within us. Impressions seem to leap over the barriers within our associative and deliberative memory. Yet impressions too are bounded by ignorance. Through them we are privileged to feel again as a child, but we experience a sensory fullness strangely unreal, oddly abstracted from the events it must once have contained. We cannot for long tolerate such a rich, but abstract, experience. Our memory, our logical, reflective, calculative memory reconstructs for us a plausible narrative of events to support such spontaneous impressions of childhood, and provides them with a 'rational' content that, properly speaking, never belonged to them. That wonderful, but fleeting, anticipation that comes with the first incipient recognition of a taste or smell that is about to 'trigger' an impression quickly fades in the disillusionment of concrete memories that come to crowd around it and rationalise for us an otherwise inexplicable pleasure.

Memories and impressions do not work together to provide for us a fuller picture of our early experience. It is not as if each were a faculty adapted to the recollection of different branches of experience. They work separately, they point, so to speak, in opposite directions and remain fundamentally opposed.

The great work of memory is to sustain the present. It convinces us of the reality of our own past and our sense of a continuous personal identity. And it is just this attempt to procure our continuity and selfhood that lends intellectual fascination to the game of early recollections.

Impressions however, in retaining an aspect of the genuinely childish world, recall a subjectivity anterior to this personal identity. A subjectivity that still luxuriates amidst countless possibilities. The more particular and specific, the more objective and precise our memory, then the more the plenitude of this original subjective world is concealed from us and the more, in consequence, the necessity of our own personal history is reinforced.

Memory in offering us a logical and circumstantial account of ourselves, a plausible 'story' that leads inevitably to ourselves as we are presently constituted confirms our current self-illusions and constitutes to use once again, Keirkegaardian terminology, a form of despair. Impressions continually threaten this work of personal mystification. They plunge us backwards into a preconceptual existence and act like an electric shock upon our inner senses, dissolving the identity we are normally at such pains to construct and protect, and dissolves it, furthermore, at the very point our memory claims to be its necessary point of origin.

Impressions, we might say, are intuitions of childhood in much the same sense that madness is an intuition of confinement. But unlike the hallucinations of the insane, impressions are extraordinarily pleasurable. This has something to do, no doubt, with their transitory nature. As in those odd states known as lucid dreams, we know, even as we abandon ourselves to the loss of time and place, that we shall return to ourselves shortly. We indulge ourselves in impressions as the luxury of a brief respite from a reality that we otherwise impose upon ourselves with undue rigour. Even in our temporary loss of selfhood we have half an eye on the way back, and we allow our memory to get to work, lessening the potency of our impressions by placing them within some objective (and probably fictional) circumstance and narrative of events.

Proust, among serious writers, remains unequalled in his ability to evoke impressions. The taste of the madeleine drenched in lemon scented tea, even if it is already a falsification of memory (as George Painter points out in his masterly biography, Marcel Proust, it was probably a crust of toast), prepares us for a description of the sensory world of childhood unrivalled in the richness of its impressionism. True to the nature of impressions, and of the childhood experiences they describe, Proust allows them, stripped of the accretions of our more calculative memory, to speak for themselves. The basic points of reference in his novel, almost all of which are present in Swann's Way, are sensory experiences that remain as unanalysable as a painting by Cezanne, or Monet, or Elstir. The taste of the madeleine rather than the occasion of its partaking; the scrape of the latch in the garden gate and its tinkling bell rather than the personality of Swann on his regular visits; the purpling tips of asparagus, rather than the domestic economy of the household; the garden on summer afternoons rather than the books consumed there, form the real subject matter of 'Combray'.

The Narrator himself draws the distinction between memories and impressions. Combray for his 'intellectual memory' was quite dead. 'The pictures which that kind of memory shows us of the past', he asserts, 'preserves nothing of the past itself.' Impressions, however, in keeping the past alive, impose their own reality upon an unsuspecting consciousness. 'No sooner,' he says, 'had the warm liquid and the crumbs with it, touched my palate than a shudder ran through my whole body, and I stopped, intent upon the extraordinary changes that were taking place.' A change in which 'an exquisite pleasure had invaded my senses, but individual, detached, with no suggestion of its origin'. More faithful than our deliberative memory whose capacity to recall the complexity of the sensuous world 'is infinitesimal', impressions carry within them a vanished reality. 'The smell and taste of things', he discovers, 'remain poised a long time, like souls, ready to remind us, waiting and hoping for their moment, amid the ruins of all the rest'; carrying in 'the tiny almost impalpable drop of their essence, the vast structure of recollection'.

Proust begins his book between waking and sleeping, with the self-deception of falling asleep and awakening suddenly at the thought it was time to go to sleep. He frequently returns to such twilight states, hovering between sleep and wakefulness, between dream and reverie; connecting them always with those impressions of childhood that act like a solvent upon personal identity because childhood, like awaking from deep sleep, arouses the senses before they are formed into a coherent image and provides us with a rich subjectivity outside of the 'self' that we later assume to be the prerequisite of all our experience.

These little self-deceptions, sleep, reverie, the impressionism of consciousness, prove to be the essentials of rest. To abandon the self to its preconceived origins suddenly or gradually; and to accomplish this without falling into the void of nothingness and retain amidst its formlessness a human sensibility is the most refreshing spiritual exercise.

Such distinctions as that between memory and impression are not, of course, so fixed and clearcut as sometimes we might wish. Vladimir Nabokov, for example, makes what at first appears a similar distinction, between the working of a cold, intellectual memory, on the one hand, and the recall of a complete sensuous image, on the other. 'There are two kinds of visual memory,' he tells us in his charming story, Lolita, 'one when you skilfully recreate an image in the laboratory of your mind, with your eyes open (and then I see Annabel in such general terms as

'honey-coloured skin', 'thin arms', 'brown bobbed hair', 'long lashes', 'big bright mouth') and the other when you instantly evoke, with shut eyes, on the dark innerside of your eyelids, the objective, absolutely optical replica of a beloved face, a little ghost in natural colours (and that is how I see Lolita).

But the distinction is not quite the same. His image of Lolita has retained some of the immediacy and richness of an impression but has succeeded in transforming her extravagant sensuousness into an 'optical replica', that can be 'evoked' like any other memory, at will.

In some instances, too, the memory will not submit to our will but runs on under a power of its own. this can reach frightening proportions. We have already met, in Bleuler, the idea of compulsive thinking, and Borges devotes one of his little epistemological stories to a man destroyed by a memory that refused to forget anything. A condition of nervous paralysis confirmed, with all the scientific precision it requires, by Luria in his fascinating monograph The Mind of a Mnemonist.

These intermediate categories — wilful impressions and spontaneous, uncontrollable memories, attest at least to the reality of the polarities between which they mediate. The polarities, at times, may even appear to coalesce. We have already noted that pure impressions rarely reach us uncontaminated by memory, so that the pleasure in finding ourselves children again is overlaid by the calculative effort of supplying details of time, place and circumstance.

And the method of memory, by an apparently inverse process may give rise at times to seemingly genuine impressions. This is, in brief, Freud's psychoanalytic method which begins always with the chain of association, dwells upon its inhibitions and in the practice of relaxed consciousness allows the truth of impressions to emerge from deceptive memories.

Transitional phenomenon, and apparent merging does not weaken however the utility of the original distinction. Intellectual effort can decompose, to some extent, the memory's rationalisations; impressions do contain memories. This coalescing, however, is itself the work of a cold, intellectual memory aimed as always at the preservation (or calculative change) in our self-image.

Gide, again, detects this rationalising function of memory. He was convinced that he could remember the entry of the Prussians into Rouen; such was the vividness of his impression, 'the walls of the houses were whipped into astonishing life by the flickering lights of resinous torches', that he felt some great historical event must be recalled by it. When he was finally convinced this could not have been the case, he says, 'I felt as if I had been a little defrauded; it seemed to me I had been nearer the truth in the first instance'. It had not been, in other words, a case of simple misremembering (that is never simple) but an effort on the part of a more developed self to bring into line the powerful swell of primitive impressions with some appropriate objective event.

Mary McCarthy in her autobiography of childhood, Memories of a Catholic Girlhood, takes advantage of the memory's misconstructions to present the same incident several times over. She juxtaposes her uncritical memory of an event with a second version more carefully thought through then with the testimony of others involved at the time, and with their recollections of the incident. The aim is less to move progressively towards a more 'truthful' account, as to expose some of the complex self-deceptions through which we look back on our own childhood. While her book does not recapture the natural attitude of the child it does carry a certain metaphorical persuasiveness, allowing the disintegrated subjectivity of so many partially overlapping accounts to stand for the unsynthesised subjectivity that it cannot more directly represent.

THE ART OF RECOLLECTION

Our interest in such books is essentially personal. The entire 'literature of childhood' is profoundly 'interesting' in Kierkegaard's sense of the term, bearing directly, that is to say, upon our personal existence. The appeal of Rousseau's Confessions, as of Proust's Remembrance of Things Past and Freud's Interpretation of Dreams, is not just in what they tell us about their authors, but in what they tell us about our own personal past. Our attraction to such literature is often narcissistic, in contrast to the voyeurism that animates our reading of the 'literature of confinement'. And although we cannot give ourselves wholly to the 'pure' sensations hinted at in our impressions, we can at least take the hint and exploit their visceral excitement as our guide to the 'literature of childhood' as nausea was our guide to the 'literature of confinement'. The sensations aroused by a page of, say, Swann's Way is not unlike those experienced in reading Metamorphosis. We feel in the latter that 'our gastric juices are flapping like a flag', and a closeness to childhood can induce, at first, a similar sense of interior dissolution. But these nervous reactions become, on longer acquaintance, clearly distinguished. A kind of pleasing vertigo runs through the whole of Swann's Way and the best of Freud's interpretations. A sense of falling in all directions at once as if we were freed suddenly from the dominion of gravity, a lightness, expansiveness, a dissolving outwards rather than inwards, an explosion of sensibility rather than a withdrawal. This effect too, is never the work of the sudden aperçu of confinement in all its ghastly purity, but the result of accumulating detail that carries, as a kind of sensuous undercurrent, the impressionism that belongs to our childhood. An undercurrent that may, from time to time, emerge into a clearer light, as in this passage from 'Combray';

> When, before turning to leave the church, I made a genuflection before the altar, I felt suddenly, as I rose again, a bitter-sweet fragrance of almonds steal towards me from the hawthorn-blossom, and then I noticed on the flowers themselves were little spots of a creamier colour, in which I imagined this fragrance must lie concealed, as the taste of an almond cake lay in the burned parts, or the sweetness of Mlle. Vinteuil's cheeks beneath their freckles.

One feels he could have spun out for ever the sensuous

condensation contained in the image of hawthorn-blossom. Indeed, he returns to it again and again and uses it as a switching point for the innumerable strands of his narrative, protecting its appearance from the 'development' that as we grow up splits asunder the multi-valenced sensory world and assigns 'objects' to places within their self-contained orders. Hawthorn-blossom, in other words, effects real sensory connections within our experience rather than merely suggest abstract, metaphorical similarities among our ideas.

The task of discovering our own childhood, then, is more difficult than it at first appears. We have not, after all, moved from intuition and indirect communication to the more straightforward problems of positive knowledge. What at first seems a kind of permeable membrane between adult and childhood experience turns out to be in fact a barrier as impenetrable as that which encloses the confined within their own world. Neither memory nor impressions really pierce this barrier. Memory stops short or pretends, for interests of its own, to have tunnelled its way through. And impressions in carrying us clear to the other side demands in the process that we forsake our selfhood so that, after a very short interval they dissolve, and we cannot anymore relive them than we can the experience of childhood to which they gave us a brief, privileged access. Impressions are, then, like some dreams the details of which fade as we awake but leave still a tantalising sense of having visited another no longer perceptible reality.

This correspondence between awakening and the spontaneous impressions of childhood has been noted most vividly, in addition to Proust, by Kenneth Grahame in the finest of all children's stories, The Wind in the Willows. Grahame's writing is, incidentally, the nearest equivalent in English to Swann's Way and shares the sensory alertness which is such a feature of Proust's 'style'. In an extraordinary chapter 'The Piper at the Gates of Dawn', Mole and Rat go in search of a baby otter that has strayed from its parents. They follow the mysterious sound of Pan's music to a small island in the river where Pan has kept the young otter in safety. The rescue complete, the vision of Pan disclosed for a moment, Mole stands in deep contemplation;

As one wakened suddenly from a beautiful dream, who struggles to recall it, and can recapture nothing but a dim sense of the beauty of it, the beauty! Till that, too, fades away in its turn, and the dreamer bitterly accepts the hard, cold waking and all its penalties; so Mole, after struggling with his memory for a brief space, shook his head sadly and followed the Rat.

It is in just such terms that the spontaneous recollections of our early years disturbs our consciousness.

A large part of our childhood, then, despite the best efforts of Freud and Proust, remains lost to us. Even they, in fact, never attempted a complete reconstruction of childhood experience. Their aim was to reinvent rather than simply to recall. In essence they created alternative childhoods to cure the adult because, as adults, they could no longer live on good terms with the childhood they had actually lived through. But having forgotten this childhood - the presumed hidden root of their unhappiness - the idea of therapeutically changing it for something better was too enticing to resist. Their aim was to create a more satisfactory future self by exploiting the weaknesses in our recollections and to fashion for us, as an image of ourselves, a new past and a fresh set of recollections upon which to base the 'development' of our personality. Our childhood, in becoming opaque to us, exercises over us a fatal attractiveness; it leaves us free to fabricate the past in accordance with our present needs. The barrier set up by childhood amnesia - as absolute in its own way as the boundary around confinement - acts as a perfect reflecting surface, so that the adult in looking back finds it difficult to discern the mirrorlike surface and easily mistakes the image it throws back for the alien being of his own early experiences.

The emptiness at our own point of origin, however, has not gone undetected. No amount of intellectual reconstruction can persuade our memory fully to reoccupy these early years. And it is this partial vacuum that has prompted the development of an extraordinarily varied array of scientific theories, literary explorations and philosophical speculations - in brief the 'literature of childhood' - to fill the void in our self-knowledge and secure us, once and for all, from falling into nothingness. The art of recollection becomes an imperative of our adult selfhood, a fact clearly recognised by Friedrich Froebel, who himself contributed significantly to the development of such an ideology; 'By the remembrance of childhood', he writes in his influential Pedagogics of the Kindergarten, 'we live our best life'.

Childhood has become then, for us, a screen upon which we can project an image of ourselves, and behind which the secret of our own personality can lie safely hidden. The 'problem' of childhood in this sense – of discovering and securing our own origin – is not universal and depends for its emergence upon a form of social life which embodies, in a secular form, the myth of the self-subsistent individual, thus conceived, as his 'sacred' duty and the key to his personal happiness, the task of unfolding his 'true self'. It is only recently, of course, that such a conception of individualised selfhood has become institutionalised, and relatively even more recently, therefore, that childhood has been 'discovered' by academic historians and social scientists. James Sully, thus, – one of the finest pre-Freudian writers on childhood in his Studies of Childhood (published in 1896), says, 'There is good reason to suppose that it is only within recent times that the more subtle charm and deeper significance of infancy have been discerned.' And as an historical problem it is only since Phillippe Ariès' pioneering Centuries of Childhood, that the enormous cultural shifts in our early forgotten experiences have become obvious.

His work, despite criticisms – especially his over-reliance on the diary of Heroard, court physician in charge of overseeing the early 'development' of the future Louis XIII – remains fundamental to all academic discussions of modern childhood.

What has particularly aroused interest is Ariès' claim that 'there was no place for childhood in the medieval world'. Medieval artists, for example, painted children simply as small adults, without any distinguishing physical or emotional features of their own. The young lived, according to Ariès, in the midst of adults without the 'benefits' of all those special institutional arrangements – their own dress, own pastimes, their own language and culture – which reached effusive proportions by the end of the nineteenth-century. Arrangements which themselves have now become the object of sentiment and nostalgia as a presumed 'Golden Age' of childhood.

Ariès attempts to trace the emergence of childhood and its achievement of a separate status, which

came, in time, to be regarded as 'natural'. The
historical process was, of course, complex and many-
sided; the shifts in cultural ascriptions never duplicate
the neatness or completeness of rational categories.
The 'age' of childhood, for example, is only one
element in the total conception of the child, and
was, Ariès shows, relatively late to emerge from
within the general configuration that defined it.
The 'inappropriateness' of children to adult concerns
and activities was characterised initially (and
accurately) by their dependent status and not by
their age alone. It was their lack of independence
from adults that defined children. Ariès argues that
this confused children with what we now term
adolescents, a distinction which depends upon the
introduction of purely temporal criteria. Commonly,
though, throughout the sixteenth and seventeenth
centuries the 'age' of childhood was prolonged well
beyond what we think of as natural to children.
Less common, but a more telling illustration of his
thesis, were those children of the privileged who
could enjoy a wider range of independence than
either the children of the lower orders of the time,
or of the majority of children today. They possessed
what appears to us a quite extraordinary freedom
and license. They behaved, in fact, as little adults.
They ate with adults, relaxed with them, joined
in common pastimes and sports, jointly flaunted
their sexual curiosity and participated in all the
major undertakings of the adult world. 'Youngsters'
of twelve or thirteen were frequently in responsible
positions as soldiers or ship's officers, and could
freely enter into contractual obligations on the same
footing as any 'adult'. The life of such independent
youngsters largely by-passed what we now think
of as essential to childhood years; though, in fact,
such 'essentials' were the product of later nineteenth
century cultural preoccupations. They avoided, therefore,
the shock of discovering their own difference from
and subordination to, adults: the discovery so
beautifully recalled, later, by Proust in the tormented
longing for his mother to desert, for a moment,
her adult duty at the evening dinner party and
impart upon him the ritual of the goodnight kiss.
And remembered also by Gide in the dawning realisation
as he overlooked from the shadow of a staircase
an adult's party where 'a mysterious, differently
real, more brilliant, and more exciting life, which
began only after little boys had gone to bed' was
being enacted. It was a sight that put his brain

in a turmoil, so that 'before sinking into sleep I thought in a confused way – there is reality and there are dreams: and there is another reality as well'.

Ariès illustrated the 'development' from the end of the fifteenth century to the middle of the seventeenth century of an essentially new notion of childhood. One not only rooted in a specific age category but, even more significantly one which regarded particular physical, behavioural and psychological characteristics as 'natural' to this age. Concomitant with this conceptual distinction came new emotional relationships. What Ariès terms the 'coddling' attitude to children became respectable; an attitude in which 'the child, on account of his awareness, simplicity and drollery, became a source of amusement and relaxation for the adult'. Though such indulgence, as Ariès is quick to point out, attracted its critics and along with the 'coddling' attitude there developed as well new demands, and new techniques, of discipline and control. The new institutions of childhood, he is surely correct in realising, were not simply a recognition of the separate reality of childhood but a means, as well, of exerting control over its alien impulses.

Ariès stops short of contemporary society, but suggests that the 'age of childhood' has already passed, and that the 'problem' surrounding adolescence has become a new focus for much of our cultural life. The fact, however, that children 'enjoy' a less separate life today than in the nursery of a bourgeois Victorian household does not mean that we have ceased to be preoccupied by the essential mystery of childhood. A limited rapprochement between the adult and child world has, indeed, come about, for the most part under the commercial impetus of the extension backwards of the 'pop culture's' marketable commodities to ever younger age-groups.

We have not yet, however, outgrown the problem of our own childhood. It has changed in significance rather than importance. The emergence of childhood as a separate reality provided first of all the opportunity for indulgence and pleasure and then posed, for adults, the problem of control. But it provided also, and in this sense childhood continues to be fascinating for us, a hiding place for the self. The re-integration, to a limited extent, of children within our adult society, then, is the corollary of the internalisation of childhood within ourselves. And in consequence children as a separate species have become less an object of interest as our own personal childhood, our lost past, has been made into the recipient of our impassioned self-curiosity.

This, from the child's viewpoint, is doubtless a mixed blessing. It has been suggested - by Lloyd de Mauss in a collection of useful essays The History of Childhood - that 'the history of childhood is a nightmare from which we have only recently begun to awaken'. He is no doubt correct in his contention that, for the most part, past ages have treated children with scant regard. Very often they have been lucky to be merely neglected. But it may be premature to announce the wakening from the nightmare, de Mauss is rather too quick to assume that our conception of childhood, backed by the scientific authority of psychology, developmental studies, pedagogy and medicine, is more civilised and 'correct'. Children, from having to protect themselves from our neglect, or our simple exploitation as a source of labour, now have to shield themselves from the dissecting knife of our tormented curiosity and the emotional 'ambivalence' generated in our hectic efforts to 'find' ourselves through them. They have to survive, in other words, what in a more general sense we call 'loving' them, and this too often leads to its own special kind of cruelty.

Childhood is a universal phenomenon. It appears also to contain some universal features as, for example, the young's dependence on adults, or the manner in which they learn to walk and talk. But beyond that it is subject not just to changing fashions, but to radical shifts in its cultural meaning.

Where confinement is absolute but contingent - that is to say it does not (yet) exist everywhere, but where it does it is everywhere the same - childhood is universal but without a fixed significance. The experience of childhood, therefore, is both historically and individually variable. What is peculiar to 'modern' childhood is the new significance which has been found in the universal feature of its being forgotten, and the transcendental function this amnesia has come to play for us in the development of our mature selfhood.

It is as if we were attracted by ignorance. If there is something about ourselves that we do not know, that we cannot know, then must it not be the most important aspect of ourselves? Does it not still contain, disguised in our memories and impressions, our deepest nature? And does its spirit not continue to animate, albeit unconsciously, all our actions?

Is it surprising that we continually look back and devise tricks to tempt childhood from its reticence? D.W.Winnicott, one of the leading spokesmen for the modern ideology of childhood, put it, echoing Froebel's sentiments, thus; 'People want to know about the beginning of their lives, and I think they ought to want to know'.

It was the 'objective' description first applied to children in general, as an 'alien' species, that was later re-absorbed, individually, as a personal history. During the period that stretches approximately from the first publication of Alice in Wonderland (1857) to the appearance of The Wind in the Willows (1908) childhood was accorded a cultural objectivity it lacked before and has since been denied; and it is from the diverse productions of this period that many of the most significant works of the 'literature of childhood' can be drawn. And it is in these works also that we can discern the changing significance of childhood within the dialectic of self-knowledge. It was during this period that the majority of literary 'classics' written for children were composed; that educational experimentation attained epidemic proportions; that child psychology was 'invented' and the new autobiographical calculus of Freud and Proust was conceived.

It was also, of course, the period of 'high capitalism' which saw the fullest development of its individualistic culture. Self-assertion reached, apparently, its peak of confidence and dynamism. The problem of self-knowledge and the maintenance of a self-sufficient identity prompted, none the less, many anxious inward glances. The 'discovery' of childhood was one of the 'symptoms' of this unfashionable introversion, and a species of reflection that created more additional worries than it calmed irrational fears. Childhood and its investigation plays a similar role, in the culture of the times, as the study of the newly discovered 'savage' tribes. Both psychoanalysis and anthropology sought, in their different ways, for the completion of self-knowledge which secular individualism demanded. It was, however, psychoanalysis and all other sciences of childhood, as well as the even greater bulk of non-scientific reflections upon childhood, that proved, by their greater intimacy with the publicly unacknowledged but privately agonising trials of self-doubt, the more lasting influence.

6　The Golden Age

How can we give substance to the early years of our lives?

It was an ambition common to many writers during the 'golden age' of childhood to do just that, an ambition that extended far beyond the self-imposed boundaries of the new academic study of child psychology.

It would be possible to describe childhood experience by the method we used to describe confinement; that is, by following the transformations in the sense of time, space and the body which differentiates early experience from what we take for granted as 'normal' to the adult. Indeed this, to a large extent, is the method adopted by Piaget, whose books provide a very detailed description of the child's conception (if not experience) of all those categorical frameworks that order the adult, rational world. This description, however, and the method of supporting it is, for our purposes, too rigorously unsubordinated under a paradigmatic 'development' of reason. Not only are the 'cognitive' faculties of the child singled out for special attention, but the ordered and necessary 'progress' (in the sense of a rationally understandable development). In these faculties towards the standards of abstract logic, becomes the guiding thread of the entire project.

In this, Piaget was the first to take the study of children beyond the 'age of childhood' which imparted to such investigations their original impetus. The interests of contemporary thought is once again in 'mediation'. Childhood must be connected to adult experience, adult experience must itself be a species of reason, the whole comprehensible through a 'structure' common to all. The writers of the 'age of childhood' took a different view. They were concerned with the profound 'otherness' of childhood, and, as already stressed, above all with the otherness of their own childhood. The vanished world of childhood could not, therefore, be described in terms that shared, simply through a natural process of 'development' in our own framework of truth. The 'golden age' described its children variously, but common to this variety was the bewildered admiration with which they beheld the mysterious business of 'growing-up'. Many no doubt conceived, or misconceived, children's activities through a romantic disregard for many of the obtrusive 'facts' of child-life, and allowed a nostalgic longing for its presumed simplicities and pleasures to colour their perception. But these 'errors' are themselves indicative of the separation that had been brought about between the adult and child world, and the very real intellectual difficulty involved in accounting for the regular passage, in one direction only, between them.

It is more profitable, then, to describe childhood directly in terms of its own 'categories'. Its overriding principle is, in opposition to confinement, motion. We first recognise confinement through immobility; but in childhood nothing is still, movement is its essential mode of being. The child never remains unmoved. It is exactly this perpetual motion, shifting boundaries, multiplicity of points of view and forms of organisation, variety and changeability of experience, that defines childhood. The experience of childhood is of continually changing states. It is a kaleidoscopic world that obeys its own laws of motion rather than the interests or will of individuals. Children are caught up in its movements and childhood is contained within, rather than expressed by, its perpetual dynamism.

It is the denial of this principle of motion (among other things) that so angered Maria Montessori and prompted her educational experiments. She quotes for example, in her Advanced Montessori Method a particularly grotesque official regulation in respect of the manner in which the schoolchild should be made to sit. 'The child', it insists, 'seated at the table, should have his feet planted flat upon the ground, or upon a foot-rest. The legs should be at right-angles to the thighs, as should the thighs be to the trunk, save for a slight inclination of the bench itself' and so it runs on in meticulous detail, finishing 'the forearms, two-thirds of which should be laid upon the table, should rest on it, but without leaning upon it.' This imperative to 'correct' posture was re-enforced by specially designed workdesks that prevented all superfluous movement. Montessori later wrote, in The Discovery of the Child, 'the bench is made in such a way that as far as possible the child is left motionless'. And such unnatural constraint, according to her, not only made school a nightmare for most children and made learning almost impossible, it gave rise also to a whole medical speciality to deal with the 'school diseases' (particularly malformation of the spine) to which it gave rise. Remember too the harnesses in which the young Schreber 'learned' correct posture. He, and the children Montessori rescued, were hardly children at all but little captives denied the motion essential to their nature.

The principle of motion is itself a necessary feature of the fullness of childhood experience and this is conceived most clearly in direct opposition to confinement. Constraint is the natural sign of confinement, but it is only a sign of which confinement 'in itself' is not the means and technique of imposing immobility but the void in experience concommitant with such immobility. Childhood, in contrast, is indicated by motion, by a ceaseless inner dynamism. But this too is only its sign, the outward show of its inexhaustible inner fullness. The childhood world presents a prodigal richness and variety and consists, indeed, in a veritable plenitude of subjectivity. All childhood lacks is the individual identity which will come in time to destroy it. Where confinement takes the individual and, in placing him in the midst of nothingness, allows all his particular identifying characteristics to evaporate, childhood, as yet innocent of the synthesis of individuality, is composed of an infinite variety of such particulars. In childhood the subject, rather than the world, is empty, or at least unformed, and in being unformed is still able to contain, in its continuous inner-movement, the world's abundance. Such a vision of the world, if it is rediscovered in later years, can be irresistibly entrancing. John Cowper Powys, one of the greatest writers to articulate such a childish vision, both through the extraordinary sensuous density of his 'Dorset' novels and in his equally profound Autobiography regarded its loss as tragic. 'It is a criminal blunder of our mature years', he writes in the latter work, 'that we so tamely, and without frantic and habitual struggles to retain it, allow the ecstasy of the unbounded to slip away out of our lives'.

The 'golden age' of childhood is then a subjectivity of unbounded possibility and richness, in contrast, on the one hand to the absolute tranquility and emptiness of confinement, and on the other to the rigorous individuality of adulthood with its unifocal point of view and exhausting search (its peculiar and unvarying form of motion) for its own selfhood.

Such terms however as motion, plenitude, possibility,

though accurate in their way describe childhood at a too general level. Before the significance of such abstract terms can be fully grasped, some more detailed description of childhood experience is necessary. Such a description is best made in terms of those 'categories' which while bearing upon our own problems of self-development participate also (as purely 'rational categories' do not) in the pure motion and sensory abundance of childhood. These terms are formed so to speak at the meeting points of the child's and adult's world. They are Play, Anxiety and Desire. Such terms cannot be intended too rigorously. They are useful as descriptive labels rather than formal analytic tools, but their interconnections suggest quite accurately the underlying conception of childhood common to so many writers of the 'golden age'.

PLAY

Here are some examples of children's play.

Firstly the opening passage from Arthur Ransome's Swallows and Amazons. 'Roger, aged seven, and no longer the youngest in the family, ran in wide zigzags, to and fro, across the steep field that sloped up from the lake to Holly Howe . . . each crossing of the field brought him nearer to the farm. The wind was against him and he was tacking up against it . . . He could not run straight against the wind because he was a sailing vessel, the Cutty Sark.'

And from Leon Garfield's, The Ghost Downstairs, 'along the pavement ran a little boy in a sailor's suit, banging a makeshift iron hoop. His bleached, almost transparent face wore an intense expression as he kept the hoop rolling with his stick.'

Or from Piaget's Play, Dreams and Imitation in Childhood which, even if its interpretations cannot be directly borrowed provides a fund of useful illustration; 'J. put the doll's head through the balcony railings with its face turned towards the street, and began to tell it what she saw: "You see the lake and the trees. You see a carriage, a horse." etc.' And from the same source: 'J. said to L.: "Let's be two sisters reading a book, shall we?" and both of them sat down (L. was 14) and each looked at her book.'

A description of a game, 'cigarettes', provided by one of the young informants in the Opie's Children's

Games in Street and Playground:

> Cigarettes is a game where you all stand on the pavement and one person stands in the middle of the road. The people pick the name of a cigarette and tell each other what they have picked, but the do not tell the person in the middle of the road . . . Then the person in the middle thinks of all the different cigarettes and if she says your one you try to run across to the other side of the road without her or him tigging you.

Lastly a lovely example from Dostoevsky's The Brothers Karamazov: 'And so it was decided that they should go in the evening to a spot about half a mile from the station, so that the train might have time to gather full speed after leaving the station. The boys assembled. It was a moonless night, not just dark but almost pitch-black. At the fixed time Kolya lay down between the rails.'

The purpose of such a listing, and it could be indefinitely extended, is not to anticipate some systematic 'classification' of play, with each item carefully chosen to illustrate one of its particular leading 'characterisitcs' (the element of fantasy, skilled use of the body, absorption and attention, use of tools and toys, its incipient social learning, inner organisation or element of daring and danger), but simply to take notice of the great variety of activities which we do not hesitate to designate by the term play.

The ease in designation is not matched, however, by any certainty in its definition or classification. We can say without difficulty that all those examples are of children's play; it is less easy to find the underlying unity that encompasses their diverse forms within this single term. We recognise, in other words, that play distinguishes itself from other activities, attitudes or feelings, but we cannot precisely define the nature of this difference.

Play has, for this reason, proved an analytic embarrassment to many philosophers and psychologists. Innumerable attempts at defining clearly the boundaries of play have failed. Johan Huizinga, in his classic essay on play Homo Ludens, admits the difficulty, 'the fun of playing, resists all analysis, all logical interpretations'. And even more clearly he states, 'Play lies outside the antithesis of wisdom and folly, and equally outside those of truth and falsehood, good and evil. Although it is a non-material activity, it has no moral function. The valuations of vice and virtue do not apply here.' And although play effects this categorical separation it yet remains attached to all other human activities. It shares a broad and ambiguous boundary not only with work (a fairly recent distinction) but more generally with art, reflection, sexuality – in fact with any human preoccupation.

Huizinga preferred, therefore, to define play as a particular attitude to life, rather than a specific set of activities. With summary neatness he declares, 'Play is the direct opposite of seriousness'. This method, however, raises difficulties of its own. Such subjective predispositions vary independently from the many different criteria through which we recognise play. Many of the early students of child psychology, thus, noticed the seriousness with which children played. James Sully, again, remarks upon their intentness, 'their absorption in the present moment', the high seriousness with which they play. It might be objected that this absorption is not genuine seriousness but a species of naivete; no more than a simple lack of self-consciousness or self-awareness. Is this not, in fact, one of the attractions in watching children play, the source of their charm? Even admitting this we cannot say either that their play is 'unserious' or frivolous. This distinction is as inapplicable as any other.

A good deal of the difficulty arises, apart from our love of overly neat definitions, from a wish to reabsorb children into the adult world. This did not appear as a pressing need for many of the writers of the 'golden age', who accorded, in contrast, a separate reality to childhood, and made play natural to it. Instead of attempting to define play through the application of categories which describe adult experience, they simply accepted its irrationality and used it to define the world, or a large part of the world of childhood.

Although in retrospect this appears to be the underlying idea of more especially writers of children's stories, particularly Kenneth Grahame and Edith Nesbitt, play was regarded by some as something of a problem, both intellectually and practically. The separation of childhood emphasised the irrationality of play, and for those unwilling to let it rest there two different methods of assimilating its oddness proved to be of some significance historically.

The first was to 'animalise' play. That is to say play was defined as an instinct and belonged

essentially to the animal world. This idea, much
influenced, of course, by the spread of Darwinism
during the latter part of the nineteenth century
and Darwin's own pioneering study of child development,
reached full bloom in Karl Groos's famous book The
Play of Man. Conceived as an instinct play enhances
our chances in the struggle for survival; without
it our faculties, especially our physical faculties,
could not develop with the strength or, more importantly,
flexibility that we require of them. Play is a 'practice'
of our skills before they are needed in earnest,
and is therefore primarily an adaptive function.
The originality in Groos's book lay in attempting
to show that the fantasy and make-believe aspects
of play could be understood in just the same way,
as the pre-practice of mental faculties. In spite
of this, however, he could not accord any significance
to the subjective dimension of play; such functional
theories had to ignore the child's own account of
his play, it was of no importance that he was 'building
a house' or 'being the captain of a ship'.

The second method of rationalising play, what
might be termed its 'domestication', seized upon
this subjective dimension and injected into it the
purposes and aspirations of the adult. This, the
main impulse behind Friedrich Froebel's Pedagogics
of the Kindergarten, was less to liberate the young
child from the drudgery of instruction, than to subvert
his spontaneous play to the higher aim of education.
Froebel saw play in spiritual terms. The child contained
'life in itself' and through his own activities indicated
a 'slumbering apprehension' that the educator could
stimulate and channel according to the needs and
desires that would ultimately shape his life. In
play the child himself does not aim at anything
beyond the present moment, to play is 'to busy
one's self' but this 'impulse to action' is capable
of direction and control. Froebel developed a complex
technique of such control which consisted in a graded
series of 'plays' which were introduced in the correct
sequence and under supervision, to the child. This
began with the ball, which is the first natural
plaything of the child, in which 'quite unconsciously,
it can see its own self-dependent, stable and yet
movable life, as it were, in a mirror'. This Hegelian
conception was not uncommon, James Sully offers
a similar 'explanation' for the attraction of the
hoop: 'the child', he suggests, 'controls a moving
thing which in the capricious variations of its course
simulates a free will of its own'. Froebel, having

aroused the 'slumbering apprehension' of the young child, proceeded to develop his cognitive abilities by allowing him to 'play' next with a cube, then subdivided cubes, moving objects and so on, all organised with mathematical nicety to impart, by the age of five or six, a complete course in Aristotelian logic. A supervised progression which was necessary so that the child's faculties and qualities 'may not be carried on by arbitrary and accidental exercises'.

Froebel's kindergarten movement spread rapidly and his conception of play as self-motivated activity going to waste unless captured for adult, educative purposes still underlies the pre-school playgroup and nursery school practices of today. A more modern, representative statement can be taken, for example (and there are many such examples), from The Significance of Children's Play by Joan Cass in which play, we are told, 'brings about understanding, warmth, and sympathy towards others' and if the focus has shifted away somewhat from the development of cognitive faculties towards the fostering of a more diffuse social competence, this in no way alters the aim of giving to play a legitimate adult purpose which it might otherwise lack.

Karl Groos himself criticised Froebel, and more especially his followers, in rather stern terms, 'At school', he argues, 'one should learn to work, and he who does everything playfully will always remain a child.' But interestingly, and consistent with his own conception of play he charged them with spoiling play for the child. This interference and supervision means only that 'spontaneity' and 'naivete' are almost totally destroyed undermining, in the long term, the biological function of play.

Despite criticisms, Groos shared with Froebel in a common ambition to defeat the purposelessness of play. The only way to do this, however, is to join it either with the functions of Nature, as ethologists still attempt to do, or the purposes of Society; and claim for it self-improving possibilities if it is accepted as intrinsic to child-life then it must be accepted as it is, unreachable by abstract reflection or conceptual acrobatics.

In supposing play to be natural to childhood, however, the representatives of the 'golden age' were not suggesting, even implicitly, that play belongs somehow to the state of nature anterior to social life. This naturalness of play is a spontaneous activity that flourishes only when its preconditions have already been met by a particular organisation of adult society. Play, in other words, depends for its existence upon the tolerance of social life. This is illustrated most clearly by the dramatic, though usually poorly documented, cases of 'wolf children'. Those children, abandoned, deprived of all association, do not play at all – they struggle to survive. In one of the best accounts of such a case, The Wild Boy of Aveyron, Harlan Lane has carefully reconstructed from unusually full documentary evidence, a picture of the most 'unnatural' of childhoods. Captured after apparently spending several years alone in a forested region of Southern France, the Wild Boy, despite the dedicated efforts of Itard (the physician who made himself responsible for his education) did not succeed in learning properly. Lane makes a convincing case for supposing the Wild Boy's general intellectual and social immaturity was a consequence, and not a cause, of his abandonment. Nothing shows more clearly the emptiness of social isolation – that the most perfect 'freedom' from social constraint is a form of imprisonment. The Wild Boy never had a childhood, and so never grew up. He lived his entire life in confinement, his immobility was striking, his passivity interspersed by occasional frenzies in a symptomatic oscillation noted, it will be remembered, by Dostoevsky in The House of the Dead. His lack of sensitivity is quite disturbing; he could tolerate extraordinary ranges of temperature without complaint and refused warm clothes or bedding. He had suffered in confinement to an irreversible degree. He was thought by some experts at the time to be insane. He certainly displayed many of the classic symptoms of insanity; symptoms that had themselves prompted certain 'therapeutic' measures (subjection to extreme cold, isolation, removal of clothes, etc.) as if an intensification of their suffering might relieve, in a grotesque parody of innoculation, the patient of the cause of his illness. In any event the Wild Boy, neither in a state of nature, nor later when introduced into human society, had any time for play. Itard was surprised that he destroyed the toys he was so generously given for his amusement.

Play in fact, when it is solitary, is not asocial because society must procure the means for its existence. The 'golden age' was the period when children were, for the first time, as a general rule, removed from the process of labour and protected from the struggle for survival. Freed from this necessity play became seen as the natural medium of the child's existence.

This does not imply that play can be defined simply through its opposition to necessity, only that its existence depends upon the 'protection' of adult society. A liberal sufficiency of 'provender' – to use Kenneth Grahame's magical word – must be provided so that the playworld can establish itself according to its own inessential needs. Nor does this imply that children were accorded a new freedom so that they might simply enjoy it. In a complex industrial society children became more valuable as 'inputs' to the educational system than directly, as labour power, and not just because technical training became so important but because the new organisation of work demanded a discipline that could be easily and reliably taught in schools. Although children were subjected to this new regime of discipline, and learned to adapt to the rhythm of 'schoolwork' their elders, especially their favourite uncles such as Kenneth Grahame, chose to observe, as a kind of objective support for their own nostalgia, the life of children on holidays and weekends.

The writers of the 'golden age' saw only children's freedom and envied their natural playfulness. So that Froebel was displaying remarkable foresight in inaugurating, at the very moment when children became free to play, a new technique of ludic exploitation to spoil it.

In claiming play to be natural to childhood they were not attempting to put childhood beyond the reach of social control. It is natural to children, when freed of necessity and left to themselves, to play and we can see more clearly now that children are very rarely allowed such freedom.

The naturalness of play to childhood is, however, much their indulgence in it is restricted, the central idea of the 'golden age'. This naturalness is revealed, for example, in the extraordinary physical and mental agility, the social competence and emotional composure of children at play; a far greater 'maturity' than they seem, on other occasions, to be capable of. Flora Thompson remarks upon this in a passage from her evocative memoir, Lark Rise to Candleford, 'most of the girls when playing', she tells us, 'revealed graces unsuspected in them at other times; their movements became dignified and their voices softer and sweeter than ordinarily'. And more recently John Holt, in his book How Children Learn has drawn attention to the encompassing skills and aptitudes all young children demonstrate in their play, making their subsequent 'failure' to learn in school more a form of resistance to its demands than a reflection of their natural abilities. Holt found that even quite young children could, if left quite to themselves, learn - by playing with it - how to 'work' a typewriter.

Children's greater skill and competence at play seems, however, to be restricted to their spontaneous, self-organising pastimes. As the Opies noticed the craze for organising and supervising children's play often results in a 'regression' or deterioration in their behaviour. 'We have noticed', they write, 'that when children are herded together in the playground, which is where the educationalists and the psychologists and the social scientists gather to observe them, their play is markedly more aggressive than when they are in the street or in the wild places.' And there are markedly fewer accidents in 'adventure' playgrounds and unsupervised play-sites than in those overseen by 'responsible' adults.

Left to themsleves children not only devise new variations of old games, they take care to initiate the younger generation into the culture of the playworld. On their own, as Piaget has shown so forcefully in his classic research The Moral Judgment of the Child, they are scrupulous in their observation of fairness, are intolerant of cheating and expect straightforward honesty from their friends; exercise, in other words, among themselves, a morality their teachers usually fail to impose.

They behave in this way less from any abstract considerations of justice than because it is integral to their play, and play, as an end in itself, is neither instinctual behaviour nor purposeful activity. The 'golden age', therefore, saw children as a human but unfamiliar species who were most truly 'themselves' when at play.

Play in this sense is an 'existential' rather than a conceptual 'category'. Play is the mode of existence proper to childhood, or one at least, of its appropriate modes. This is what is meant, ultimately, by claiming play to be natural to childhood. And in play the child exists neither for instinct (Nature) nor purpose (Society), but for possibility. Play takes place, as it were, under the sign of possibility. In play all things are possible, even, we might say especially, what we normally regard as impossible. And before the infinity of particular possibilities may be realised, one after the other and, sometimes, simultaneously, in play, the possibility of play itself must be accepted and welcomed. Play, in which everything becomes possible, is not always itself possible, it does not always 'work'. There is an irrational element in its very existence. Kenneth Grahame, as the young narrator of the quintessential Dream Days, remarks, 'Life may be said to be composed of things that come off and things that don't'. By life, the narrator being the distillation of a particular childhood, he means play, and play may or may not 'come off'. It has no rationale beyond this possibility of 'coming off'. The narrator, for example, chose the wrong moment to become a black puma, launched himself at his younger brother, Harold – and started a 'real' fight. It may just as unexpectedly terminate as in the beautifully contrived transition that more illustrious Narrator recalls, that marked the boundary between his childish game of wrestling with Gilberte in the bushes of the Bois de Boulogne, through sudden sexual awakening, to a 'playfulness' of a quite different kind.

When it does 'come off' play's absorbing possibilities create a fluid and unpredictable world. A ship's captain one moment, a shopkeeper or pirate the next. An upturned chair and a piece of cardboard change imperceptibly from a castle under siege to a motor car, an aeroplane, a hospital then become once again a fortress. Each in its turn does not destroy, merely returns as it were to the stock room of possibilities that went before. The child can play 'at' anything without this 'choice' carrying with it any of the consequences of 'real life'. Play, we might say, in existing in possibilities, rather than selecting from among possibilities, indulges in absolutely indecisive choices. And in choosing without consequence it both secures an existence for itself and, at the same time, holds in abeyance the self which will come in time to choose much more painfully. Play seems to escape the penalties invoked by a more individuated existence. It lies outside of Kierkegaard's 'spheres' or 'stages' of existence. It is at once the enjoyment of immediacy without the threat of boredom, the exercise of choice without the guilt associated with responsibility for its consequences, and faith (what might be better termed here 'trust') in the transcendental beings that allow its multitudinous realities to form without exacting, in anticipatory payment for its pleasures, an apprenticeship in spiritual suffering. Play has a relationship with, but escape from, the aesthetic, the ethical or the religious spheres of existence. It is curious that Kierkegaard never considered play within his complex description of existence.

He was, of course, concerned above all with the existence of the individual, with the formation of a self by way of a deepening subjectivity potentiated, through a series of discontinuous 'leaps' towards 'a single one'. Play requires no leap, it invites the child and refuses to be determined by a wilful act; it 'happens'. From this point of view play can be more clearly seen as an obstacle (rather than a medium) of 'self-development'. It offers everything and takes nothing; it does not demand the exercise of selfhood. In positing endless possibilities the potential 'self' can hover above itself for ever without being required to alienate its infinite plasticity in exchange for a single, determinate identity.

It is from this point of view that we can perceive an homology between play and philosophy. Kierkegaard's strictures against metaphysical 'systems' are well known: his polemic against Hegel in particular, charged abstract reason with denying existence its own medium. The philosopher's abstractions miss the very point of real life – the self – and describe experience through a 'system' of categories interrelated through the application of transformative rules which allow of no impassable barriers. Philosophy's idea, as he remarks in a Journal entry, is mediation, unhindered, free movement among its own categories as the 'representation' of experience. This system of representation Kierkegaard claimed to be not only false, but dangerously so because its powerful unifying appeal seduced the unwary into believing the real problems of life could be solved philosophically, by reflection, without the risk and suffering of committed action.

Play duplicates on the other side, so to speak, of the spheres of existence this unbroken chain of mediation. Play contains within it no impenetrable barriers, all its forms flow together, no metamorphosis is beyond its capacity. And just as the mediations of philosophy can be reversed, so in play children return to their starting point for all the world as if they had not moved at all. Play and philosophy are alike, then, in being inconsequential, in escaping the irreversibility and intransitivity of an existing selfhood. But where philosophy's 'trick' is abstraction, (the philosopher literally 'thinks' himself out of existence), play succeeds by a concrete imagination that refuses in the first place to allow the self to appear. We might even guess that play is the greater obstacle to the determination of the self because the philosopher's love of mediation, of movement, and his construction of a system within which he can move freely is a kind of gigantic mnemonic device through which he can recall in another less exalted form, the absolute liberty he enjoyed as a child at play. And although we have said that play accepted in this light is unreachable through abstract categories, they possess, none the less a metaphorical likeness one to another. No particular philosophical term can 'define' or 'describe' play but the activity of philosophising and the abstract structure of thought it produces bears a skeletal similarity to playing and the play-world. Reflection and play form outer edges to our identity, the one connected to the self through memory, the other through impressions. The initial disjunction within our recollection between memory and impressions point to these two major difficulties in the 'development' of our selfhood. Both infect the self with the temptation of a greater freedom; memory seeks to dissolve the self through abstract reflection and loves philosophy, while impressions, by releasing within us a little of the sensuous expansiveness of childhood, momentarily transcend our individual identity in play. Their threats are, for the most part disarmed, the self subordinates and tames their fluid spirit. The memory is put to work in the service of self-recollection (rather than recollection of selflessness) and impressions, thus remaining incomprehensible, are injected with the 'secret' of our entire personality. The absolute freedom encountered in play and recollected in philosophy is thus subverted by the self, which interprets (perversely) our knowledge of both within the framework of its own, and only, existence.

Play differs profoundly from philosophy, however, in not being abstract. It is not concerned with 'categories' but with 'being' and being in its manifold variety. Play is distinct from both imagination and fantasy; it is a form of subjectivity but not simply a 'subjective vision' of our world. The created immediacy of play has only a symbolic reality but it utilises, for its creations, the objects of the real world. As Winnicott puts it 'playing is doing' and therefore engages, even before they can be seen as such, the world of objects. On the other hand, it is not action, because it is bereft of purpose or necessity, it is not, in other words, part of the process of labour, however broadly conceived, and it is this freedom from a necessary relationship with the world of nature and other people that extends to play the privilege of retaining undiminished its

inexhaustible plenitude. Play in existing for possibility
is indefinitely renewable. It is marked, therefore,
not only by its extraordinary variety, and the
unexpectedness of its inner transformations, but
also by its repetitiveness. Children love repetition.
Young children especially seem able to derive pleasure
by simply repeating some newly completed activity;
even if they appear indifferent to the initial movement,
its repetition in itself seems to carry with it the
transformative power of play. A game can be inspired
by a simple mechanical reflex.

This aspect of play has often been noted, and
is familiar to every parent who has to cope with
the endless questioning of a child of three or four
years old. The repetitive 'whys' are not to elicit
information so much as to form the basic unit of
a verbal game. Even more noticeably they demand
to be read, again and again, a favourite story
even although they know, better than we, what is
on each page. Many of the simpler children's games
also display a marked repetitiveness – some, like
skipping, bouncing a ball, throwing and catching,
rolling a hoop, have repetition as their primary
motif. The same could be said of their rhymes and
chants.

Repetition within the play world, however, has
a quite different meaning from either the deathly
tedium of confinement, or the 'leap' into selfhood.

Kierkegaard in his essay on Repetition, denies
that empirical reality as perceived and lived through
by an individual contains repetition at all. He tests
the idea by attempting to 'repeat' a visit to the
theatre in Berlin. He found the experience disappointing
and disillusioning, the enjoyment of the first performance
had somehow evaporated in the interval. Or rather
his capacity to enjoy it had been destroyed by its
changing, through the absorption of many experiences,
during the interval. The experience he had initially
cannot be repeated, nor can any other, because
the agency of experience, the self, having the power
of memory, is in a continuous state of change. The
repetition of which Kierkegaard wrote was the willed
movement of the self towards a more concrete realisation
of its own inner nature. In 'repetition' the self
'raises itself to a higher power', appropriates its
own meaning and ultimately takes the 'leap' into
faith. But in this categorical inward transformation
the self discovers that only it and not the world
has altered. In repetition, as he never tires of
repeating, 'nothing is lost'. Repetition for Kierkegaard

has a purely inward significance, in it the self appropriates its own truth.

The repetitions of the playworld are, in contrast, part of its plenitude. By a strict logic, known to Giordano Bruno, but more familiar to us from Leibniz, repetition is included within its fullness. Play has before it everything, including therefore, the repetition of itself, endlessly. And as no possibility is lost or completely abandoned in play, repetition has exactly the same significance as novelty. The first time is commensurate with its second, its third, its hundredth repetition. And as play is a form of selflessness – does not demand a choice from possible alternative selves – repetition has no 'meaning' for the individual at play. The fact of repetition in the playworld, indeed, is another sign of its refusal to tolerate individual identity. A characteristic recognised by Hans Georg Gadamer. in his important book Truth and Method, who links the essence of play with its repetition. 'The movement which is play,' he writes, 'has no goal which brings it to an end; rather it renews itself in constant repetition.' In play repetition, then, is just another game which can itself, of course, be repeated. The ending to the story is just as exciting when it has been read a dozen times as it was on the first occasion.

The repetitions of play and selfhood are quite distinct and, for the sake of completeness, we can recall the repetition of confinement. The awful sameness of each prison cell, the unvarying daily routine, the likeness of each prisoner to his neighbour – all those enforced empirical repetitions that are no fun at all but the instrument of self-abandonment. Confinement, we have said, is an inverted repetition, its uniformities decompose the self and force the captive always to act against his own interests, till he can no longer act at all.

Play avoids the self, its repetitions never lead to 'self-development' nor to 'self-destruction'. It stands between the inward repetition of the individual subject and the outward repetition of life confined to a cell. Put another way, play has as one of its preconditions (along with the ready supply of provender) and as one of its effects, a collective rather than an individuated subjectivity. It is in this that children's play shares in a common prehistory with adult life. Breugel, for example, painted pictures in which adults and children played together with tops, little windmills, at leapfrog and 'tig'. Ariès has taken some care to establish this commonality of games and pastimes which, he argues, was just one aspect to the lack of distinctiveness in the childhood of earlier times. They shared with adults a common world of symbols, work and recreation. It was just one of the consequences of the growth of individualism, as a concomitant to the market economy and the destruction of domestic production, that children no longer found a place in such a common world, inheriting, as a mark of their inferior status, the exclusive use of many of the cast-off rituals of the pre-modern age. The carnival, which was only the most extravagant form of play, became a merely 'quaint', incomprehensible relic of a world of common experience, and its festive mood is still more accurately caught in children's spontaneous play than in the laboured zest of any modern adult 'performance'.

Michail Bakhtin, in a strikingly original book Rabelais and his World, describes the culmination of the carnival tradition in European culture. It was embodied and reflected above all, he claims, in the writing of Rabelais. His is truly a literature of the play-world before it was consigned to being merely childish. The enjoyment of a spontaneously created immediacy, the enormously enriched and extended sensuality, the grotesque exaggeration, the fascination with bodily functions, the reversals in normal social roles, sudden switches in persona; all testify to a common experience in play. Rabelais belongs to a different world and many people cannot any longer read his work with immediate enjoyment. John Cowper Powys detected something of Bakhtin's more fully developed insight when, in his Rabelais, he calls his master 'the most purely childish writer in the world.' What appears to us as an outrageous mixing of the adult and the childish, the serious and the frivolous, the grotesque with the realistic, is beyond our compass psychologically. Bakhtin shows beautifully how the carnival tradition, the world of play, provides a common cultural life and a collective subjectivity within which these disjunctions are dissolved. The social and cultural separation of children from adult life left them with the historic remains of this culture; with the clothes adults of an earlier period wore, then with their toys – the swing, the spinning top, the hoop – with their games of hide-and-seek or leapfrog, finally with their tales of witches, demons and fairy princesses. What had been the expression of a common life became the activities that both distinguished and subordinated child-life. It is, furthermore, in this separation that the adult, forgetful of his own childhood and ignorant of its history, can regard the play world with such nostalgic longings.

Children have, however, maintained this tradition, this culture of a collective subjectivity. As the Opies among others point out children are not taught how to play. They learn for themselves the basic plays, first with their own bodies, then with a ball, or bricks or a rope. And from other children they learn the games adults as well as children played some hundreds of years ago.

This common, collective subjectivity that play requires and, in its turn, fosters, has an infectious quality about it. Children want to 'join in' a play that others have begun, numbers are rarely fixed in advance and even where specific roles are assigned they are, after all, only temporary and change, with the game's repetition when someone else will be 'it'.

This common subjectivity is even more evident in the 'absorption' with which children play. It is just this 'concentration' displayed during play which puzzled the early psychologists who had been trained to expect a short 'attention-span' among those not yet far advanced in 'self-development'. Yet at play children seemed more immersed in their own activities than at any other time. This, however, is not a phenomenon of 'attention' at all. Robert Roberts for example, tells us, in the memoirs of his childhood in Salford, A Ragged Schooling, that after heavy rain one day he found a flooded area and built a small island, where his father finally found him after searching till after midnight. And Jimmy Boyle reports in his A Sense of Freedom that children in the Gorbals regularly played in the streets till that time. Play, like the carnival, however energetic, is always effortless. It is not a matter of the self 'engagng' in play, for amusement or diversion, and therefore having to exert itself in one way or another, in 'trying' to have a good time; it is rather that play, being natural to childhood, engages them and makes them part of its world. Hans-Georg Gadamer, again, has put the matter concisely; 'play', he tells us, 'has its own essence, independent of the consciousness of those who play.' A child is more absorbed by play than he is absorbed in play. Concentration, effort, the arduous fatiguing, exertions of the day is expended in trying not to play, because, for some unaccountable reason, it has for the time being been forbidden.

Even where play is solitary, then, it participates in this common subjectivity, it becomes part of the play-world in which separate identities are of no consequence; and enjoyment of immediacy the expression of an unrestrained nature.

This subjectivity, we have already seen, is fluid and given to unexpected transformations. More quickly and completely than confinement the 'normal' experience of space, time and the human body are altered. Where the metamorphosis of confinement leads always in the same direction, in play, such changes are bereft of order or purpose. Objects change their function, and the space appropriate to them is created – mountain range, the rolling ocean, a battlefield – instantly. Time also escapes both the forward momentum, however conventionalised, of 'normal' life and the pure duration of confinement – as in a dream it can be suddenly yesterday or last year, next Christmas, night time – as the play makes it. The human body, neither a physical camouflage of ourselves, nor yet part of the uniform substance of being, is a play-object like any other. As such, it is neither more nor less sentient than any other object. A precarious tower of wooden blocks, for example, shares in the collective exercise of play, and has to be talked to and cajoled into its appropriate form; its failure, as when it falls at the wrong moment, is the sign of a recalcitrant and perverse spirit – a kind of 'individualism' that 'spoils' the game. On the other hand, the body has no special privilege as an object, it can enter into play in every possible way, as someone else's horse, the fingers can fire bullets, and arms turn into the branches of a tree, the whole body a ship or an aeroplane. Wilhelm Preyer reports again from his The Mind of a Child, a nice example of this cavalier attitude to the body. He asked his son, at nineteen months, to hand him a shoe that had fallen from his foot – 'Give me the shoe'. His son obliged. 'Give me the foot', he asked and the infant, just beginning to enjoy the game, was bewildered to discover he could not hand it to his father. Bodily boundaries, like any other, change and change again, definable for the purposes of play in an indefinite variety of ways.

Though we cannot claim for such a view of children's play – self-sufficiency, infinite possibility, absolute liberty, the enjoyment of immediacy and repetition, the conquest of despair – any general validity, it describes for the 'golden age' not only the natural freedom they accorded childhood but a kind of dimly perceived irrationality carried still within the spirit of each adult and exercising, in its half-glimpsed presence, a disturbing fascination. We have become, over the years, less sensitive to this feeling and allow children now very little more freedom than we (foolishly) allow ourselves. But for the 'golden age' childhood, and more particularly the playworld if often (wrongly) conceived as exhaustive of childlife, was the mirror for a hidden human reality.

The boundary between play and non-play was thus seen as something rather peculiar. It was viewed from one direction only. Play itself did not acknowledge the existence of any boundary to its world, only from another point of view altogether could play be distinguished as a 'category' or differentiated as a specific form of life. This, at its most general level, is the reason for the 'absorbing' quality of play. When it 'comes off', play abolishes all limits and with it, therefore, the type of existence from which it could be viewed as one, among other, kinds of activities. Here again we meet one of the paradoxes built into our thinking about boundaries. Play in becoming authentically infinite must remain blind to any other kind of existence and, in consequence, from another point of view, is not infinite at all. Confinement is constituted by a reverse movement. In being exclusively bounded it creates for itself, on the inside, an infinite existence from nothing. Infinity only exists, in other words, within a bounded space, and it is only through the imposition of an absolute barrier that infinity as a 'real category' – a form of experience – can exist.

This unsettling vision of play was relieved eventually by a more academically respectable view. Children play, not to enjoy what is natural to them, but because they lack the ability to do otherwise. Yet in play a certain sharpening of human skills could be observed and this had to be taken into account. Instead of attempting to define the nature of play, or have play define for us the nature of the human, a kind of condensation of Froebel and Groos was effected in which play became seen as the medium, above any other, of 'self-development'. Not only were physical skills practised in play, even more significant was the introduction it afforded to the practical complexities of social life. Play became defined as games, or incipient games; and games in being constituted through conventional rules were social activities of an 'advanced' sort. Play performed, that is to say, a critical socialising function. In a modern overview, therefore, Play, Catherine Garvey is concerned exclusively with what she calls the 'systematic and rule-governed nature of play'. In this she follows Piaget's lead. Take, for example, the game of marbles so illuminated in his The Moral Judgment of the Child. Piaget is quite correct, of course, in treating the 'rules of the game' as conventional social rules and seeing them as an important feature of the play. What he perhaps fails to stress sufficiently is the function of such rules. 'Play rules' exist to protect the playworld, they are there above all to allow play to commence and to be repeated. Unlike, then, the rules by which adults play, they are not primarily concerned with defining winners and losers and establishing a competitive spirit. Children indeed are very little concerned with winning such games, they always think it 'unfair' if one child, however skilful, wins all the time. And adults realise as much when, at children's parties, they blatantly 'bend' the rules to ensure everyone 'wins' a prize.

Much has been made also of Piaget's observation that children up to the age of seven or so treat the rules of the game as 'sacred'. They refuse to play except in strict conformity to their rigorous standard of correctness. Only after that age do they come to accept the conventionality of such arrangements, and regard as legitimate its many variations. This 'development' is, however, of a highly ambiguous nature. It is normal to regard the growing complexity and conventionality of rules of play as indicative of a great differentiation and individuation of the psychological world. An 'identity' is established capable of both comprehending a complex outer reality and monitoring its own inner reactions and needs. Playing then becomes a matter of playing a 'role' appropriate to the game, and the game becomes more complex and stylised to indicate to other children and to themselves that they are 'only' playing. Play comes to be 'expressive' and 'significant' in new ways; it becomes permeated with social intentions. Some writers, notably Brian Sutton-Smith, in his Dialectics of Play, have pointed out that, as well as constituting a medium of socialisation, play can also satirise, oppose and innovate. That in becoming self-conscious through play children are not necessarily brought to that state of 'development' which is most wished for by their 'responsible' parents and teachers. If play socialises it can as well socialise children into delinquent as into conforming 'roles'. Indeed, play can come to appear as the expression of a 'counter-culture', something hinted at by Piaget himself in his description of the moral community of children's games. And from this point of view some of the elaboration of play-rules seems to be a kind of protection against the adult world and what it expects. But whether their play expresses the formation of a conforming selfhood – as when they begin to want to win or impress others, or fulfil their duty – or whether it expresses some form of resistance, in games of destruction, or role reversals, their absorption within the playworld has ended.

If children resist growing up by playing, then the use of play to express wishes and demands that run counter to the imperatives placed upon them by adults can have only a limited success. In resisting they have already been defeated, because the demand above all others is that they should grow up, cease playing and become 'selves'. To resist through play is to transform play into something else. To resist, a recalcitrant self must have already been brought into existence and the real possibility of play denied. Their only successful form of resistance is to play without thereby expressing anything, to give way completely to its purposelessness.

Play itself cannot, then, be a socialising 'agent'. It is the socialisation of children, rather, that comes in time to undermine the privileged freedom of play. The temporary and unpredictable duration of 'playtime' makes it, in addition, vulnerable to decay. The continuous oscillation between play and other 'activities' eventually comes to define a boundary which remains visible from within the playworld itself. It becomes more and more difficult to ignore this boundary and enter completely into the infinity of play. The identity imposed upon us by social life is carried over the boundary and 'spoils' many games that were perfectly absorbing at an earlier age. Play eventually becomes impossible as it is domesticated to 'secular' purposes that allot it a particular time and place, conventionalise all its moves and institutionalise all its practices until it becomes like any other social activity. The play world remains on the fringe of our memory – though it may be given to us again in impressions – something vague from the other side of the looking glass or deep within the rabbit burrow where, now that we are grown-up, we cannot go.

ANXIETY

Only children play; but they do not only play and, even when released from compelling adult attentions sometimes find, quite inexplicably, that they are unable to play. Our personal reconstructions of our own childhood tend to avoid this unpleasantness and prefer to dwell on those Dream Days that Kenneth Grahame has described for us – 'Those memorable days that move in a procession, their heads just out of the mist of years long dead – the most of them are full-eyed as the dandelion that from dawn to shade has steeped itself in sunlight'. Yet Grahame – and this is one of the qualities which make him such an exceptional writer – recognised that some days were, none the less, 'blind with the spatter of misery uncomprehended, unanalysed, only felt as something corporeal in its buffeting effects'.

Anxiety is not the privilege of adults in the way that play is the privilege of childhood. Indeed most people, however much they might 'worry' as adults, experience genuine anxiety only as children. Oddly, though we have come to think of anxiety as a rather 'grown-up' disease, something exacted as payment for maturity and worldly wisdom, at the same time we admit that it is a complaint 'rooted' in some mysterious way in our early experience.

Children may even appear anxious while engaged in play. Kolya, in Dostoevsky's novel, about to prostrate himself in the path of the oncoming train, the game of 'chicken' which from time to time attains an epidemic popularity, or, more simply, the strain in building a particularly high tower of wooden blocks or an intricate card house, might all seem to precipitate 'anxious' moments. But fear, or excitement, and the tension of 'bringing off' a particularly difficult play should not be mistaken for anxiety, which contradicts its essential nature.

Anxiety is the antithesis (one of them at least) of play. It is, to begin with, unpleasant, immediately unpleasant, and spreads its painfulness through everything. Where play delights in nothing in particular, and can enjoy everything that 'turns up', anxiety equally finds everything distasteful. Anxiety, too, is motionless, it is apprehended in inactivity. Yet anxiety and play belong together; they both exist for possibility and are, therefore, both intrinsic to childhood. The typical sensations of anxiety allude to this; the feeling of panic, a desire to run in all directions simultaneously but, at the same time, to remain to the spot, appalled by the sheer awfulness of possibility.

Play is possible because of a certain irrational trust in its own reality that secures the enjoyment of its freedom in the intuition that nothing will come of its choices, nothing be lost in its creation and no consequences flow from its actions. Anxiety exists in the same world – faced with undiminished plenitude – but it distrusts immediacy, is fearful of its own choices. Anxiety is a kind of anticipation of the self, or rather the reaction to such an anticipation. It overvalues, where play undervalues, the consequences of action. And just where play ignores (for as long as it can) the real consequences which flow from its choices; anxiety cannot choose because it posits as absolute (even where no real commitment is made) the result of each and every choice. Anxiety supposes the whole future to be decided in an instant, every instant, worse than that, it is not a future chosen from fixed alternatives, but a choice from infinity.

Anxiety, which is felt as a species of fear, is fear of nothing in particular, but a fear of possibility and what it might contain. Kierkegaard defines it, in his book The Concept of Dread, as 'fear of nothing' and regards it as inward equivalent to original sin, a fear which is unfounded in our experience but conditions, none the less, all our experience. Fear without a source leaves us nowhere to turn and we remain helplessly immobile. More than that, we are attracted as well as repelled by it and cannot help flirting with its presence.

This fascination, allied to its unpleasantness, provides powerful rationalising incentives. What is really unbearable, Kierkegaard points out, is the absence of an appropriate 'object' for our feelings. And rather than acknowledge its inwardness, we 'cope' more adequately by embodying anxiety in objects more or less suitable to reflect it. There is a satisfying completeness in the way in which we have offered to children such objects as have already failed us as rationalisations in the past; to complement their anachronistic clothes, toys and pastimes. We have even come to think it 'normal' that children should fear the dark, or to be alone, or spiders and other crawling things. Yet what is absurd for us is equally so for them and is just as powerless, to still their irrational fears or calm their distraught nerves.

When the world refuses to support, in a concrete image, the turmoil in our anxious state (and do not forget the far greater intensity and genuinely infinite extent, of such anxiety for children), we often resort to obsessive, compulsive behaviour in an effort to circumvent the open possibilities that appear so alarming. Obsessions, as much as phobias, are common in young children. It no longer excites our curiosity (let alone our compassion) to see a child compelled to touch every second railing as he walks (or more likely runs) past a particular fence. And the care which they take not to step on a crack in the pavement is regarded as a 'mere' game. Or, when awakened in the night, to have to be back in bed, the covers arranged in a particular fashion and eyes closed (against the dark) before the flush of the toilet has completed its noisy cycle – that too is a merely childish 'game'. What would be in us phobias and obsessions, and qualify us as obviously neurotic, is no more than appropriate to children, as natural to them as their play and, though as little likely to appear so, just as incomprehensible.

Kierkegaard, in his extraordinary Journals, at one point writes, 'all existence makes me anxious'. No one, I doubt, has tolerated so much anxiety; indeed, in his Journals, he created its art form. Yet his anxiety was already diminished and restricted to a particular problem. How to realise his 'true' selfhood, how to become a determinate identifiable person without losing, in the process, the infinite riches of inwardness the self should contain. He even knew, or thought he knew, the solution to the problem of anxiety. It was to become a Christian, for the Christian self related itself 'infinitely to the infinite'; through the 'leap' into faith the infinity of the self was realised in a single individual. Even so, he was anxious, could not make the 'leap' and created instead, in his effort to 'explain' his painful experience, the first 'depth' psychology of modern times. How much worse for the child faced, even beyond the possibility of choosing a 'true' self, with the choice of whether to have a self at all. Existence does not make the child as an individual anxious, rather existence is, for him, an anxious reality whose never-ending variations, on some days, cannot be trusted.

Freud, after a long clinical experience and several reformulations in his theoretical views, came to hold a similar view of anxiety. Coming from within a medical-scientific tradition, he first sought a 'rational' foundation for anxiety. He postulated first, in his early researches with Joseph Breuer, a 'trauma' or 'seduction' theory. Some unpleasant event occurring in childhood had been, to alleviate the suffering it imposed on our consciousness, denied by our memory. Anxiety was the fear of remembering it again, a kind of intuition of the forgotten incident. He was forced to abandon this view, however, by the frequency with which he encountered such cases, and the apparent ubiquity of such 'traumatic' events. The memories, though difficult to arouse to consciousness must, in the vast generality of cases, be false; recollections of fantasies rather than memories of real events. Anxiety, then, could not be rooted in particular childhood events but must have its origin in some more general phenomenon; and the fantasies that emerged during therapy must point, albeit in an indirect manner, to this source.

Freud, for many years, considered the solution to the problem to have been given in his concept of repression. The child was born without anxiety, only with needs and appetites. But to become properly human the system of appetites had to be brought into alignment with social demands. Certain values had to be denied and repression was the unconscious process of denying those wishes. They did not, however, simply disappear. The process of repression created a reservoir of unfulfilled and unconscious wishes. In this form they exerted a continuous 'pressure' on consciousness and action, breaking through in disguised form in dreams and neurotic 'symptoms'. Symptoms were, in fact, a language of repressed desire, and not the memory of specific events. Anxiety remained, however, as a kind of fear of the unconscious, and was perfectly rational because a return of repressed wishes, on a large scale, would be quite destructive. The basic method of dealing with anxiety was effective repression. Repression both caused and cured anxiety; and anxiety was only the result of inadequate repression, a kind of leakage which was itself a symptom or an indicator of a neurotic temperament.

Freud, however, late in his career, came to alter this view drastically. Two difficulties in particular caused him to reformulate his theory. The first was that, in childhood, anxiety seemed to precede the first and, most decisive, phase of repression. Secondly was the phenomenon he termed 'repetition-compulsion', the practice he found in many of his patients of repeating failed or unpleasant activities. Such repetition,

even Freud in the end, admitted could not be traced
to the covert working of the pleasure principle.
Repetition-compulsion pointed, in Freud's view, to
an excess of anxiety over repression but not in
itself to inadequate repression. Anxiety was not
the result of repression, a fear of the unconscious;
but repression, rather, was the primary method
of dealing with the anxiety which is given as a
datum of experience. This later view, expressed
in his Inhibition, Symptom and Anxiety, brings him
very close to Kierkegaard. Anxiety is admitted as
part of the 'energy-system' of existence and to alleviate
the 'nameless dread' repressed wishes were 'blamed'
for causing it. This is an astonishingly economical
and elegant method of realisation. Instead of
appropriating for itself, in other words, some external
'object' anxiety is 'explained' and thus domesticated
by attaching it to disreputable (but desirable) parts
of ourselves.

Again, the situation for children, expecially young
children, is both an intensification and a generalisation
of adult suffering. In the absence of repression,
without the unconscious and the powers of rationalising
which this differentiation in psychic functioning
allows; anxiety is given much greater scope.

More recently John Bowlby, in his Attachment and
Loss, has also recognised anxiety to be a central
experience in the life of children. Unlike Freud,
who reconstructed his picture of childhood from his
patient's recollections, Bowlby begins with the
observations of children directly. In attempting,
however, to relate all 'later' forms of anxiety to
'separation-anxiety' he has attempted to tame the
'irrationality' of anxiety in much the same way
as Groos attempted to 'animalise' play. He offers
'separation' as the rational foundation of anxiety
and brings the armoury of modern biology to bear
in support of his contention that it is part of our
species life. He attempts really to transform anxiety
into fear, into something more 'real' than dread.
It does, however, create special difficulties of
interpretation. If anxiety, instead of being irrational,
is a kind of perverse expression of a 'real' fear
then it is difficult to see why the fact should be
disguised in the first place. Children, in fact, often
fear separation and say so, without this eradicating
the anxiety which so unreasonably troubles them
as well.

Strangely, however, children do not appear to
suffer from anxiety, at least not very often; despite

the arguments of Freud and Bowlby childhood anxiety remains invisible while we daily suffer its torments. this is because children still possess the most powerful antidote – play. Anxiety, it is true, denies the possibility of play, but, equally, play destroys anxiety.

Children have no more 'reason' to be anxious than they have to play so their world is very much divided between them; their whole subjective life moves in crazy oscillations between them. Between, that is to say, delight in his own creative powers, and abject misery at his impotence.

Anxiety and play, though mutually exclusive, come on many occasions near to a head-on collision as they struggle to impose their own version of the meaning of repetition. This strange phenomenon which gives a clue to the forms of subjectivity outside of individualism is a kind of primitive battleground. Childhood anxiety and the first mechanisms of play both emerge within repetition. We have already noted that repetition is an apparently simple device imminent in play, which contains everything including duplicate copies of itself, in principle, and indefinitely extended series. We have seen too that one method of 'coping' with anxiety is to deny the existence of the world of possibility, resulting in obsessive repetition, the benefit of which resides in its apparent lack of choice. As a 'tactic' this, of course, fails because its denial of choice is itself a choice and carries anxiety, undiminished, with it. This is, however, a very 'adult' interpretation of compulsive repetition. It might also be viewed as an effort to arouse the world of play whose more perfect release from anxiety is always tantalisingly close. Children, when anxious, turn to their most 'familiar' toys and games; but it is difficult to see what 'comfort' this can bring unless it is in the invoking of pleasure already experienced in just such a repetition when at play. And what 'security' can be embodied in familiar objects except the irrational safety of play? As Winnicott has put it, 'Children play to master anxiety' and repetition is an instrument of such mastery.

Even so this ritualisation of play cannot succeed. It subordinates play to a purposeful end and repetition to its means, which the child cannot, any more than Friedrich Froebel, accomplish.

Indeed the essential distinction between the neurotic and the normal 'solutions' to the problem of anxiety is precisely the neurotic's insistence on continuing the struggle by these deficient means. In this sense the neurotic refuses to grow up. He does not aim merely to 'cope' with anxiety but seeks, above all, a return to the perfect liberty of the playworld and the banishment within it, for ever, of dread. Repetition lets him down. Used thus as a tool it becomes saturated with the anxiety it is intended to destroy, transforming the neurotic's most cherished weapon (a mechanism, we might say of attack rather than defence) into an instrument of torture turned against himself.

Tactical avoidance of anxiety, like the purposive seeking of play, is a contradictory device that introduces the subtle calculations of individual identity into a subjective world which refuses to acknowledge them.

In childhood, anxiety and play succeed one another with incomprehensible completeness. Erik Erikson expresses a similar idea in his classic study Childhood and Society, when he characterises the young child as caught within the dualism of trust/distrust of the world. It is not just a matter of one establishing a predominance over the other depending upon the personality of the child and the circumstances of his life; but of a continuous inexplicable movement from one to the other and back again.

Even though children are protected from anxiety in play, they cannot utilise play as a basic defence against its attacks. Play cannot be subordinated to any instrumentality and this is why anxiety comes to gain the upper hand. The unpleasantness of anxiety seems to carry with it more potential for 'development' than the enjoyment of play. It induces a calculative attitude and a defensive posture that, much more than the freedom of play, proves to be a mechanism of 'self-development'. The basic 'solution' to anxiety is found in this self-development. Identity drastically reduces the world of possibilities and its anxious choices, but does so in an apparent non-arbitrary and unfrivolous way. The bottomless pit of anxiety is not finally filled in, but its terrors are restricted and contained within the forward motion of the self. We grow up because we cannot tolerate the anxiety which is the reverse side of the absolute liberty we so much enjoyed at play. And in choosing the self as a weapon against the anxiety that plagues the selfless world we do not even rid ourselves completely of its terrors. We impose upon ourselves as a duty, a continuous striving towards an ultimate self-realisation that is never accomplished. In this ceaseless striving we will always be anxious; it is almost a sign that we are still trying. Such an account of our inner-life carries just sufficient conviction to make the struggle bearable.

Growing-up puts us in touch with necessity and this alleviates to a large extent the anxieties indigenous to childhood. It is when we impose necessity upon children that we can observe a quickened pace in the oscillations between anxiety and play. We recognise this in emotional 'stress', in sudden changes in mood and disposition. Freud has classically described the first such period, the Oedipal crisis through which the child is made to recognise, in a rough and ready fashion at least, reality outside himself. To put it another way, he is forced to recognise himself as a reality separate from others. Both play and anxiety, existing as aspects of infinite possibility, deny any determinate status to particular individuals and resist the imposition of a structure of experience that falls short of plenitude. The child, in a sense, takes refuge in both play and anxiety, for anxiety, too, is a defence against growing up. It is not so much the experience of anxiety, as the techniques deployed in its 'solution' that trick the child into 'self-development'. But no refuge can be secure. Complete dependence on the adult world cannot be avoided and in the end, therefore, its view of reality becomes 'natural'. This takes time, however, and the Oedipal crisis imposes only a skeletal reality, a limited necessity and a selfhood as yet incompletely individuated. This leaves, during what Freud termed the 'latency period', the possibility still to play.

The second, and more complete, imposition of necessity brings childhood to a close and with it the world of play. It transforms a rudimentary identity into an individual, comlex personality, and the world of infinite possibility remains only as the anxiety the self carries within itself, as despair.

Confinement, it might be noted, moves to an extreme in the radicalisation of necessity. It closes all possibility and finally relieves the subject of even that reminder of childhood.

DESIRE

Play and anxiety belong together, each colouring in different hues its inexhaustible variations. They are separately constituted subjectivities, each defining a different relationship of possibility. One in which all things are possible, and all possibilities pleasurable, the other in which all possible things are available but must somehow be kept at a distance.

Children also experience a relationship to the non-immediate world. This relationship is most generally termed desire, which is a choice that goes beyond what is immediately available and implies, therefore, some activity, striving or effort to close the gap between the chooser and his choice.

Hegel had already pointed out, in a famous passage of The Phenomenology of Spirit, that desire was the relationship of identity and self-consciousness. Only the 'I' could desire and experience desire. Desire was, thus, the fundamental point of transition from animal consciousness to human self-consciousness. Desire opens up the subject to himself; it always has an inner point of reference, however 'objective' its aim. Kierkegaard took up this idea and made desire (what he terms passion) the fundamental relationship of 'inwardness'. The point, however, is not just to distinguish between the consciousness of animal needs and human self-consciousness, but to differentiate through passion forms of the different selfhood. For the most part 'Christianity' had destroyed passion and most people most of the time simply accept unthinkingly the conventional arrangements of their social life and a conventional identity as an image of themselves. Kierkegaard's aim was to inspire passion, to arouse desire. More than that, he was concerned to show that passion once aroused always sought, through the objects of its choice, the person of the chooser; so Kierkegaard urged the more fundamental and less hypocritical choice - the self. The self chosen passionately transforms the inner life of the subject and condenses within him a genuine, personal rather than conventional, social, identity. The secret of selfhood, then, is properly to desire the self, to dissolve within ourselves the distinction between subject and object.

Desire, then, appears to be a structure of selfhood and not an aspect of childhood subjectivity. The tradition of philosophical psychology, from Hegel and Kierkegaard to Dostoevsky and, above all, to Proust, assumes desire to be a basic modality of self identity. It ought, therefore, to be a relationship absent from childhood in which the 'self' has not yet emerged beyond a 'primitive' level.

Indeed in this sense desire is absent from childhood. What is noticeable in children is that they wish rather than desire, and that wishing is as easy, and inconsequential, as playing. To wish for something does not mean, for children, that the self is being 'projected' into the object of the wish. The relationship that Hegel described as the basic process of developing self–consciousness – of alienating the self into 'otherness' then reassimilating it in its new form – is absent in childhood.

Wishing is quite typical of childhood and is the characteristic least attractive to adults, who 'over-interpret' its significance. As children experience themselves without the benefit of that passionate distance between self and other, their wishing is quite harmless and, we might say, playful. Typically children wish to possess things they do not have, because their friends have them, or they just happen to see them in shop windows. Or they wish to go to the cinema or the swimming pool, to play with their friends; that it would stop raining, that they could fly, or become a princess. They do not distinguish in their wishes between the possible and the impossible. They can recognise well enough, if they reflect upon it – though without this diminishing their longing for the exotic – the limits of practicability. They do not generally wish, however, to be loved, or to be admired by their friends, or to be better or richer than anyone else. They are not concerned with these 'qualifications' of the self; their wishes are for provender and a good time, that their play world might become permanent and that they be left alone to enjoy it.

Where play expresses – if it expresses anything – an unrestricted liberty; wishing is the subjective side of children's dependence upon adults. Dependence leaves them no option but the wish; it is their fundamental mode of action upon adults. The character of wishing (as distinct from desire properly speaking) is that its satisfaction is entirely contingent upon others and its outcome, therefore, completely unpredictable. Hence, even if children had genuine identities they would not risk expressing them through wishes; and as it is they cannot even take such a chance. The self has no investment in a wish. A wish, we might say, is all 'otherness' where desire is ultimately all 'self'. Hence, the mobility of children's wishes; they are subject to the wild pulsations of whim and fashion, negated in a moment without a trace of grief.

Children do not wish for some specific 'thing' (any more than adults desire some particular object); it is rather that in wishing they attempt to broaden the boundaries of play and accommodate practical life within its comfortable domain. An effort to disarm by absorption the power of adults over them. To do this they must wish for everything – but not seriously.

But is there a more serious side to the wish? Did not Freud show, beneath the superficiality of wishing, something that could more properly be termed desire?

Freud argued that there is no initial need to wish. All pleasure comes from the manifold satisfaction of bodily processes in the meeting of physical needs and appetites. Pleasure in the infant is not differentiated according to source or form; it is 'polymorphously perverse'. this is a way of describing, at its most general level, the 'selflessness' of infancy, is total absorption in the sensuous playworld. The demands adult society places upon children, however, sets up an internal mechanism of repression which selects from the polymorph range of pleasures those deemed to be 'inappropriate'. The creation of an unconscious stocked with unfulfilled possibilities of pleasure is reflected in consciousness as wishing. The unconscious, as Freud describes it, is composed of wishes. Conscious wishes in their turn no doubt express in a disguised, acceptable form the longing of forbidden pleasure. More generally all innocuous conscious wishing is an acknowledgement of the wish for the freedom of sensuous play. Interestingly enough Freud talks always of sensuous gratification, rather than play; limiting himself ultimately by this to a biological conception of pleasure. Play, however, is more general than gratification and reflects more appropriately the subjectivity of 'libido'.

This in itself is not desire, merely the replacement of unnaceptable with innocuous wishes. The mechanism of this repression, however, depends upon the formation of an intense relationship with an adult. The Oedipal crisis shakes the child from his 'original narcissism' and forces upon him the first 'object choice'. This renunciation of the absolute freedom of the sensuous playworld is effected through the condensation, within an image of the adult, of all the child's sources of pleasure. The child thus 'falls in love' with the adult simultaneously with the conversion of immediate pleasure into unconscious wishes. Desire and wishes are, then, born together. Wishes (which are the sign of repression) are the corollary of the desire aroused in the child for an adult. This desire, in its turn must be repressed, attracting the wishes of the unconscious towards it so that, when we grow up, our unconscious and conscious will reinforce each other in their object-choice.

It is doubtful, however, if the Oedipal crisis creates desire. It is the character rather than the intensity of the feeling which is at issue. It is not a falling in love according to the modern romantic theory, not a striving together of two independent selves. The Oedipal stage still reflects the extreme imbalance between adult and child. Forced from his immediate enjoyment of the playworld the child has no option but to identify with the aggressor and adopt, as a temporary measure at least, the identity which fills his world. It is not that the child 'chooses' the adult but the adult who chooses himself through the child. The child still only wishes, but in wishing to be like the adult reflects, for the adult, his mature desire. The child's desire, then, is borrowed – and returned. He becomes the point of 'mediation' for the adult's self-identification.

Freud, in describing the origin of 'desire' in children has shown the completeness of the adults' domination. The Oedipal crisis imposes upon the child a premature, counterfeit identity, and the child cannot help but allow this image of himself to flow through him. The mechanism gains a foothold in the child's wishes. His powerlessness is reflected in the way in which his wishes very often express only what is approved by adults.

Childhood wishing is, therefore, a complex affair. What originally appeared to be desire is better termed wishing, and wishing is of two fundamentally different sorts. Firstly there is wishing which reflects the child's pleasure in play; the wish, expressed in countless particular and frivolous longings, to be left alone in play. These can be distinguished, 'analytically' at least from those wishes which have their origin in a superior adult's needs and desires and, although also expressed in a variety of forms, always amount to a wish to grow up. This second form of wishing should more properly be termed compulsion. Desire, properly speaking, belongs to the adult world; in childhood wishing is its 'play form' and compulsion the presence within it, already, of adult interests.

Although wishing and compulsion are distinguishable for us, children more often experience the two together. Both are relationships of dependence which, within a non-individuated world, can hardly be separated. Whether the child acts upon the adult, or the adult upon the child, or upon himself through the child, is almost never clear. Such a series of subjective illusions is caught beautifully in a story, A Child's Heart, by Herman Hesse.

Children, despite 'living' on wishes, do not know how to wish 'properly'. They either wish for the impossible (to remain for ever at play) or in wishing for the possible (to grow up) wish on an adult's, rather than on their own, behalf. This could hardly be otherwise; they have nothing to wish with, no self that seeks to aggrandise itself with tokens of its own importance or 'discover' itself through its own restless striving.

CHILDHOOD SUBJECTIVITY

Play, anxiety, wishing, compulsion constitute together the basic realities of childhood experience. Play and anxiety are mutually exclusive forms of what is immediately possible; wishing and compulsion are only analytically separable and are experienced more often as an indeterminate longing, often a kind of melancholy, in the child's relation to non-immediate reality.

However, these 'categories' are not synthesised and childhood subjectivity should not be understood as a 'structure' of these terms. The experience of the child is unpredictably mobile, a continuously shifting mêlée of feeling. Nor can these terms be organised hierarchically according to some presumed sequence of 'development' one to the other. The child moves continually through this circuit of differing 'orientations'. Hardly surprising then, that James Sully, giving way as he does from time to time, to a charming Scottish expression, calls his child 'the wee amorphous thing'. Amorphous, nowadays, is perhaps two strong a word; experience, after all, does not seem possible outside of some form, but childhood is rich in such forms and has not yet abandoned them all in favour of the myth of individual identity.

These movements of childhood can be suggested, but no more than suggested, with the aid of a diagram.

The limitations of such a diagram are obvious. What should be stressed, above all, is the fundamental disjunction between play and other 'categories'. Play is not a 'category' at all but a world to itself and once within its domain all else ceases to exist or, rather, everything is transformed by its power into another reality.

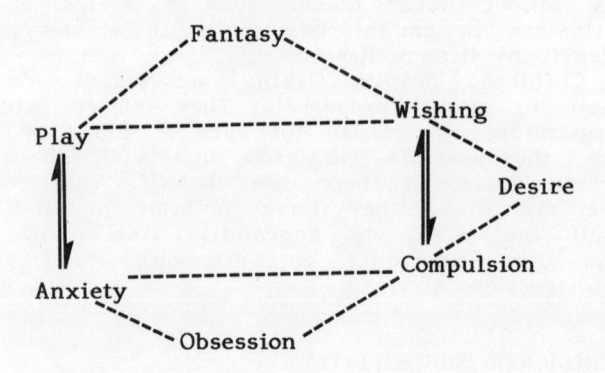

```
          Fantasy
       ╱          ╲
    Play ─────────── Wishing
     ↕                 ↕    ╲
                            Desire
     ↕      ────────────  ↕
    Anxiety              Compulsion
       ╲                ╱
          Obsession
```

What must also be borne in mind is that outside it as a condition of its entire 'structure' exists the world of necessity; of adult social organisation. It is the removal of children from this field of action which opens up these possible forms of subjectivity. Even in their relationship through adults to the non-immediate world, children are not brought directly into touch with any 'necessary' reality. Hence, the form of wishing, and its obverse, compulsion, which is the imposition of adult desires and not of necessity (the process of labour), directly. We can see in this compulsion (to make children still) an attempt by adults to restrict the reality of childhood freedom, to define it as utopian and thus (for they were also children once) restrain within themselves childish dreams of liberty.

A 'development' of sorts none the less comes to overrule the oscillations within the child's spirit. Wishing/compulsion, which is founded on the adult's refusal to leave children alone, eventually turns children away from play, or, making them somewhat self-conscious, closes off the world of play as a refuge. Then 'growing-up', 'development', the emergence of selfhood, become the only means of defeating anxiety.

Some, none the less, refuse the trade and do not – or try not to – grow up at all; but in refusing self-identity they must find some less successful solution to the problem of anxiety. We can attempt, if we are allowed (through neglect), to escape anxiety by coalescing wishing and playing, by living, in other words, in fantasy. This leads, however, not to a prolongation of childhood but to the world of confinement. Play is again destroyed by the attempt to make it conditional upon a wish, and the wish cannot come true because it is not directed towards a superior power capable of satisfying its craving. Fantasy refuses, certainly, to allow the self to come into existence but in doing so destroys as well the world of play and leaves the subject, literally, with nothing.

The alternative to fantasy is calculative repetition, indulgence in compulsive, obsessive behaviour. This however, as we have seen, fails to overcome anxiety and does not even succeed in avoiding the formation of a self-identity which hides in the very actions which were designed to evade it.

In the overwhelming majority of cases, however, growing up is the only real possibility. Then we waken some morning to discover we can no longer remember what it was like to be a child. Like Kenneth Grahame, as he tells us in The Golden Age, 'the trackless meadows of old time have shrunk and dwindled away to a few poor acres' and with him we wonder, 'Can it be that I also have become an Olympian?'.

7 The Prehistory of Nostalgia

The 'golden age' of childhood was remarkable most obviously for its creation of a special literature for children. Such a literature, written specifically to be read by, or more frequently to be read to, children, denotes not simply the new significance accorded childhood, but a self-conscious reflection upon it. Such a literature naturally enough expresses more accurately adults' preoccupations with childhood, especially with the memory of their own childhood, than it does children's spontaneous conceptions of the world.

The 'classics' of children's literature belong almost exclusively to this period, from the transmutation of the traditional folk tale and the new inventions of Lewis Carroll to George MacDonald's magical tales, Kipling's adventures and the flowering of naturalism in the stories of Edith Nesbit and, above all, in the subtle genius of Kenneth Grahame. At its best a culture of determined individualism, during a period of dynamic self-assertion and expansion, unquestioningly committed to the logic of capitalist growth, produced imaginative reconstructions of child-life which remain unsurpassed in their sensitivity and psychological alertness. It is true, of course, that the stature of such 'classics' gains by comparison with the host of lesser works written during the same period, uniformly dull and now unread, that shared in a complacent view of children as the passive recipients of their stifling morality. Yet this mass of 'improving' litertature responded to the same, new situation - the separateness of childhood with its special educational needs - as did the far fewer inspired works that succeeded in describing the world from the child's point of view.

It is, oddly enough, largely due to the uncritical, ahistorical acceptance of the relationship between adults and children as 'natural' and fixed for all time (despite the fact that they were responding to something essentially new in just this relationship) that lend to their writing a characteristic vigour and lack of condescension which has since become even rarer. Children's literature has been infected, to a greater or lesser extent, by an element of self-

THE PREHISTORY OF NOSTALGIA   155

consciousness and guilt, an uneasiness at least in attempting to 'entertain' those who are so completely dependent upon us. Relationships between children and adults are avoided as much as possible, yet the dominant literary orthodoxy of realism makes this squeamishness absurd.

A clear example of this tendency can be seen in the deterioration of Arthur Ransome's stories. Swallows and Amazons in the 'classic' mould of Edith Nesbit's books on the Bastable children. The children's own playworld is accepted at face value and their 'adventures' described from their own point of view. His later books, however, become increasingly fantastic but retain a quite inappropriately realistic style. There is all the difference in the world between 'playing' pirates with Uncle Jim in Swallows and Amazons and the 'real life' adventures in Peter Duck or the excruciating Missee Lee.

Another significant sign of uneasiness in writing for children is in the historicising of morality common to much contemporary children's literature of the more 'serious' kind. Joan Aiken's Midnight is a Place, for example, is one of the best examples of transposing the uplifting moral from the character to the setting (early factory life) of the story. Well-intentioned moralising is taboo for modern writers, but historical 'realism' remains perfectly acceptable and the tradition of 'improving' literature is kept alive under its aegis. The morality of the setting has even penetrated a tradition of purer fantasy, beginning with Frank Baum's Wizard of Oz (escape from the Kansas dustbowl during the depression) to Roald Dahl's Charlie and the Chocolate Factory (escape from the poverty and boredom of routine factory production). It is almost surprising to find Pippi Longstocking, Karlson and Emil - whose only value is to have fun - still alive and well and Astrid Lingren among the most popular of children's entertainters.

There is even something suspicious in the continuing 'popularity' of the classics, for they no longer describe the real world of childhood and have themselves become (for adults) exemplary historical documents, read still to children as an 'introduction' for them both to their own vanished world and to 'serious' literary values. The 'rediscovery' of Edith Nesbit, for example, seems a consequence of this Froebel-like subversion of children's 'natural' choice of entertainments.

The classics (or the memory of them), exert their

fascination more for their psychology than for their historical accuracy or literary tastefulness. They described, in terms more immediately comprehensible than those offered by the philosopher or scientist, the new world of childhood. They can still serve to fill out the skeletal framework of childhood experience which we have derived, largely, by implication from Kierkegaard's descriptions of adult self-identity.

Children's literature could make its appearance only when childhood had been accorded an identity separate from (though contained within) adult society. Once such a status had been conferred, the fairy-story quickly achieved within it, an unquestioned priority. This association between child-life and the fairy-story has remained, more or less intact, to the present. It was not that fairy-stories were written or collected specifically for children – neither Perrault nor the Grimms had any intention of recounting vanishing folktales to the very young; it was more simply that as an unfashionable and dying literature it could be safely given to children to 'play' with. Tolkien, admirably anticipating Ariès in a passage from his important essay 'On Fairy-Stories', remarks, 'Actually, the association of children and fairy-stories is an accident of our domestic history. Fairy-stories have in the modern lettered world been relegated to the 'nursery', as shabby or old-fashioned furniture is relegated to the playroom, primarily because the adults do not want it, and do not mind if it is 'misused'. And, interestingly, he makes the point that this association depends upon a view of children 'as a special kind of creature, almost a different race'. The fairy-story, that is to say, in its modern form, is a survival of a pre-modern popular tradition of folk tales. Those tales were originally part of that culture of common subjectivity, shared by adults and children alike, that, as Bakhtin shows, culminated in Rabelais's literary carnival.

It is tempting, nevertheless, to see the fairy-story as peculiarly 'suitable' for children. The folk-tales from which they are derived themselves expressed, as Jack Zipes in his Radical Theories of Folk and Fairy Tales has pointed out, a dependent relationship; a world of non-individuated subjectivity in which unnamed fears oscillated inexplicably with unbelievable good fortune and where, above all, the primacy of the wish and the efficacy of wishing had not yet been superseded by self-reliant action. It is not that children 'suited' such stories because they were, in any romantic sense, keeping alive the traditions of a more 'innocent' age – though such a view was not unknown among the writers, pre-eminently George McDonald and Andrew Laing, of the 'golden age' – but because, like the masses in pre-modern society, children live in a world of extreme dependence upon other, more powerful, beings. This subordinate position leaves them no alternative but 'magical' thinking, the cognitive equivalent of the wish.

The 'characters' in the tales are queens, kings, princesses, witches, the embodiment of the superior powers which in some mysterious way conditioned the lives of the readers who, themselves belonging to the masses, never appeared in the stories themselves.

It is odd, therefore, that Bruno Bettelheim, in an influential study, The Uses of Enchantment, finds it possible to interpret fairy-stories in terms of psychological 'needs' for development. The fairy-story, in his view, provides symbolic material upon which the child can 'work' to represent to himself his own experience. It relieves anxiety and encourages a kind of security which is essential to 'growing-up'. But this is a 'meaning' which they only assumed after their relegation to the nursery, and a meaning given to them not by the children who listened to them but by the adults who read them aloud. Originally, the problem of inducing in the young a kind of teleological governor, a self-controlling and self-directing device, had been unknown and the folk-tale performed a more exalted, and no doubt more complex task. Like the carnival, which as a licensed event was an afforded luxury that remained innocent of its own preconditions, the folk-tale extended a subtle oppression. It expressed longings contained, aspirations denied, desire domesticated and suppressed. And today the child and adult presumably listen to the same story from very different points of view and find in it equally desirable, but opposite, meanings.

Bettelheim seems even more to confuse his defence of childhood with his defence of the fairy-story as the 'best' of all stories for children. He sees in Hans Anderson's deliberately written stories, the first signs of the deterioration of children's literature towards unrealistic and trivial. Yet it is in Anderson that the self-conscious here first emerges from the collective spirit of the folk-tale. If his stories are more ambivalent psychologically and less pure stylistically than the Grimm's collection, they are at least clearer thematically; development towards a determined self-indentity is their recurring motif. His inclusion of death, which Bettelheim dislikes, and its transcending significance for the inward subject makes his stories, in fact, models for Bettelheim's thesis. Their difficulty, of course, is that 'development' necessarily entails anxiety and dealing with anxiety which Bettelheim (as a responsible adult and model parent) conceals from his young listeners. As developed for a child audience, paradoxically, the fairy-story has ceased to be 'rooted' in the experience of a dependent, collective subjectivity and has come to serve the maieutic art, continually pointing beyond itself to the necessity of growing up and assuming adult responsibilities.

The traditional fairy-story, like the carnival, none the less illustrates liability between wishing and compulsion. The deceitfulness of desire which is not yet free. The fairy-story, particularly its modern development which reaches its peak with Oscar Wilde and, in particular, with Antoine de Saint-Exupéry's The Little Prince, became a highly ambivalent indicator of childhood experience. Saint-Exupéry combines the greatest sensitivity to the autonomy of childhood experience and, at the same time, makes individuation, growing-up, and the death of childhood, the basic theme of his story. Other writers from the 'golden-age' provided a more naturalistic description of child-life, each tending to one or other element within the 'structure' of children's experience; Edith Nesbit, for example, was fascinated by the phenomenon of wishing and the inter-relationship between wishing and play. One of the earliest and clearest examples is her story The Five Children and It, in which five children holidaying in the country discover a sand fairy who can grant them one wish each day. She incidentally complains of London as a place for children, there is nowhere to play, it is 'like prison for children', too regular and geometric, everything 'the wrong sort of shape' – confusing by her criticism the view of play as natural to children and the idea of 'nature' as 'animal' freedom. Her story is not, however, a fairy-story. It is neither about Faerie (Tolkien's criteria) nor is it about the superior powers that really control their lives (kings, princes, etc.). It is about their own wishes, and their incapacity to wish in their own interests. They always wish compulsivley, unthinkingly and with unpredictable results. They find the fairy a mixed blessing. They wish, for example, to be beautiful then find they are unrecognisable; to be rich and then find they cannot spend the gold pieces they are granted; they wish for adventures, which become all too-frighteningly real. There is a fundamental difference, Nesbit notices, between the fantastic realisation of wishes in play, which are free of any immediate consequences, and the granting of wishes by some more powerful and independent being. They come to mistrust the fairy, that is to say, to mistrust their own wishes, to disbelieve their own desire. They are continually trapped by the wish, rather than making it their instrument. They do not know what to wish for, because they have not yet attained that settled self-image which fixes ahead of itself equally settled objects of its desire.

The wish becomes something more to be avoided than welcomed; but cannot be absolutely banished, sooner or later one of the children will inadvertently say, 'I wish . . . ' and find it too easily granted. The wish, thus, automatically granted, is not a wish at all, but an aspect of immediacy. No distance is opened up within the subject that can be experienced as a vague melancholic longing. Children must distrust wishes too easily granted because it removes from them the possibility of wishing properly, that is to say, of experiencing real desire. It, thus, weakens their powers of self-development. A version, in other words, of the popular theory of 'spoiling' the child.

In a sophisticated extension of her basic theme, Nesbit brought compulsion, as well as play and wishing, into a naturalistic narrative. The Wouldbegoods not only wish, but wish for themselves, what the adults wish for them, to be 'good', to keep out of 'mischief', to be 'well behaved'. Wishing and compulsion perfectly coalesce in their minds, they have no wishes of their own. However, this successful (from the adult viewpoint) 'synthesis' within their budding character is continually undermined by the subversive freedom of play. Once they begin to play, their good intentions – which have not in fact been 'internalised', not become part of their identity – vanish and they enter completely into its world and accept completely its reality. Play, refusing to recognise anything beyond itself, pays no regard at all to their sober wishes which are activated again only when an outraged adult intrudes upon some unruly, playful scene. The opening chapter of the book describes in some detail an elaborate play, the consequence of which precipitates their wish to be good. The play, 'Jungles', is a spontaneous adaptation of stories from their favourite writer, Kipling. The game takes off in a big way. 'We all thought of different things,' reports Oswald, 'Of course, first we dressed up pillows in the skins of beasts and set them about on the grass to look as natural as we could. And then we got Pincher and rubbed him all over with powdered slate-pencil, to make him the right colour for Grey Brother.' The 'props' became quite extravagant, 'even so all was not yet lost beyond recall. It was the stuffed fox that did the mischief.' They incorporate their uncle's stuffed trophies into the game.

> Then Dicky had an idea . . . He just got the hose and put the end over a branch of the cedar tree. Then we got the steps they clean windows with, and let the hose rest on the top of the steps and run. It was to be a waterfall, but it ran between the steps and was only wet and messy; so we got Father's mackintosh and uncle's and covered the steps with them, so that the water ran down all right and was glorious.

The play was highly successful. 'The lawn under the cedar was transformed into a dream of beauty'. And Oswald reflects, 'Taking one thing with another, I don't know that we ever had a better time while it lasted'.

Of course it did not last. Play has no consequences within its own world, but can have dramatic effects on the 'real' world, populated by powerful adults, beyond. Uncle returned, with visitors. 'Oswald saw, in a flash, exactly how it would strike the uncle, and his brave young blood ran cold in his veins. His heart stood still.'

Nesbit's stories, however, fall short of total realism through her omission of anxiety as a constituent of children's experience. The protectiveness of adults is reflected too directly and one-sidedly, removing from childhood not just the insecurity that might be aroused by imperfect care, but the anxiety proper to its brimming potentiality. Where she does attempt, as in The Railway Children, to record less playful aspects of child-life, anxiety is borrowed entirely from adults and has its source in a disruption in the adult world (their father has been wrongly accused of spying). The result becomes in consequence increasingly sentimental.

Kenneth Grahame, whose work provided a model for Edith Nesbit, not only recognised the primacy

THE PREHISTORY OF NOSTALGIA

of play and described its transformations with particular care, he accords to anxiety an independent existence in childhood. His early stories especially, those collected in The Golden Age and Dream Days, each stress some particular element in childhood experience, or the movement among its various forms. A passage from 'Dies Irae' has already been quoted, the day, 'blind with the spatter of misery uncomprehended' had, like the underlying despair of The Railway Children, an ostensible cause in the adult world. In this case Martha (a servant) had suffered the loss of her brother, a sailor, popular with the children, drowned at sea. Yet the young narrator cannot really conceive of her grief. Anxiety which on that particular day had broken through to infect everything with its misery, is felt as something palpable that she also shares. Fantasy, however (a playful wish), proves a sufficient antidote. He indulges in extravagant images of himself as a heroic soldier, turning the tables on all his hated relations, lording it over their pitiful servility before affording himself the ultimate luxury of appearing magmanimous in their eyes - though not without the enjoyment first of all of giving them 'a good talking to'. His fantasy perfectly inverts his normal relation to the adult world and this is just sufficient to break the spell of anxiety and allow in its wake a more perfect refuge in play. He repeats a favourite walk, returns to immediate pleasures and restores the world to its proper proportion by tramping over the fields, avoiding the bridge to splash through the stream. On his return, now playful, cheerful, he is mystified to find Martha still plunged in the gloom of her 'real' despair.

If play is a 'cure' for anxiety it is also a partial protection against growing up. Selina, the eldest of the children in Grahame's Dream Days is already in a dangerous condition of advancement. She had 'just become a subscriber to the Young Ladies Journal' and allowed herself 'to be taken out to strange teas with an air of resignation palpably assumed'. Yet it is Selina who gives way to the exuberance of a really good play. She 'commemorated' Trafalgar Day (naval history was her 'special subject') by mounting a huge bonfire that consumed in addition to pea-sticks the 'sacred' fuel for the hothouse. Selina undergoes a kind of 'regression' during play; 'hatless and tossing disordered locks, all the dross of the young lady purged out of her, she stalked around the pyre of her own purloining, or prodded it with a pea-stick'. Even so play cannot restore her childhood to her. The transformation is only temporary and as her 'brief inebriation' dies down with the fire 'she could see herself as a plain fool' while her young brother Harold, a partner in her villainy, is more fortunate: 'youth and a short memory made his case less pitiful', still innocent of a selfhood to which he must remain faithful.

Grahame also makes clear the primacy of the wish to play over the wish to grow up. He does not simply ignore, or romaticise, the superiority of adults. Far from it, the curious 'Olympians' are at once boring and mysterious. How perverse that, 'free to fire cannons and explode mines on the lawn', they chose instead to remain indoors and merely talk; that having finally achieved an 'absolute licence to indulge in the pleasures of life, they could get no good of it'. Subordination to them is keenly felt, as in a ravishing story 'The Magic Ring' in which a 'promise' to take the children to the circus is, for no reason but absolutely characteristically, betrayed. Their wish, on this occasion, is redeemed by a generous gipsy-like stranger who can still share with them in the excitement, the sensuous ecstasy and, significantly, the miserable impotence, of childhood. Their wish is not to be like grown-ups, only that grown-ups should look after them unobtrusively and leave them alone to enjoy themselves.

Grahame's astonishing psychological precision (approached more recently only by Philippa Pearce, especially in her collection What The Neighbours Did) is coupled with an 'impressionistic' style, reminiscent in its interruption of narrative, its sensuous density, its nostalgia, with Gérard de Nerval's Sylvie; the only precursor Proust acknowledged to his own masterpiece.

This impressionism and his complete grasp of the subject matter makes Grahame the finest of writers for children. A view accepted very shortly after the publication of The Golden Age in 1895. His reputation, oddly enough, was not enhanced by the appearance of The Wind in the Willows some thirteen years later; a view now difficult to credit. But our reversal in favouritism and critical acclaim in instructive. The Golden Age was a perfect description of the separate reality of childhood, for a particular period, and was easily understandable, despite the sophistication of its language, by both adults and children. It expressed by and large an adult's view of this separate reality and its superiority over its successors and imitators rested on the subtlety and accuracy of its observations rather than in any fundamentally unconventional image of childhood at its core. Oswald Bastable reckoned The Golden Age to be 'A1 except where it gets mixed up with grown-up nonsense', and this allowed the grown-ups a certain sense of superiority in reading it, and it was the grown-ups, after all, who bought the book and made Grahame's reputation. But they enjoyed no such privilege in The Wind in the Willows, which succeeded in concealing the 'grown-up nonsense' from the grown-ups as well as from the children. In it Grahame explored not only the adult's view of the child's world, but the child's view of the adult's and even more their mutual misunderstandings and misconceptions.

The transposition in The Wind in the Willows into animal society allows this double, synchronised illusion to be explored. Rat and Mole behave both as adults believe children 'play' when left on their own; and as children believe they would behave if they were suddenly transformed into adults.

The false independence of the 'latency' period suffuses all their activities. Friendship undisturbed by passion is the particular mark of such a period and Rat and Mole, inexhaustibly devoted to each other, are the most perfect of friends. They would agree with another fictional Water Rat, one in a story of Oscar Wilde's, 'The Devoted Friend', who says, 'Love is all very well in its way, but friendship is much higher.' Interestingly enough the 'moral' of that story is the transcendence of love over friendship (of growing up over staying as a child) but Grahame adopts friendship, and the children's world which alone supports true friendship, as the ultimate value of his story. This friendship, though centered on Rat and Mole, embraces in its wider ambit Badger and Toad as well.

Their friendship, and the 'seriousness' of their playworld, is heightened and more 'realistic' in animal society. Where children could only play 'make-believe' games of building houses and dens or going on dangerous adventures, Ratty and Mole set about such business with matter-of-fact realism. They live there after all. But they live still in a playworld. The seriousness of their occupations reflects their deep absorption in play, not the struggle with nature, the labour of necessity. 'Provender' (how significant this word to Grahame's vocabulary of childhood) is always on hand and is provided with magical ease. No-one at River Bank 'works' or even hunts, they just go to the amply filled larders to re-stock yet another picnic hamper. Even when shortages threaten, as when Mole and Rat unexpectedly find themselves overnight at Mole-End near Christmas when the carol singers call, a way is always found; in this case Rat sends one of the young singers off to the shops. The shops, like the money he gives him for the purchases, belong presumably to another reality, connected in some undefined way to the 'real' world of play at River Bank.

The story is constructed, indeed, upon a series of loosely connected anxious adventures and upon the more solid foundation of provender. Rescued in Wild Wood by the discovery of an entrance to Badger's House, for example, 'they gathered round the glowing embers of the great wood fire, and thought how jolly it was to be sitting up so late, and so independent, and so full'. A quite typical passage which beautifully combines the adult's nostalgia for the 'simple' sensuous pleasures of childhood and the child's eye view of the independent luxury of adult existence. Rat and Mole live in both worlds at once, in the best of both worlds at once. They enjoy not only the freedom of play, but freedom from adult interference. They could never become 'Olympians' but they have gained the power of the 'Olympians' to do as they please. They are in the happy position of the all powerful adults for whom as he says in the 'Magic Ring' from Dream Days, 'Life lies at their feet, a parti-coloured india-rubber ball', without having lost the capacity to enjoy it. Mole adds a final flourish, a grown-up pose in which only a child could take pleasure, 'cocked up on a settle and basking in the firelight, his heels higher than his head'. Their feasts retain some of the excitement of the raided larder without the threat, normal to such escapades, of being discovered.

The domestic ideal, as well, should not be taken too literally. The primary significance of 'home' for all the main characters is not to be safe and secure, protected by more powerful beings – not in general terms to be 'looked after' – but a place, rather, in which it is safe to play. The 'domestic architecture' for example of Badger's home, which he delights in showing off to his visitors, is an elaborate adaptation of ancient human 'workings'. That is of homes abandoned by adults who grew out of their possibilities for comfort and warmth. It is not a house but a 'den', an ambitious work of 'bricolage' in which Badger can take refuge from the adult world above. Rat's house, even more, possesses this quality of playful transposition, a naturalised house, part tunnel, part building, stocked with 'real' but diminutive furniture. The kind of construction, in other words, children build when they play at 'houses'.

The double vision that runs through the entire book makes Toad and Badger rather complex figures. They are the switching points, so to speak, of the author's (and reader's) point of view. They are at times unmistakably part of the same world of childhood friendship as Rat and Mole, but they never belong there absolutely.

Badger retains a certain aloof authority. But he can always be counted upon in a tight corner. He has grown up but without losing his childish qualities. His adulthood has simply been added on rather than destroying his childhood. He is more a favoured uncle (like Grahame himself) able to enter spiritually into the games of children, than a responsible adult who will complain of 'mischief' or mess or both.

But it is Toad, as a meeting point of the less desirable qualities of children and adults, that most fully embodies Grahame's subtle variation in viewpoint. Toad belongs, rather ostentatiously, to the adult world. He alone lives in a 'real' and rather grand house, full of real furniture, and owns a boathouse full of real boats; all built by craftsmen and not the makeshift constructions of the child. Furthermore his money is 'explained' by inheritance where Ratty's appears magically from nowhere.

Even more he is psychologically an adult in being possessed by desire – an unquenchable lust for motor cars. And one of the explicit themes of the story is the danger of such uncontrolled desire; the extent to which it corrupts the innocence of childhood friendship and gathers around it an unsavoury constellation of characteristics, deceit, boastfulness, treachery. It is not, however, simply a matter of dangerous passions, or that such desire should not be part of child-life, but rather that in Toad, who is in other respects still a child, such passion is ruinous. Toad's longing is only, after all, a caricature of desire, wishing that has grown beyond normal bounds because, freed from adult restraint, it can satisfy his every whim. Car after car ends on the rubbish heap without satisfying Toad's demonic passion. He is possessed of a 'fixed' idea, if he could just find the 'right' machine, he could free himself but, like any other child, he does not know how to wish properly and every machine is the wrong one.

He is the only character in the book who prefers talking to eating and looks forward to banquets for the opportunity it affords for boastful speeches. He is the only one in fact with a self-image sufficiently crystallised to require the supportive role of speech. He has gone beyond the point where play can offer any real relief to the rigours of selfhood. His plays 'fail' because they too have been tainted with desire. While locked up by Rat and Mole (they too believe confinement can 'cure' the subject of his passion), he tries to 'play' at cars. 'When his violent paroxysms possessed him he would arrange bedroom chairs in rude resemblance of a motor-car and would crouch on the foremost of them, bent forward and staring fixedly ahead, making uncouth and ghastly noises, till the climax was reached, when, trying a complete somersault, he would lie prostrate amidst the ruins of the chairs, apparently completely satisfied for the moment.' It was, however, a temporary calm, his passion was only briefly assuaged. But genuine play has no climax, no desire, no rhythm of tension and release, it is sensual but not erotic.

Toad has been transformed by his passion, his wish gone crazy, into an adult, but without growing up. Badger, in contrast, has grown up without losing his 'solid qualities' as a child. And Rat and Mole live permanently in a playworld expanded beyond its normal boundaries where it has gained the dignity and seriousness otherwise denied it by its merely tolerated existence within adult society.

Rat, too, suffers briefly from passion and almost loses this playworld, but is saved by the friendship of Mole. His is not, like Toad's, a childish whim grotesquely enlarged, but a desire borrowed from a source outside himself. The birds begin to talk of migrating to the Sunny South and, his interests aroused, Rat meets a seafaring member of his species whose lyrical talk fills him with a longing to travel to distant places and to indulge a more adventurous freedom. He wishes, in fact, to grow up and move beyond what suddenly appears as the narrow confines of River Bank. But he has formed only the wish, more general than childish whimsy, no longer to be a child; he has not yet formed for himself the object of a more mature desire and borrows it from the migrating birds. But he can gain nothing but despair from this borrowed desire and the restraining hand of Mole 'saves' him till his fit passes and he returns to the peace of River Bank.

The privileged playworld at River Bank accepts, in the end, even Toad's premature old age. His wandering beyond Wild Wood had put Toad in touch with the real adult responsibilities, with the cause and effect of social life; with the law. But back at River Bank all that vanishes again. He is persuaded, it is true, to compensate the washerwoman and gipsy and make recompense for one or two of his other misdeeds. But the police never come to Toad Hall to drag him off, once again, to prison. We remain, however, distrustful of Toad's restoration to the playworld, he has 'seen sense' and knows who his friends are, but he cannot ever join with them in the collective pursuits their playworld offers to them. In the end reason in him triumphs over his passion and his future one imagines to be similar to Badger's, as an elder statesman within the child's enchanted domain.

The enjoyment of unrestrained freedom is the misconception adults have of children, they do not 'enjoy' it in the sense adults give to the term; they are absorbed by the freedom of play with nothing held back to provide a platform from which they might recall the reality of their pleasure. Nor does this absorption save them from anxiety. And the enjoyment of unlimited independence is the error children make in relation to adults, because they ignore (having been kept in ignorance) the necessity of labour. Their image of the mature 'self' is then of a monstrous 'absolute ego' such as Toad, rather than that of an individualised subject.

Grahame exploits these misconceptions and builds upon them a vision of 'real' childhood friendship, selfless devotion and loyalty undisturbed by erotic pride.

An interesting 'development' of Grahame's stories can be found in The Hobbit. Tolkien's indebtedness to The Wind in the Willows is explicit. Bilbo Baggins lives at Bagend, a residence structurally similar to Mole's home. The opening pages of both are strikingly alike (and both, for that matter, like Kafka's The Burrow, though without any direct influence), beginning as they do with an irrational 'leap' into the adventure. The Hobbit is structured upon a series of adventures and an undercurrent of provender – the same word, in fact, is used. He remarks later, in Lord of the Rings, that 'bringing up young hobbits took a lot of provender'.

The resemblances, however, are superficial. Tolkien's story is a 'modern' fairy tale rather than an internal defence of childhood. Bilbo is the hero of anxiety who sets off upon his adventurous journey, unsure of the result but knowing it will issue in real consequences. He 'realises' his full hobbit potential and is awakened to self-consciousness, returning to find the Shire folk he left still cocooned in their playworld, while he has become a grown-up independent person. They do not even realise what Bilbo has come to understand, that the very possibility of their tranquil, pleasing existence depends upon their borders being protected by more powerful beings, most importantly by Gandalf the Wizard. Only their indulgence allows the hobbits freedom to play as they like.

The 'golden age' of childhood occupied a relatively brief period, bounded on one side by the integration of children and adults directly through the process of labour and the sharing of a common culture and ritual life; and on the other by the 'absorption' of childhood into the adult 'unconscious'. The period between was marked by the decisive separation between adult and child that allowed a particular child 'psychology' to take shape.

The 'classics' of children's literature are still the classics because they first described the separate world of childhood for us, making later examples of the genre imitative and, very often, crude by comparison. Their appeal to adults who, after all, choose to read them to their children, is not historical but nostalgic. They express for us a childhood which, though altered in circumstantial detail, was once our own. We are at one with their psychology because it is their vision of childhood which we have adopted for ourselves to stand in for the deceptions of our memory, and the brevity of our impressions. They create for us the illusion of moving backwards in time to restore to us the secret of our own existence; the recreation of those early forgotten years. The nostalgia, for such is the appeal of these stories, is compounded of a double impulse. The desire to 'find' ourselves, to glimpse our own origin more completely than our unaided recollection allows, and, at the same time, to wish to be rid of the struggle for self-development. These oddly contradictory impulses are held together, however improbably, in Kenneth Grahame's masterpieces. In them we can relax, confident in his powers of creation, his accuracy, his insight. We can give way to the stories without feeling we are 'escaping' from our own reality, we are giving way only to our own innermost nature. And how delightful to discover the highest and most difficult task we set ourselves (to 'discover' our 'true' selves) can be accomplished so simply and easily. This is the irresistible promise of nostalgia. Like play it is effortless, you need only to admit to it and everything follows. You can surmount the struggle with yourself; be done with the troublesome and tiring journey towards complete individuality and instead find your 'authentic' nature in this intensified recollection of the sensuous fullness, the pure friendship, even in the anxious moments and mysterious compulsions of your own childhood. The 'secret' of the self is nothing else than its own negation and we can relax again in the Dream Days that Grahame wrote, not about his, but about our own childhood.

We no longer conceive of childhood as this separate reality. We assume, all too easily, that the greatest need of the child is the need to 'grow up', so that it never surprises us when he does. Yet the vision of the 'golden age' is still very much with us in another, and more intractable, form. It is this view of childhood as a self-sufficient reality defined by incompatible irrationalities - by play, anxiety and desire - that we have 'internalised' as a description of the 'secret' of our own selfhood, as our personal unconscious. We have transposed the 'golden age' from a vision of childhood into a revelation of our own individuality.

Secular versions of 'individual' psychology had to face the problem of solipsism, and not as an intellectual puzzle alone, but as the real suffering of despair. If the 'self' was nothing more than the construction of itself by itself, if it was indeed a self-moving synthesis, then the 'security' of external conditioning norms was lost. The 'real' self had to be defined actively and progressivley with only itself as a point of reference and standard. This difficulty is present in fact, in an acute form, in some religious views of selfhood. Kierkegaard, the most audacious and consistent religious thinker of the nineteenth century, withdrew the conditioning norm of selfhood to an infinitely remote point. God was buried so far within the subject that faith could be defined only as a 'secret' between the self and God and the religious life was rationalised in the concept of the 'single one' rather than in any collective enterprise. This inner loneliness of the individual – His withdrawal to an infinite distance – was symmetrical with his outward helplessness – God's relationship to Nature as an infinitely remote First Cause – and both permitted and encouraged the development of a secular psychology of the self, on the one hand, and scientific theories of the natural order, on the other. However much the individualism of the 1840s appears still to be a development of religious principles, the transition to secular theories had already taken place, leading irresistibly from Kierkegaard's Training in Christianity to Dostoevsky's Notes from Underground.

The 'solution' to the problem of solipsism – of the self-defining self – was found in childhood, especially in the fact of our forgetting what our own was like. Individualism provided the precondition, culturally speaking, of the 'golden age' of childhood, and the 'golden age' in its turn offered a stable point of reference for a theory of 'self-development'.

The separate existence of childhood offered an ideal screen upon which to project both the 'origin' and 'secret' of the self. The conditioning norm of selfhood was now internalised, part of the structure of the individuated subject, but a part which remained unconscious, infinitely interior, buried in our own past. The self was a secret we had with ourselves, rather than 'with God'. The task of life was to realise this secret, not indeed to bring it into the open (we can never experience the unconscious directly, any more that we might see God) but to bring our consciousness into harmony with its ultimate wishes. The ideal, simply stated, was to become at one with our own innermost nature. A feat possible by the subtle sign language of the unconscious which in gestures that conceal for ever its real substance alerts us to disharmonies within the relationship of selfhood.

This movement, without altering the decisive impulse to activity and prescribing for us still an endless quest, secularised its own mythology; internalising God as the Unconscious and incorporating His telos within ourselves as the forgotten determinant and initial cause of our own restless striving.

The nineteenth-century Christian Self, the bourgeois 'projective' theory of childhood, and the modern Unconscious belong together as aspects of modern individualism, and are defined by the same language of irrationality. The self, Kierkegaard demonstrates, cannot be described with abstract consistency, its existence is a paradox and logical contradiction is one of the few linguistic devices at our disposal to indicate its true form. Absurdity, too, is the mark of childhood. The playworld knows no contradictions, accepts no logic but its own momentary fancy. The child moves, in addition, not simply within its irrational 'sphere' but oscillates among the more general absurdities of anxiety and desire. It is this more particular language of childhood which has become indicative of the unconscious.

Childhood and the Unconscious continue, in an implicit form, to acknowledge those religious sentiments expressed more openly in Kierkegaard's Christian writings. There is what might be termed a 'religion' of childhood. This is, in part, a quite open 'worship' of freedom and innocence that makes childhood the touchstone of creativity and pleasure. Edith Cobb's The Ecology of Human Imagination in Childhood is an interesting and comprehensive expression of such a sentiment, in which childhood is sought as 'the creative principle in human personality and the source of cultural evolution'. But it is also, more covertly, the location of our 'personal-sacred' images. It is in the practice of the art of recollection that we remain most under the sway of older religious myths; and our efforts to recall our childhood is the only technique in which we can 'relate ourselves infinitely to the infinite'. This nostalgia, expressed perfectly by Kenneth Grahame, is a moment in the long and painful history of the self. And the attractive melancholy of nostalgia is founded upon ignorance, its longings are all fundamentally hypocritical. Childhood is useful to us psychologically because we have forgotten it, not because we can remember it with affection. It is only because it has disappeared that it can take up and solve for us the problems of identity our social life poses for us.

Childhood then, like a Divine Being, is a form of 'otherness' in relation to which we define ourselves. But unlike the Divine Being, it can be internalised within the self under the cover of 'natural' processes.

PART THREE
Conclusion

'The world of possibilities has always been more open to me than that of real events.'

Marcel Proust, *The Captive*

8 Metaphysical Polarities

Confinement and Childhood are the two faces of selflessness in modern times. The one empty, void, absolute; the other brimming, unformed, universal. The experience of either in a pure form is 'preconceptual' and available to us only as an intuition of its particular species of 'otherness'. Both, then, constitute worlds to themselves that have their own poets and philosophers to describe for us their intimate, alien, presences.

A culture of 'advanced' individualism defines the nature of the self in opposition to these other forms of subjectivity; viewing its emergence either as a continuous struggle against the nothingness that surrounds and attracts it, or as a process of progressive differentiation from the plenitude into which it was born. Both nothingness and plenitude are regarded generally as abstractions, as concepts more or less useful to the process of reflecting upon our experience. Since Marx's The German Ideology, however, it has been impossible to speak of abstractions as 'merely' tools of thought. However abstract, such concepts are and remain part of the social world with which they simultaneously develop. what is peculiar to these conceptions of selflessness is not (as in other 'ideologies') their symptomatic value within a general process of alienation, but their significance, as indications of life outside of the necessity of labour. They do not reflect directly, in other words, the distortion of human nature consequential upon a particular mode of production and division of labour (though their origins are bound up with such specific forms) but suggest to us images of human nature undisturbed by any necessity. They appear, that is to say, uniquely 'philosophical' in substance and remain attractive in their purity to the philosophically inclined mind.

It is not surprising then that philosophers – who have aspired to deduce, from a single principle, the structure and appearance of our everyday experience, and account, through a single term, for the diversity and contradictoriness of perceived reality - should have tended towards, as their master concept, a notion of either Confinement or Childhood; nothingness or plenitude. Though metaphysicians were not themselves concerned to describe either Confinement or Childhood, they were driven, by their ambition to circumscribe everything within a consistent monism, to reflect in quite literal sense either the one or the other.

Anticipating to some extent the fully fashioned social forms of selflessness, speculative philosophy could be said to have 'discovered' for us the real meaning of both Confinement and Childhood - as E. B. Carnochan has already established for the case of Confinement in his masterly essay Confinement and Flight. Such philosophical reflections, as has already been suggested, are somewhat like play and, like play, abolish the self. This retreat from the self into speculative philosophy ends either with Spinoza's metaphysics of Confinement, or Leibniz's philosophy of Childhood.

Spinoza's pre-conceptual 'category' he termed the conatus, the reflective equivalent of simple undifferentiated substance. All appearances were aspects of this single conatus. There were no exceptions to this simple rule. This featureless substance is the starting point for thought, and is wholly abstract. He has, none the less, discovered the real principle of confinement, whose underlying undifferentiated substance is all too concrete. And it is in confinement that the conatus becomes a palpable reality, forcing the differences we are capable of experiencing into a kind of cosmic black hole that renders all things indistinguishable.

Spinoza himself lived a solitary, isolated life. It is hardly surprising that it was he who discovered confinement, or that he should have been the philosopher whom Bernard Malamud has the hero of The Fixer contemplate during his long incarceration.

Leibniz is the greatest philosopher of Childhood. The monad, is the 'proto-self' brimming with possibility. His method is to include all of reality within the monad, a plenitude developing towards its own specific identity through self-sufficient laws. Continuity, identity, plenitude, the laws of sufficient reason, Leibniz's vocabulary (though not his philosophical ambition) can be taken over in its totality to describe the 'golden age'.

Metaphysical theories, however seductive in their generality and consistency, are usually abstract and, therefore, cruel, denying as they do, the human subject matter of thought.

The temptations of such abstraction, especially where it can be more properly attached to some empirical 'reality', is great in comparison to the hard anxious struggle with the self. This has even received some 'official' acknowledgment in the contradictoriness of our values. Above all we are given the task of 'discovering ourselves'. But we are given licence, as particularly 'sensitive' souls or as religious 'virtuosi' to go 'beyond' the self in a spiritual immolation; or, on a lesser scale, to fall in love and temporarily 'lose ourselves' in thought, in admiration, in sympathy. These temporary 'aberrations' however are only the play forms left to us as recreation from the harder road. We refuse to take them very seriously, unless we admit to being 'freakish'.

There are two fundamental forms of 'selflessness' in our society and they can quite easily be mistaken one for the other. Confinement can be 'misunderstood' as a form of childhood and childhood all too readily regarded as a kind of confinement.

The first 'mistake' is typical of Genet's literary perversions. He has expressed a philosophy of childhood within a confined world. The real nothingness of confinement is denied by projecting upon it this other form of selflessness. Hence the innocence of Genet's characters, their spiritual purity, the lyricism of his writing, the seductive variety of its moods. The confined world is rendered disturbingly attractive by thus masquerading as a reclaimed childhood. It is a more refined and a more 'modern' illusion than de Sade's, exploiting as it does our impressions, and borrowing nostalgia in creating its false image.

The representation of childhood as confinement on the other hand is not far enough from the truth. Now that we have 'progressed' beyond the 'golden age', and because of our efforts to wrest from childhood its secret, and through the control of our own children discover our own inner nature, we often subject them to an emotional tyranny from which they withdraw into an interior, but empty, world of their own. However much cruelty to children remains at odds with our conception of a 'natural' relationship it is not implausible to regard some case of child battering as an intensification of this self-curiosity.

Misapplications and elisions within the peculiar dimension of selflessness are, in fact, quite commonplace. Less frequent is their direct confrontation, or attempted synthesis. There are two major examples of each – one in Tolkien's Lord of the Rings and the other in Proust's incomparable work of fiction.

The development of Tolkien's fantasy is in the opposite direction to that of the modern fairy story. Tolkien begins in The Hobbit with a tale of self-discovery. Bilbo discovers at the end that his adventure has irreversibly changed him; as Gandalf remarks to him 'you are not the hobbit you were'. The Lord of the Rings is conceived, however, along more traditional lines; owing more to the saga, and ancient folk-tale than the modern children's fairy story. Individual identity is reabsorbed, in its long, elaborate adventure, into a common, collective culture. It is conceived more as an anthropology and history of Faerie than as Frodo's adventure. The 'repetition' of Bilbo's journey by Frodo is not a device to reveal Frodo's individual talents and character, but a means of exploring the common tradition and lore of Hobbits and related creatures. The Dark Lord is defeated more by this collective tradition than by Frodo's personal heroism.

The opposition at the heart of Lord of the Rings is not that of Good against Evil or even of Life against Death, but of Childhood against Confinement. The childlike character of Hobbits is obvious. The dependence upon The Wind in the Willows as a model is again quite clear. Frodo and Sam are related, as Water Rat and Mole, by the devotion of true friendship, which is a phenomenon restricted to childhood. It is the hobbit weakness, naivete and love of freedom that in the end overcomes Confinement, or at least allows Frodo to penetrate the mighty enclosure of Mordor.

Frodo embodies all hobbit-like characteristics and learns, as the journey progresses, from Gandalf and the powerful heroes of Elfinland, more and more stories of the 'history' of Middle Earth. As he reaches the Gates of Mordor he has concentrated within him the oral traditions of many generations.

Mordor, on the other hand, enclosed behind impenetrable barriers (originally to prevent escape rather than entry), is the power of Confinement. The Dark Lord himself has no personality, he never appears and works, at a distance, by the power of suggestion. The pure nothingness of confinement is contained within 'his' empty tower. His servants too are freakishly invisible and assume a form, when pursuing their enemies only as an outward sign, and their black cloaks conceal, literally, nothing. The lesser servants of Mordor, the frightening battalions of obscene orcs, enslaved by the Dark Power, have lost their human qualities. They are now without traditions, without memory or culture, reduced to an undifferentiated mass, a uniform, nasty substance.

This opposition between Childhood and Confinement is made explicit at times. The Lady Lorien, for example, tells Frodo, 'I do not fear pain or death' but 'a cage'. And Frodo, carrying within him the plenitude of childhood brings into Mordor what he terms 'the doom of choice'.

The ring 'mediates' between the 'cage' of Mordor and the 'choice' of the Shire. Ultimately even a child can be corrupted. The power of the ring, the power of nothingness (it makes the wearer invisible), slowly deprives Frodo of the will to discard it. His task is to carry it to the volcanic mountain in which it was originally wrought and cast it into its great natural furnace. In the end he cannot do it and the Shire is saved only by the playful intervention of pure chance. Frodo has been followed by the Gollum, a goblinlike creature who once possessed the ring. In the final scene he snatches his 'precious' from Frodo's grasp, and overbalances carrying it with him into the flames. The astonishingly moving climax to the long tale is perfectly consistent with its underlying theme. Childhood cannot win the victory by the open use of power, certainly not by summoning up a will greater than that of any adult. It is precisely because the adults lacked sufficient self-determination that the 'innocent' Frodo was entrusted by Gandalf with the task. He can win only by being an instrument of the principle of play and must give himself to the pure freedom of chance by surrendering to its possibility. The fact that an adult reader might find in the conclusion to the story an anti-climax indicates just how faithful Tolkien has been to the spirit of his Hobbits. Frodo, no more than Bilbo, likes adventures and he returns, his task accomplished, or rather the task accomplished through him, to live for many years in peace.

If The Hobbit defended the desirability of growing up, or at least the necessity that some should grow up to protect the freedom of childhood, The Lord of the Rings more completely sides with the child and views his world as the only safe protection from nothingness. Unlike The Golden Age, in which childhood is viewed as a defensive measure against growing up. Tolkien here defends childhood as a permanent cultural value. The price of this, of course, is prolonged and unconscious dependence - the 'humility' that strikes a religious note in his otherwise flamboyantly pagan romance.

Tolkien's defence of childhood, like Grahame's, has to be made from outside of childhood itself, in his case through the falsification of experience in fantasy rather than the latter's deceptive certainty of personal recollection. But for either method, once childhood has been lost, it cannot simply be re-invoked, to invite such a backward leap leads to inevitable distortion. The more you side with Childhood against Confinement the more you fall into fantasy and, hence, fall victim to the very power you oppose. Tolkien's opposition - between Confinement and Childhood - in other words, becomes a diabolical alliance. You cannot resist Confinement with Childhood because Childhood no longer exists and, when it did, was a dependent, powerless condition. Such attempted resistance is a form of self-deception that begins the disintegrative work of Confinement's negative synthesis.

This almost irresistible collusion is even more marked in Proust's entrancing fictional synthesis. Confinement and Childhood depart from individual identity in opposite directions but Proust, in effecting an artistic synthesis between them, makes it too easy to move from one to the other.

It would be a caricature to call Proust's work a novel of childhood, thought it contains the most significant of all literary explorations of childhood. It is obviously more than that. Yet it begins with childhood, and not with childhood as an 'objective' fact, a 'logical' starting point of conventional biography, but as a deeply problematic and ever-present portion of our experience. He begins in Combray not from any interest in its 'objectivity' as an historical recollection or out of mere curiosity - but as an urgent matter of self-discovery.

The unexpected pleasure he discovered in his childhood impressions haunted him. He keeps returning to their sensuous fullness in renewed efforts to discover their secret. The memories that came to him in the wake of such impressions finally obscured the path to a clearer apprehension of the reality they seemed to contain. His 'problem' at first appears conventional enough - to discover himself; choose decisively and lift himself out of the boredom of the merely aesthetic. The two 'Ways', however, signified by the alternative routes of his Sunday walks, of Nature and of Social Life, are found not to contain the material from which the 'self' can construct its appropriate image. The whole enterprise founders and the Search becomes a search to transcend the conventional images of selfhood and reach the universal substance intimated in his childhood recollections. These recollections had shown, in an empirical sense, only that his 'origin' was empty. At the beginning of his life there was no 'blueprint' of himself, only a dazzling richness of possibilities, all of which have been lost, traded for the despair of selfhood.

The emergence of this unreasonable and painful 'self' is caught beautifully in the history of its love affairs. In the entrancing passages at Balbec, the 'Seascape with Freize of Girls' the Narrator is shaken from his introversion. 'I had seen,' he says, 'alight from carriages and pass, some into the ballroom of the casino, others into the ice-cream shop, young women who at a distance had seemed to me lovely.' The embodiment, collectively, of a perfectly abstract beauty, from which, through a process of gradual differentiation, Albertine emerges as his 'object-choice'. A girl whose superficial oppositeness to himself created an objective distance that could be filled by his desire; and through desire secure for him a firmer recollection of himself. He seems at first to expand beyond himself, to fall in love with Albertine, simply by being attracted to her own qualities. But even as this occurred he realised her attractiveness depended upon her capacity to arouse in him more of those impressions the recollection of his childhood had allowed him to glimpse. 'I had in me a store of old dreams,' he confesses, 'memories dated from my childhood, and in which all the tendencies (tendencies that existed in my heart, but, when my heart felt it, was not distinguishable from anything else) were wafted to me by a person as different as possible from myself.' This difference that allowed a new recognition of his deeper, hidden self, recalls Kierkegaard's doomed passion for Regine Olsen. Proust declares, 'our most intensive love for a person is always the love, really, of something else as well'. That is to say, a love of the self. Kierkegaard had similarly viewed love as a form of self-reflection, and despaired over his failure in it, which was nothing but a form of self-doubt, of self-torment.

None the less in falling in love Proust irretreivably loses his childhood. 'Those years of my earliest childhood are no longer part of myself', he regrets, 'they are external to me.'

He returns again to Combray, no longer to rediscover his childhood, the secret of himself, but to go altogether beyond the trials of identity. He recognises now, through this 'repetition' into higher aesthetic categories, the 'real' meaning of the pleasure he found in childhood recollection. 'And even my most carnal desires,' he insists, 'magnetised always in a certain direction, concentrated about a single dream . . . at the innermost core of which, as in my day dreams while I sat reading all afternoon in the garden at Combray, lay the thought of perfection.' It is the essence of this perfection which he touches in the strange pleasure afforded by his reminiscences, or by the sight of apple blossom, or the view from a particular angle of a line of trees near Balbec. It is this same essence which pervades Vintieul's sonata, especially that 'little phrase' that haunted him for years. And the same metaphysical longing to touch it that animated Swann's love of Vermeer who condensed it, for all to see, in a little patch of light illuminating the corner of a roof in his wonderful painting 'A View of Delft'.

Childhood is closer to this essence because it has not yet been taken in by the hypocrisy and deceit of a purely individual selfhood, by the trickery of its own memory. Childhood is a kind of unconscious work of art, experiencing directly that more complete sensuous reality which the artist can only suggest to us.

He equates childhood, therefore, with sleep and dreams; not through the romantic notion of their similar longings and charm; but more rigorously through the denial of selfhood entailed by both. To seek our childhood it is of no use to revisit, in the waking world, the houses and gardens in which we played, we must look deeper within ourselves, beyond memory, in the dissolution of the dreamworld. In the deepest sleep, he contends when we 'descend into the subterranean galleries' that we discover 'the garden in which as a child we used to play'.

The recollection of childhood, then is not an end in itself and is not itself responsible for the undeniable pleasure such recollections afford. Childhood is a stepping stone only to that more perfect reality expressed in art. Proust moves then from the art of recollection into a 'golden age' of his own childhood before transforming its nostalgia into a higher art form and a new metaphysical theory of art. Perfection – that is to say the essence of things – becomes more and more distanced from us through our struggle to appropriate and maintain a self-identity. Childhood, and the recollection of childhood for us, frees us from this burden and enables us to approach this perfection more closely. If we are lucky we may, like Swann just before he dies, touch it through the inspiration of a great work of art.

The search which begins as a journey of self-discovery ends by dissolving itself in a higher and more extensive reality. What begins in childhood ends in nostalgia, not indeed in a simple longing for the past, but in a longing for what the past held within its grasp without realising it. He dissolves himself in the end in a metaphysical theory, in a search for an essential reality, in the substance of the spirit. He has moved, in other words from monad to conatus and this is matched in the more visible aspects of his life and work: his withdrawal from society, his living for the most part during the night, his isolation, his abstraction and love of cruelty. And as a great artist he is able to bring together, as analytical thought would never allow, the pleasing fullness of childhood and the metaphysical perfection of confinement. The most alluring of all invitations to self-abandonment. Nowhere else has confinement been given such a human face, or childhood been so charged with the potency of the absolute.

He cannot succumb completely, however, to the illusion, or be so dishonest as to pretend it. No more than Kierkegaard could be rid of himself in the final repetition into faith, Proust cannot live in the reality foreshadowed in childhood and recaptured in art. 'Man', he admits, 'is the creature that cannot emerge from himself, that knows his fellows only in himself; when he asserts the contrary he is lying.' He cannot shake off his selfhood, neither can he determine upon it absolutely as his identity. He has no option but to meet his fellow humans as images and extensions, as reflections, of his own inner reality, however unfounded such a reality might be, and accept as a consequence the self-torment of despair. Thus, with Albertine he writes, without complaint, as a matter of observation alone, 'I felt that my life with Albertine was, on the one hand, when I was not jealous, mere boredom, and on the other hand, when I was jealous, constant suffering'. He longs therefore for the metaphysical dissolution of all self-doubt, and longs, therefore for confinement, which is already to anticipate its nothingness.

Even so he had not entirely abandoned the Search, as a purely personal exploration. 'Could life console me for the loss of art,' he asks rhetorically (its being rhetorical indicates how far he has moved out of the psychological world of childhood and into the subjectivity of confinement) and goes on, 'was there in art a more profound reality in which our true personality finds an expression that is not afforded it by the activities of life.' The 'essential self' might still be revealed to him through art which is a kind of generalisation from those scattered moments of privileged impressions – 'those impressions which at remote intervals I recaptured in my life as starting points, foundation stones for the construction of a true life'.

But to find the 'true self' only in its own dissolution is the final 'repetition' from nostalgia into confinement. Nostalgia, then, is a kind of mid-point between childhood and confinement. It is rather like irony that 'hovers' above the aesthetic without yet being part of the ethical.

Proust constructs, in fact, more faithfully than Freud, the secular continuation of Kierkegaard's Christian psychology. To find the self is to renounce yourself into infinity. The conditioning telos of subjective 'self-development' is not Faith but Art. Where Freud uncovered the unconscious as the interiorisation of our own childhood, Proust externalised it once more as an essential transcending reality.

Childhood cannot, any more than Confinement, provide for us a consistent and whole image of human nature. In offering a permanent resting place for the self, Confinement and Childhood deny the real nature of the self, which is to be continually struggling against its own resistance. Not, of course, that this need always be the case. It is however our inheritance, and only one aspect of our inheritance, from the individualising tendencies of a market economy, and the cultural forms that developed within it. To 'overcome' the self implies overcoming, also, those other basic forms of social organisation. To think we have overcome them otherwise is an illusion, and an illusion 'rooted' either in Childhood or Confinement, which are the metaphysical polarities which still define the limits of reflection upon our experience.

Bibliography

Aitken, J. *Midnight is a Place* (Johnathan Cape, 1974).
Ariès, P. *Centuries of Childhood* (Jonathan Cape, 1962; Penguin, 1973).
Artaud, A. 'Fragments from a Diary in Hell' in *Collected Works of Antonin Artaud*, vol. 1, tr. V. Corti (Calder & Boyars, 1968).
Bachelard, G. *The Poetics of Space*, tr. Maria Jolas (Beacon Press).
Bakhtin, M. *Rabelais and his World*, tr. Helene Iswolsky (M.I.T. Press, 1968).
Bao Ruo-Wang (Jean Pasqualini) and Rudolph Chelminski, *Prisoner of Mao* (Andre Deutsch, 1975, Penguin, 1976).
Baum, F. *The Wonderful Wizard of Oz* (Dent, 1965).
Bettelheim, B. *The Uses of Enchantment* (Thames & Hudson, 1976).
Bleuler, E. *Dementia Praecox: or the Group of Schizophrenias*, tr. J. Zinkin (International Universities Press, 1966).
Bowlby, J. *Attachment and Loss*, 2 vols (Hogarth Press 1969, 1973).
Boyle, J. *A Sense of Freedom* (Cannongate, 1977).
Brown, N.O. *Love's Body* (Random House, 1968).
Buca, E. *Vorkuta*, tr. M. Lisinski and K. Wells (Constable, 1976).
Canetti, E. *Crowds and Power*, tr. C. Stewart (Victor Gollancz, 1962).
Carroll, L. *Alice in Wonderland* (London, 1865; Puffin 1946).
Carnochan, E.B. *Confinement and Flight* (University of California Press, 1977).
Casanova, J. *The Memoirs of Jacques Casanova de Seingalt*, tr. A. Machen, vol. II (Putnam, 1958).
Cass, J. *The Significance of Children's Play* (Batsford, 1971).
Chekhov, A. *A Dreary Story* in *Chekhov Seven Stories*, tr. and ed. R. Hingley (Oxford University Press, 1974).
Chekhov, A. *Ward Number Six* in *Chekhov Seven Stories*, tr. and ed. R. Hingley (Oxford University Press, 1974).

BIBLIOGRAPHY

Cleaver, E. *Soul on Ice* (McGraw, 1968).
Cobb, E. *The Ecology of Imagination in Childhood* (Columbia University Press, 1977).
Dahl, R. *Charlie and the Chocolate Factory* (Allen & Unwin, 1967).
Dolgun, A. and Watson, P. *Dolgun* (Fontana, 1978).
Dostoevsky, F. *The House of the Dead*, tr. H. Sutherland Edwards (Dent, 1962).
Dostoevsky, F. *Notes from Underground*, tr. J. Coulson (Penguin, 1972).
Dostoevsky, F. *Crime and Punishment*, tr. D. Magarshack (Penguin, 1951).
Dostoevsky, F. *The Brothers Karamazov*, tr. D. Magarshack (Penguin, 1958).
Douglas, M. *Purity and Danger* (Routledge & Kegan Paul, 1966).
Ellis, A. E. *The Rack* (Heinemann, 1958).
Erikson, E. *Childhood and Society* (Paladin, 1977).
Erikson, E. *Toys and Reasons: Stages in the Ritualization of Experience* (Marion Boyars, 1977).
Ford, Ford Maddox *Memories and Impressions* (Bodley Head, 1971).
Freud, S. *Inhibition, Symptom and Anxiety*, vol. XX of *The Standard Edition of the Complete Psychological Works of Sigmund Freud*, ed. J. Strachey (Hogarth Press, 1959).
Freud, S. *The Interpretation of Dreams*, vols IV and V of *The Standard Edition*
Froebel, F. *Pedagogics of the Kindergarten* (London, 1897).
Gadamer, H.-G. *Truth and Method* (Sheed & Ward, 1975).
Garfield, L. *The Ghost Downstairs* (Longman Young Books, 1972).
Garvey, C. *Play* (Fontana/Open Books, 1977).
Genet, J. *Miracle of the Rose*, tr. B. Frechtman (Anthony Blond, 1965).
Gide, A. *If It Die*, tr. D. Bussy (Penguin, 1977).
Golding, W. *Free Fall* (Faber, 1959).
Grahame, K. *The Golden Age* (Bodley Head, 1895; 1979).
Grahame, K. *Dream Days* (Bodley Head, 1898; 1979).
Grahame, K. *The Wind in the Willows* (Methuen, 1908; Magnet, 1978).
Groos, K. *The Play of Man* (Chapman & Hall, 1901).
Hegel, G. *The Phenomenology of Spirit*, tr. A. Miller (O.U.P., 1979).
Hesse, H. 'A Child's Heart' in *Klingsor's Last Summer* (Jonathan Cape, 1971).
Holt, J. *How Children Learn* (Penguin, 1970).
Holt, J. *Escape from Childhood* (Penguin, 1975).
Hughes, R. *A High Wind in Jamaica* (Chatto & Windus, 1929; Penguin, 1971).
Huizinga, J. *Homo Ludens* (Paladin, 1970).
Huysmans, J. K. *Against Nature*, tr. R. Baldick (Penguin, 1959).

BIBLIOGRAPHY

Jackson, G. *Soledad Brother: The Prison Letters of George Jackson* (Penguin, 1970).
Jackson, G. *Blood in My Eye* (Random House, 1972).
Kafka, F. 'The Burrow' in *Metamorphosis and Other Stories* tr. E. Muir (Penguin, 1961).
Kafka, F. 'Metamorphosis' in *Metamorphosis and Other Stories*, tr. E. Muir (Penguin, 1961).
Karp, D. *One* (Victor Gollancz, 1954).
Kavan, A. *Asylum Piece and Other Stories* (Peter Owen, 1972).
Kierkegaard, S. *Either/Or* 2 vols, tr. W. Lowrie (Princeton University Press, 1971).
Kierkegaard, S. *Repetition: An Essay in Experimental Psychology*, tr. W. Lowrie (Harper & Row, 1964).
Kierkegaard, S. *Fear and Trembling*, tr. W. Lowrie (Princeton University Press, 1941).
Kierkegaard, S. *Stages on Life's Way*, tr. W. Lowrie (Schocken 1967).
Kierkegaard, S. *The Sickness Unto Death*, tr. W. Lowrie (Princeton University Press, 1941).
Kierkegaard, S. *The Concept of Dread*, tr. W. Lowrie (Princeton University Press, 1944).
Kierkegaard, S. *Concluding Unscientific Postscript*, tr. D. Swenson and W. Lowrie (Princeton University Press, 1941).
Kierkegaard, S. *Training in Christianity*, tr. W. Lowrie (Princeton University Press, 1941).
Kierkegaard, S. *Søren Kierkegaard's Journals and Papers*, 7 vols, ed. and tr. H. Hong and E. Hong (Indiana University Press, 1967-78).
Koestler, A. *Darkness at Noon* (Penguin, 1964).
Lane, H. *The Wild Boy of Aveyron* (George Allen & Unwin, 1977).
Lewin, H. *Bandiet* (Penguin, 1978).
Lindgren, A. *Pippi Longstocking* (Puffin, 1976).
Lindgren, A. *Karlson on the Roof* (Methuen, 1977).
Lindgren, A. *Emil Gets into Mischief* (Hamlyn, Beaver Books, 1978).
Luria, A. *The Mind of a Mnemonist*, tr. L. Solotaroff (Jonathan Cape, 1969).
McCarthy, M. *Memories of a Catholic Childhood* (Heinemann, 1957).
Malamud, B. *The Fixer* (Penguin, 1966).
Malcolm X, *Autobiography of Malcolm X* (Hutchinson, 1966).
Mandalstam, N. *Hope Against Hope*, tr. M. Hayward (Penguin, 1975).
Mandalstam, N. *Hope Abandoned*, tr. M. Hayward (Penguin, 1976).
Mann, T. *The Magic Mountain*, tr. H.T. Lowe-Porter (Penguin, 1960).
Mann, T. *Death in Venice* (Penguin, 1966).
Marchenko, A. *My Testimony*, tr. M. Scammell (Pall Mall Press, 1969).

Marx, K. and Engels, F. *The German Ideology* (Lawrence & Wishart, 1970).
de Mauss, L. *The History of Childhood* (Souvenir Press, 1976).
Montessori, M. *The Advanced Montessori Method*, 2 vols (London, 1917/18).
Montessori, M. *The Discovery of the Child*, tr. M. Johnstone (Kalakshetra Publications, 1966).
Nabokov, V. *Invitation to a Beheading* (Weidenfeld & Nicholson, 1960).
Nabokov, V. *Lolita* (Weidenfeld & Nicholson, 1959).
de Nerval, G. 'Sylvie' in *Gerard de Nerval: Selected Writings*, tr. G. Wagner (Panther Books, 1968).
Nesbit, E. *The Five Children and It* (Unwin, 1902; Puffin, 1959).
Nesbit, E. *The Wouldbegoods* (Unwin, 1901; Puffin, 1958).
Nesbit, E. *The Railway Children* (Dent, 1975).
Nin, A. *The Journals of Anais Nin*, 4 vols (Quartet Books, 1973).
Opie, I. and P. *Children's Games in Street and Playground* (O.U.P., 1969).
Painter, G. *Marcel Proust*, 2 vols (Peregrine, 1977).
Pearce, P. *What the Neighbours Did* (Longman Young Books, 1972).
Pell, E. *Maximum Security* (Bantam Books, 1973).
Piaget, J. *The Moral Judgment of the Child* (Penguin, 1977).
Piaget, J. *Play, Dreams and Imitation in Childhood* (Routledge & Kegan Paul, 1962).
Poe, E. A. 'The Cask of Amontillado' in *Selected Writings of Edgar Allan Poe*, ed. D. Galloway (Penguin, 1967).
Poe, E. A. 'The Pit and the Pendulum' in *Selected Writings of Edgar Allan Poe* ed. D. Galloway (Penguin, 1967).
Powys, J.C. *Autobiography* (Picador, 1982).
Preyer, W. *The Mind of the Child* (New York, 1895).
Proust, M. *Remembrance of Things Past*, tr. C.K. Scott Moncrieff and A. Mayor, 12 vols (Chatto & Windus, 1966).
Ransome, A. *Swallows and Amazons* (Puffin, 1962).
Ransome, A. *Peter Duck* (Puffin, 1968).
Ransome, A. *Missee Lee* (Puffin, 1971).
Roberts, R. *A Ragged Schooling* (Manchester University Press, 1976).
de Sade, D.A.F. *The Complete Marquis de Sade*, tr. P. Gillette, 2 vols (Holloway House, 1966).
de Saint-Exupéry, A. *The Little Prince* (Pan Books, 1974).
Schatzman, M. *Soul Murder* (Allen Lane, 1973).
Schreber, D.P. *Memoirs of My Nervous Illness*, tr. and ed. I. Macalpine and R. Hunter (Dawson, 1955).
Serge, V. *Men in Prison* (Writers and Readers Publishing Co-operative, 1977).
Sinyavsky, A. *A Voice from the Chorus*, tr. K. Fitzlyon and M. Hayward (Collins and Harvill Press, 1976).

Solzhenitsyn, A. *The First Circle*, tr. M. Guybon (Collins, 1968).
Solzhenitsyn, A. *The Gulag Archipelago*, 3 vols, tr. T. Whitney (Collins, 1978).
Solzhenitsyn, A. *One Day in the Life of Ivan Denisovich*, tr. R. Parker (Penguin, 1963).
Soyinka, W. *The Man Died: Prison Notes of Wole Soyinka* (Penguin, 1975).
Sully, J. *Studies of Childhood* (London, 1896).
Sutton-Smith, B. *The Dialectics of Play* (Verlag Hoffman, 1976).
Thompson, F. *Lark Rise to Candelford* (Penguin, 1973).
Tolkien, J.R.R. *The Hobbit* (Unwin, 1975).
Tolkien, J.R.R. *The Lord of the Rings*, 3 vols (Unwin, 1974).
Tolkien, J.R.R. 'On Fairy Stories' in J.R.R. Tolkien *Tree and Leaf* (Unwin, 1975).
Tolstoy, L. *The Death of Ivan Ilyich* in *The Cossacks*, tr. R. Edmonds (Penguin, 1960).
Winnicott, D.W. *The Child, the Family and the Outside World* (Penguin, 1964).
Wollstonecraft, M. *Maria, or the Wrongs of Woman* (Norton, 1975).
Zipes, J. *Breaking the Magic Spell: Radical Theories of Folk and Fairy Tales* (Heinemann, 1975).
Wilde, O. *The Happy Prince and Other Stories* (Puffin, 1962).

Index of Names

Aiken, J., 155
Andersen, Hans, 156
Ariès, P., 112-13, 114, 132
Artaud, A., 80-1, 86

Bachelard, G., 12-14, 16, 17
Bakhtin, M., 133
Bao, R-W., 18
Baum, F., 155
Bettelheim, B., 157
Bleuler, E., 81-2, 87, 91, 92, 94, 107
Borges, Jorge Luis, 107
Bowlby, J., 143-4
Boyle, Jimmy, 35, 51, 134
Brown, Norman O., 31
Bruno, Giordano, 132
Buca, E., 32, 35, 36, 73
Burton, Robert, 87

Canetti, Elias, 96-7
Carnochan, E.B., 176
Carroll, Lewis, 154
Casanova, J., 6-10, 17, 20, 31, 35, 36, 45, 62, 69-70, 72, 93, 94
Cass, J., 124
Chekhov, Anton, 15, 79, 82-6
Cleaver, Eldridge, 49, 61, 78
Cobb, E., 171

Dahl, R., 155
Daniel, Y., 20
Dolgun, A., 26, 35, 39

Dostoevsky, Fyodor, 6, 15, 17, 25, 26, 33, 34, 35, 53, 57, 61, 77, 78, 81, 121, 125, 139, 147
Douglas, Mary, 30

Ellis, A.E., 26, 27, 34, 36
Erikson, E., 145

Ford, Ford Maddox, 101
Freud, Sigmund, 46, 79, 80, 94, 108, 109, 111, 141-4, 146, 149, 150
Froebel, F., 112, 116, 123, 124, 126, 136, 144

Gadamer, Hans-Georg, 132, 134
Garfield, Leon, 120
Garvey, C., 137
Genet, Jean, 6, 15, 23, 25, 26, 50, 58, 61, 71-3, 78, 82, 177
Gide, André, 102-3, 108, 113
Golding, William, 23, 49, 50, 82
Grahame, Kenneth, 99, 110, 122, 126, 128, 139, 153, 154, 160-7, 169, 171
Groos, Karl, 123, 124, 136, 143

Hall, G.S., 101
Hegel, G., 66, 69, 129, 147-8

INDEX OF NAMES

Hesse, H., 151
Holt, J., 126-7
Hughes, Richard, 101
Huizinga, J., 121-2
Huysmans, J.K., 13, 14

Jackson, George, 4, 6, 33, 35, 36, 43, 61, 63, 64, 66, 83
Jung, Carl, 94

Kafka, Franz, 13, 14, 42, 43-8, 167
Karp, David, 18, 22, 23
Kavan, Anna, 86, 88
Kierkegaard, S., 51-9, 61, 62, 64, 66, 68, 74, 75, 85, 94, 95, 105, 109, 128, 129, 131, 140, 141, 143; 147, 156, 170, 171, 181
Kipling, Rudyard, 154
Koestler, Arthur, 25, 33, 60

Laing, A., 157
Lane, H., 125
Leibniz, G., 132, 176
Lewin, H., 16, 18, 21, 27, 32, 33, 35
Lindgren, Astrid, 155
Luria, A., 107

McCarthy, Mary, 108
MacDonald, G., 154, 157
Malamud, Bernard, 176
Mandelstam, N., 15, 21, 28, 29, 49, 81
Mandelstam, O., 15, 36, 47, 57, 58, 91
Mann, Thomas, 25, 85
Marchenko, Anatoly, 19, 32, 35, 36, 38, 39, 40, 66, 67, 73
Marx, Karl, 175
Mauss, L. de, 115
Medvedev, Z., 84
Michaux, Henri, 11
Miller, Henry, 14
Montessori, M., 118-19

Nabokov, Vladimir, 18, 107
Nerval, G. de, 162
Nesbit, E., 122, 154, 155, 158
Nin, A., 13, 14

Opie, I. and P., 102, 120, 127, 134

Painter, G., 105
Pearce, P., 162
Pell, E., 18, 32, 43
Piaget, Jean, 117, 120, 127, 137, 138
Poe, Edgar Allan, 5, 17, 23
Powys, John Cowper, 119, 133
Preyer, W., 101, 135
Proust, Marcel, 105-6, 109, 110, 111, 113, 116, 147, 180-3

Rabelais, F., 133
Ransome, A., 120, 155
Roberts, R., 134
Rousseau, J.-J., 109

Sade, D.A.F. de, 50, 69-70, 71, 73, 74, 79, 82
Saint-Exupéry, A. de, 158
Schatzman, M., 97-8
Schreber, Daniel Paul, 80, 88-94, 95, 96, 97, 98, 119
Serge, Victor, 18, 24, 25, 26, 38
Sinyavsky, A., 20, 21, 22, 27-8, 33, 37, 42, 43, 49, 50, 58-60, 65, 66, 78, 81, 92, 94
Solzhenitsyn, A., 4, 34, 39, 50, 58, 63, 64, 65, 66, 94
Soyinka, Wole, 16, 19, 28, 29, 35, 37, 38, 39, 42, 43, 49, 61, 65, 72, 78, 81, 94
Spinoza, B., 176

Sully, J., 112, 122, 123, 151
Sutton-Smith, B., 137

Thompson, Flora, 126
Tolkien, J.R.R., 158, 167, 178-80

Tolstoy, Leo, 85
Wilde, Oscar, 163
Winnicott, D.W., 116, 130, 144
Wollstonecraft, M., 27, 33
Zipes, Jack, 156